Robert Burns and the United States of America

Arun Sood

Robert Burns and the United States of America

Poetry, Print, and Memory 1786–1866

Arun Sood
University of Plymouth
Plymouth, UK

ISBN 978-3-319-94444-9   ISBN 978-3-319-94445-6   (eBook)
https://doi.org/10.1007/978-3-319-94445-6

Library of Congress Control Number: 2018947410

Cover credit: Hulton Fine Art Collection/Getty

This Palgrave Macmillan imprint is published by the registered company Springer
International Publishing AG part of Springer Nature
The registered company address is: Gewerbestrasse 11, 6330 Cham, Switzerland

ACKNOWLEDGEMENTS

Thanks to support from the Arts & Humanities Research Council (AHRC) I was able to spend three years working with—and learning from—experts at the Centre For Robert Burns Studies, University of Glasgow. I would like to thank my supervisors Nigel Leask and Kirsteen McCue for their guidance and continuing inspiration; without it this book would not have been possible. By extension, I would also like to thank several other staff, friends and colleagues including Gerard Carruthers, Rhona Brown, Murray Pittock, Pauline Mackay, Jonathan Henderson, Craig Ronald Lamont, Joe Ryan-Hume, Marenka Thompson-Odlum, Michael Morris, Stephen Mullen and Andrew Hook. Thanks to the editors of *Symbiosis: A Journal of Transatlantic Literary and Cultural Relations* for granting permission to use previously published material in Chapter 7, and to James Quinn for designing and finessing the Appendix maps with such expert precision. An important thank you, also, to my new colleagues at the University of Plymouth for providing such a warm welcome.

Part of the pleasure of researching historical transatlantic links has been forming new ones along the way. My postdoctoral Fulbright Fellowship, spent between the Library of Congress and Georgetown University, permitted access to valuable resources and also led to treasured new friendships. Long may the Fulbright Commission receive adequate backing to foster dialogue, intelligence, collaboration and friendships across borders and between cultures. Thanks to Mary-Lou Reker, Travis Hensley and all my friends and fellows at the John

W. Kluge Center in Washington, D.C. for facilitating such a stimulating environment; to Patrick Scott of the University of South Carolina, whose meticulous eye for detail is invaluable; to Corey Andrews of Youngstown State University for providing sage advice as reader; to Larissa P. Watkins for being so hospitable during my visits to the William R. Smith Collection; and to Brian K. Mabry of the St. Andrews Society of D.C. for his kind welcome—I am grateful to you all. A special thank you to Duncan Wu for being such a continuing source of inspiration, encouraging mentor and friend during my time in the USA.

Finally, I am blessed with the support of family and friends, who have shaped various aspects of both my work and personal life. My Father, an Indian emigrant in Scotland, inherently sparked an international intrigue at an early age, while my Mother, *Mo Máthair*, made everything possible, always. For the unwavering support, belief, humour, humility and loyalty over the past few years, Ashley, Chris, John, "Sweet Street" and, of course, Elsa—you have all helped me to find the words that follow. Love to you all.

CONTENTS

PART I

Burns Beyond Scotland

CHAPTER 1

Introduction

Ae night, at tea, began a plea,
Within *America*, man:
—Robert Burns, "A Fragment" (3–4).[1]

In 1784, Robert Burns wrote a satirical ballad about the American Revolutionary War. Over nine stomping verses, Burns's speaker lampooned British military figures, heralded revolutionary heroes and reflected on the political chaos that engulfed Britain in the wake of America's successful revolt. Such biting satire was timely given the Congress of the Confederation had ratified the Treaty of Paris, officially ending the war, earlier that year on January 14. Indeed, Burns's "Fragment", first published in the 1787 "Edinburgh edition" of *Poems, Chiefly in the Scottish Dialect*, serves as a pertinent reminder of his engagement with contemporary transatlantic affairs and international politics.

For much of the twentieth century, however, Burns was considered a poet of limited linguistic range and geographical significance. His poetry rarely appeared in Romantic anthologies or university English curriculums, resulting in a literary reputation habitually reduced to archaic, sentimental and popular Scottish contexts. Critical approaches have dramatically evolved over the past decade, with the 250th anniversary of the poet's birth motivating fresh scholarly interest. In 2009, the Scottish Government tied the Burns bicentenary celebrations, along with other key themes of the nation's perceived culture and heritage,

© The Author(s) 2018
A. Sood, *Robert Burns and the United States of America*,
https://doi.org/10.1007/978-3-319-94445-6_1

to the widely publicised "Year of Homecoming"; an incentive that encouraged the Scottish diaspora to visit their ancestral origins (Burns continues to be of great economic importance to the tourist sector in Scotland).[2] Coinciding with the Scottish government's campaign was the publication of several critical studies, essay collections and biographies that better established his cross-cultural appeal and international literary significance.[3]

This upsurge in critical attention must also be explained in conjunction with wider post-devolutionary shifts in Scottish literary studies. At the opening of the newly devolved Scottish parliament in 1999, singer Sheena Wellington led opposing politicians in rousing chorus as Burns's "A Man's a Man for a' That" echoed across the chambers, marking a symbolic moment in which Burns's egalitarian anthem helped nurture a sense of collective national virtue that transcended party politics. More concretely, however, the broader implications that devolution had on Scottish Studies have meant that Burns is finally being considered, at the very least in an academic sense, outside of the limiting parameters of strictly Scottish national frameworks.

Christopher Whyte has suggested that Scottish devolution, in inspiring a fresh sense of cultural self-confidence, might "at last allow Scottish literature to be literature first and foremost, rather than the expression of a nationalist movement".[4] A few years later into the new century, Gavin Wallace stated that post-devolutionary Scottish writing had been nourished by the "outward reaching international tap-roots of Scottish culture" and encouraged a departure from considering Scottish texts and writers as functioning to shore up a cohesive national identity.[5] In his 2009 critical guide *Scottish Literature* (notably published in the same year as the 250th anniversary), Gerard Carruthers discussed how the discipline was in a period of "self-reflexive scrutiny", claiming there had been "too much emphasis upon nationalism" at the expense of "detailed analysis of other important contexts".[6] It was surely inevitable that Burns, who for so long has been popularly labelled Scotland's "National Bard", would come under fresh academic interrogation in contexts that moved beyond the Scottish national paradigm.

The conceptual renegotiation of the "nation" and "national literature" in Scotland was also in line with, and partially a consequence of, contemporary movements in the wider fields of literary studies, history, sociology and critical theory.[7] In 2008, for example, Amritjit Singh and Peter Schmidt declared a "transnational moment" in literary studies in which "local and national narratives" could no longer be conceived apart from "our shared human histories" and "global interdependence".[8] Prominent critics of American literature such as Paul Giles and John Carlos Rowe further expanded on literary concepts of "transnationality" by revisiting canonical nineteenth-century American texts and authors that "often appear in quite a different light" when examined through a "transnational matrix".[9] Though the popular tag of "National Bard" might remain, this book—in reflecting on the relationships between Burns and the early USA—further participates in the reconfiguration of the poet as a transnational figure who, both in terms of his poetic output and posthumous legacy, transgressed and continues to transgress geographical, indeed national, boundaries.

Of course, it is vital to acknowledge that Burns's popularity in the USA did not go entirely unnoticed in the twentieth century. Andrew Hook's seminal 1975 study *Scotland and America* explored Burns's early American reception, and pointed the way to current transnational trends in Burns Studies, as did valuable scholarly insights from Anna M. Painter, Donald Low and James M. Montgomery.[10] Yet there is little doubt that the 250th anniversary, combined with the cultural effects of Scottish devolution and wider critical trends, has led to much wider attention on Burns's international significance and literary reputation.

The first spring in reconsidering Burns through a broadly transnational framework grew out of "The Global Burns Network" project, founded in 2007 by Murray Pittock in collaboration with experts spread throughout England, Scotland, Spain, the Czech Republic, France, Germany, the USA and Canada.[11] One of the main incentives of the network was to encourage scholarly publication that increased awareness of Burns's global significance and historical reception across cultures and beyond the borders of Scotland. Streams of estuary publications and projects soon followed including "Robert Burns: Inventing Tradition and Securing Memory, 1796–1909" (which provided an online catalogue of worldwide Burns monuments); the essay collections *Robert Burns in Global Culture* (2011), *Robert Burns and Transatlantic Culture* (2012) and *The Reception of Robert Burns in Europe* (2014); and the commissioning of the Oxford University Press multivolume edition of Burns's works.[12]

Laura Doyle proposes that transnational literary studies should consider how literature exists "within a world of encounters"[13] and reveal layered histories, interactions and transcultural exchanges. Adopting this lens, we might draw more attention to the fact that Burns (the man), his poetry and his subsequent cultural "afterlives" participated in an interconnected "world of encounters", particularly around the Atlantic periphery. While the focus of this book is predominantly on one nation, it also pushes for a stronger recognition of how multiple civic identities (*within* that nation) impacted upon Burns's reception and nineteenth-century legacy. The advantage of this perspective is that, in extrapolating the reasons for Burns's rise to prominence, we might identify several strains of national and civic appropriation, rather than solely attributing a uniform image of him being a "friend" to a singular, egalitarian "American" way of life, as has hitherto been the dominant critical narrative.[14] The transnational approach in this book is, then, twofold; not only does this study explore Burns's popularity *beyond* the nation of Scotland, but it also accounts for the plurality of identities existing *across* nineteenth-century America that influenced his reception and subsequent afterlives. As we shall see, though Burns might well be considered a "(Trans)National Poet" (suggested in Chapter 8) it remains crucial, when considering his writing, reception and memory, to pay heed to a plurality of nationalisms and identities *within* transnational contexts.

A transnational approach can admittedly jar with some of the more popular (and palatable) conceptions of Burns as Scotland's most treasured national icon. It is increasingly known, for example, that Burns intended to sail for Jamaica in 1786 to work on a plantation. Writing to John Moore that same year, Burns lamented his possible fate as a "poor Negro-driver"[15]; a chilling phrase that has been dissected by scholars in various attempts to determine the veracity of Burns's unfulfilled plans. Carol McGuirk has noted the significance of the letter being addressed to Moore, whose novel *Zeluco* (1786) exposed the "murderous greed"[16] and cruelty of its planter-protagonist. In writing to Moore—no supporter of slavery—and describing his nightmarish vision of plantation life, it is plausible that Burns's purpose was to emphasise his destitute circumstances, with typical dramatic hyperbole, rather than sincerely assert a future career path. On the other hand, Clark McGinn refutes the idea that Burns was not invested in the prospect of emigration, using recently found documents to suggest the poet sought to directly "prosper from chattel slavery".[17]

The troubling possibilities of what Burns "might have been" (had he emigrated to Jamaica) were seemingly not an issue for the American abolitionists who championed his works in the nineteenth century. In 1859,

Henry Ward Beecher (1813–1887) even offered up a speculative defence of the poet's unfulfilled emigration plans: "I think I see Robert Burns following a gang of slaves, and chanting "A man's a man for a' that"".[18] While Beecher, Frederick Douglass (1818–1895), William Lloyd Garrison (1805–1879) and several other activists (discussed in Chapter 6) appropriated Burns into the context of American abolitionism, the truth is that the poet had very little to do with abolitionist movements in his own lifetime. That is, Burns does not appear to have engaged with any of the widespread petitions and incentives calling for abolition in Glasgow, Edinburgh, Paisley, Dundee, Aberdeen and Ayr.[19] Moreover, as referenced throughout this book, Burns wrote several emigration poems and proleptic "farewell" pieces yet none of them deal explicitly with the horrors of black slavery; thus demonstrating what Michael Morris describes as a "major failure of imaginative sympathy".[20]

One possible exception is "The Slaves Lament", first published as part of James Johnson's *Scots Musical Museum* (Volume IV) in 1792. The speaker mourns their own trafficking across the Atlantic to "the land's of Virginia-O" (2), which is described as a hostile destination of "bitter snow and frost" (7).[21] This harsh, abrasive description is at odds with Burns's other poetic references to America—discussed in the following chapter—as the hallowed ground where liberty prevails, which might be explained by the possibility that Burns collected rather than composed the song.[22] While affirmative evidence of authorship is yet to be found, the song is further testament to the transnational "world of encounters" which Burns operated in through its transatlantic references to pastoral Senegal; mourning of the middle passage; and frosty description of Virginia—not to mention its inclusion in a volume of traditional Scots verse.

A less palatable allusion to American slavery appears in Burns's "Epistle to John Rankine", first printed in the "Kilmarnock edition" of 1786. Based on Burns's illicit impregnation of Elizabeth Paton, the speaker refuses to repent for his sexual deviancy, even though it might result in having to flee to Virginia to "herd the buckskin kye" (65).[23] Here, the term "buckskin kye" (black cattle) is a direct reference to African Americans and chattel slavery, revealing, at the very least, Burns's shrewd awareness of slave-based agricultural systems in the American South.

The ardent pursuit for the truth about Burns's opinions (or lack thereof) on slavery and abolition continues but, problematically, remains reliant on scant evidence: a handful of letters, critical speculation and creative works open to hermeneutic contestation. Nonetheless, to even question the limitations of Burns's egalitarian sympathies remains controversial in Scotland where, as mentioned, he continues to represent a unified sense of "national" egalitarianism. The point here is not to resort to postcolonial, or indeed post-national, blame nor offer up another speculative defence, but rather to underline the merits of adopting a transnational perspective. It is imperative, after all, that multiple national narratives and ideas—Scottish, American or otherwise—are rooted out and discussed in all their complexity, and indeed controversy, if we are to consider Burns and his works in the fullest sense.

The Transnational Poet

The following chapters chart the publication, dissemination, reception, literary influence and cultural memory of Robert Burns's life and work in the USA up to 1866. The starting date of 1786 corresponds with the publication of Burns's first collection, *Poems, Chiefly in the Scottish Dialect*, printed and sold by John Wilson of Kilmarnock and in which evidence of his first poetic engagements with global, specifically transatlantic, affairs can be discerned. Eighty years later, by 1866, not only were biographies of Burns commonplace on American bookshelves, but he was also being culturally preserved through various commemorative practices such as suppers, songs, speeches, political appropriations, rites and material culture.

This closing date also marks the approximate beginning of what is commonly referred to as the Reconstruction Era that followed the American Civil War, making for valuable insights into how fractured national or civic identities were influential on cultural reconfigurations of the poet. The centenary of Burns's birth, celebrated at over 60 separate locations on the cusp of Civil War in 1859, also makes for a pertinent concluding marker of how widespread and malleable his work and reputation had become by the mid-nineteenth century. That said, these dates should not be considered as absolute boundaries. In discussing statuary culture, for example, I have touched upon the significance of later nineteenth-century tributes, and similarly, my afterword discusses post-Civil War constructions of Burns with a final look forward to the current trajectory of Burns Studies in the USA.

In the following chapter, a critical re-examination and case study of three works in particular, "A Fragment" (later titled "When Guilford Good our Pilot stood") (1784), "Address of Beelzebub" (1786) and "Ode For General Washington's Birthday" (1794) will provide a sense of the complexity of Burns's own "poetic views" of America[24] over the course of a decade. The term "poetic views" is employed to acknowledge Burns's fluid adoption of poetic personae, particularly when writing on revolutionary politics. Rather than taken as unflinching biographical truths, then, the "views" extrapolated from these works should be considered more as indicators of what ideas, individuals and events relating to America had clearly stimulated or inspired the poet, whether politically, poetically or otherwise.

Part II of this book—American Print Culture and Poets—shifts attention from Burns's poetic gaze to how the American reading public would, in turn, come to know and view the Scottish poet, primarily through a burgeoning print culture on the Eastern seaboard. Chapter 3 discusses the reprinting and reception of individual poems in Philadelphia dailies such as the *Pennsylvania Packet*, before highlighting how entrepreneurial printers (often of Scottish or Irish heritage) capitalised on an absence of international copyright laws by swiftly reproducing and distributing copies of Burns's *Poems, Chiefly in The Scottish Dialect* and James Currie's *The Works of Robert Burns*. Chapter 4 discusses later biographical editions alongside a selection of critical reviews taken from pioneering American periodicals. The tendency of American editors—functioning as what Pierre Bourdieu calls "artistic mediators"—to prune source texts by Currie, Allan Cunningham and J. G. Lockhart will be revealed through analysis of widely circulated American reprints.

Having established the methods by which Burns's work became available, Chapter 5 turns attention to its influence on American poets. With Britain as the most relevant comparative model, nineteenth-century American poets faced the difficult task of attempting to set themselves apart from their transatlantic contemporaries within the boundaries of poetic convention. For many, Burns provided a subversive model to classical or hegemonic European poetry through his emphasis on locality, thematic rejection of hierarchy and fluid linguistic range. Early American "imitators" of Burns's verse such as Robert Dinsmoor (1757–1836) and David Bruce (c.1760–1830) are addressed due to their aesthetic choice to employ the Scots idiom and Standard Habbie to various ends. Leading on from this, a broader assessment of Burns in relation to American vernacular poetry is put forth with particular reference to James Russell Lowell (1819–1891). One of Lowell's earliest poems was his 1837 composition, "Imitation of Burns" which was also written in Scots. Like John Greenleaf Whittier (1807–1892) before him, it seems that Lowell's poetic apprenticeship included a playful engagement with (and imitation of) Burns's Scots language poetry. Whittier and Lowell formed part of a wider group of New England-based poets known variously as the "Fireside Poets", "Schoolroom Poets" and, less commonly, the "Household Poets". The significance and possible influence of Burns on this group will be assessed, culminating in a discussion of Ralph Waldo Emerson's (1803–1882) commemorative tribute to the "memory of Burns" at the Parker House Hotel, Boston, during the 1859 centenary celebrations.

The final part of this book—Memory and Nation—seeks to better define what might have variously constituted a "memory of Burns" throughout early to mid-nineteenth-century America. Chapter 6 begins with a broad discussion of how the popular legacy of Burns has continually straddled the blurry boundaries between myth, memory and history. Framed by Jan Assmann's assertion that "cultural memory" requires objectified "institutions of preservation"[25] (relics, books, anniversaries, statues and several other modes of objectification) in order for past experience to be conveyed, the chapter proceeds to discuss the inception and effects of several "institutions of preservation" that upheld, or rather remediated, the poet and his works in the nineteenth century. The discussion spans across a variety of material and memorial culture, ranging from the establishment of the first American Burns Clubs to the transatlantic vogue for erecting statues in the poet's honour.

Chapter 7 addresses the complex issue of whether these different modes of remembrance and appropriations might legitimately be grouped together and viewed as instances of "national" cultural memory unique to the USA. Engaging with recent scholarship on national memory, I propose that the cultural memory of Burns might best be conceived as a "palimpsest"; borrowing the term from Jay M. Winter, who argues for a more "dynamic approach" to cultures of national remembrance in transnational contexts, where sites of memory can "become reused or altered" while still bearing trace of "earlier forms".[26] Like Winter's conceptual "palimpsests" (or transnational sites of memory) commemorations and figurative representations of Burns comprised of an overlay of variable messages, but were bound together by source

(Burns), nation (USA) and period (1786–1866). The chapter concludes by underlining the importance of sectional intricacies when considering the influence, memory and remediation of literature in transnational contexts, and particularly in the nineteenth-century USA. Scholars have done much to better highlight and veer from the restrictive dangers of unifying national contexts in recent years. Yet, a greater awareness of divergent sectional, regional and indeed racial factors *within* transnational contexts remains a pertinent issue, as will be demonstrated in this book.

As Murray Pittock remarked in 2011, the study of Burns continues to prosper in a "new era" where "huge hinterlands" lay yet to be discovered.[27] I hope this book will better orientate readers in a transnational plain where fresh insights into the poet's connections with the USA will be discovered, mapped and perhaps even provide guidance for future studies. In recognition of how Burns and his works spread fluidly across and within different cultures, then, we might facetiously push for a reconsidered twenty-first-century baptism: Robert Burns, The (Trans) National Poet of Scotland.

Notes

1. Robert Burns, *Poems, Chiefly in the Scottish Dialect* (Edinburgh: William Creech, 1787), 311–315.
2. The incentive was telling of both the iconic international appeal of Burns and also his economic importance to the tourist sector in Scotland. In January 2018, Joan McAlpine (MSP) called for the economic impact of Robert Burns to be reassessed. A previous 2003 World Bank commission estimated that Burns related tourism and merchandising provides approximately £157 million to the Scottish economy annually. See "The Economic Potential of Robert Burns". Accessed 20 January 2018. https://www.scottishparliament.tv/meeting/members-business-the-economic-potential-of-robert-burns-january-17-2018.
3. See for example, Gerard Carruthers, ed., *The Edinburgh Companion to Robert Burns* (Edinburgh: Edinburgh University Press, 2009); Robert Crawford, *The Bard: Robert Burns, A Biography* (London: Pimlico, 2009); Frank Ferguson and Andrew R. Holmes, eds., *Revising Robert Burns and Ulster: Literature, Religion and Politics, c.1770–1920* (Dublin: Four Courts Press, 2009); and Johnny Rodger and Gerard Carruthers, eds., *Fickle Man: Robert Burns in the 21st Century* (Dingwall: Sandstone Press, 2009).

4. Christopher Whyte, "Masculinities in Contemporary Scottish Fiction", *Forum for Modern Language Studies* 34, no. 2 (1998): 285.
5. Gavin Wallace, "Voyages of Intent: Literature and Cultural Politics in Post-Devolution Scotland", in Carruthers, ed. *The Edinburgh Companion to Contemporary Scottish Literature* (Edinburgh: Edinburgh University Press, 2009), 28.
6. Gerard Carruthers, *Scottish Literature* (Edinburgh: Edinburgh University Press, 2009), 135.
7. See, for example, Tom Nairn, *Faces of Nationalism: Janus Revisited* (London and New York: Verso, 1997); Adrian Hastings, *The Construction of Nationhood* (Cambridge: Cambridge University Press, 1997); and Benedict Anderson, *Imagined Communities: Reflections on the Origin and Spread of Nationalism* [1983]. Revised 2nd ed. (London, New York: Verso, 1991).
8. Amritjit Singh and Peter Schmidt, eds., *Postcolonial Theory and the United States: Race, Ethnicity, and Literature* (Mississippi: University Press of Mississippi, 2008), 8.
9. Paul Giles, *Virtual Americas: Transnational Fictions and the Transatlantic Imaginary* (Durham: Duke University Press, 2002), 16.
10. See Donald Low, ed., *Robert Burns: The Critical Heritage* (London: Routledge and Kegan Paul, 1974), 44–46; Anna M. Painter, "American Editions of The *Poems* of Burns Before 1800", *The Library* 4, no. 12 (1932): 434–456; and James M. Montgomery, "How Robert Burns Captured America", *Studies in Scottish Literature* 30, no.1 (1998). Accessed 20 September. https://scholarcommons.sc.edu/ssl/vol30/iss1/25.
11. "Global Burns Network". Accessed 11 September 2015. http://www.gla.ac.uk/schools/critical/research/researchcentresandnetworks/globalburnsnetwork/.
12. In January 2011, The Centre For Robert Burns Studies at The University of Glasgow was awarded the equivalent of £1.1 million by the Arts and Humanities Research Council towards producing the first volumes of the edition. In November 2016, an additional £1 million was secured for phase 2 of the research project, focused on Burns' letters and correspondence as well as his poetry.
13. Laura Doyle, "Notes Toward a Dialectical Method: Modernities, Modernisms, and the Crossings of Empire", *Literature Compass* 7, no. 3 (2010): 195.
14. This common claim, bolstered by notable writers, poets, critics and biographers, has persisted from the mid-nineteenth century right through to the present day. Donald. A. Low, for example, suggests that "Fellow-feeling with Burns was instinctive" for Americans since his "praise of

independence vindicated their own recent historic choice". See *The Critical Heritage*, 44.

15. J. De Lancey Ferguson and G. Ross Roy, eds., *The Letters of Robert Burns*, 2 vols., 2nd ed. (Oxford: Oxford University Press, 1985), 1:144. (Hereafter referred to as *Letters*).

16. Carol McGuirk, *Reading Robert Burns: Texts, Contexts, Transformations* (London: Pickering & Chatto, 2014), 37.

17. Clark McGinn, "The Scotch Bard and 'The Planting Line': New Documents on Burns and Jamaica", *Studies in Scottish Literature* 43, no. 2 (2017): 265.

18. James Ballantine, ed. *Chronicle of the Hundredth Birthday of Robert Burns* (Edinburgh and London: A. Fullarton & Co., 1859), 580.

19. See Ian Whyte, *Scotland and the Abolition of Black Slavery, 1756–1838* (Edinburgh: Edinburgh University Press, 2006), 85.

20. Michael Morris, "Robert Burns: Recovering Scotland's Memory of the Black Atlantic", *Journal for Eighteenth-Century Studies*, 37, no. 3 (2014): 348.

21. Murray Pittock, ed., *The Oxford Edition of the Works of Robert Burns, Volumes II and III: The Scots Musical Museum* (Oxford: Oxford University Press, 2018), 2:465.

22. In the recent edition of the *Scots Musical Museum*, Pittock has devised a set of eight categories to determine the extent of Burns's authorship in the *Scots Musical Museum*. "The Slaves Lament" falls under Category I ("A song wholly by Burns, with no prior antecedents identified, or suspected") or III ("A song significantly by Burns, with only isolated lines or a combination of phrases, subject matter, and tune evident from earlier evidence"). See *The Oxford Edition of the Works of Robert Burns*, 2:12, 3:142.

23. *The Poems and Songs*, 1:61 (44).

24. All references to "America" and "American" in this book denote the USA rather than the North American continent. I use the terms "United States" and "America" interchangeably unless otherwise stated. Debates over the "imperial conflation of the United States with America" are worth noting. See, for example, Kirsten Silva Gruesz, *Ambassadors of Culture: The Transamerican Origins of Latino Writing* (Princeton: Princeton University Press, 2002), 10.

25. Jan Assmann, "Communicative and Cultural Memory", in *Cultural Memory Studies: An International and Interdisciplinary Handbook*, ed. Astrid Erill and Angsar Hunning (Berlin and New York: De Gruyter, 2008), 111.

26. Jay M. Winter, "Palimpsests", in *Memory, History, and Colonialism: Engaging with Pierre Nora in Colonial and Postcolonial Contexts*, eds.

Indra Sengupta and Hagen Schulze (London: German Historical Institute, 2009), 170.

27. Murray Pittock, "Introduction: Global Burns", in *Robert Burns and Global Culture*, ed. Murray Pittock (Lewisburg: Bucknell University Press, 2011), 13.

CHAPTER 2

"Thy Harp, Columbia": Burns's American Works, c.1784–1794

Thus in the beginning all the world was America, and more so than that is now....[1]

—John Locke (1689)

In his influential work of political philosophy *Two Treatises of Government*, first published in 1689, John Locke employed "America" as a metaphor when deliberating over the "use and value of money" in society.[2] For Locke, America was not only a geographical space but also an imaginative frame through which man's "natural rights" (to "life, liberty and estate") could be identified in the face of increasing political, economic and constitutional change. Locke's metaphorical flourish is revealing of how the very *idea* of "America" had become an integral part of self-enquiry in Britain by the eighteenth century. That is, "America" became intertwined in personal, political and, most importantly for this chapter, poetic processes of self-inquiry and disquisition. The contextual, dual consideration of "America" as both a metaphorical and geo-physical space is important when approaching Burns's engagements with the emergent Republic between 1784 and 1794. Burns not only harnessed the symbolic power of America in his creative works, but also lived in an era when it offered (as a very real geo-physical space) asylum to radical poets, activists and reformers.

For opponents of British colonial rule and political reformists, the mere mention of America was loaded with connotations of liberty, freedom and progressive constitutional reform. Accordingly, Burns's

© The Author(s) 2018

A. Sood, *Robert Burns and the United States of America*,

https://doi.org/10.1007/978-3-319-94445-6_2

American works were laced with allusions to the failing British political system and utopian conceptions of liberty "owre the sea".[3] As Andrew Noble notes, it is only recently "that the American Revolution has been granted its proper status in his poetry"[4] and close textual analysis reveals the transnational intricacies of Burns's creative practice and engagement with revolutionary politics. Initially touching upon Burns's letters and correspondence, this chapter predominantly offers a critical reassessment of (what will subsequently referred to as) the poet's "American works": "When Guilford Good our Pilot stood" (1784); "Address of Beelzebub" (1786) and "Ode For General Washington's Birthday" (1794).

Epistolary Reflections

Burns's first mention of America comes in a 1783 letter to his cousin James Burnes. In a paragraph largely concerned with the local economy, trade, industry and market valuation (he describes the current value of "Oatmeal", "white pease" and "Silk" among other goods), Burns concludes:

> In short [...] since the unfortunate beginning of this American war, & its as unfortunate conclusion, this country has been, & still is decaying very fast.[5]

Here, American victory is deemed "unfortunate" due to its impact on the Ayrshire economy. There is little sense here of America being a symbolic beacon of progressive politics, or even a geographical refuge for political activists. Nonetheless, just one year later Burns was to write "When Guilford Good" which, as we shall see, depicted American victory as far from being "unfortunate". Burns's ability to craft, invent and switch between rhetorical personae is surely of relevance here, as is the fact that the decline in trade he refers to did not endure. As an article in the *Glasgow Advertiser* concluded a few years later, "the export of English and Scotch goods from Clyde to America, has increased every year since the end of the war".[6] Burns's letters towards the end of the decade are more demonstrative of how sociopolitical discourse used the dialectical example of America as a transatlantic "other" against which Britain might define itself. In an open letter to the *Edinburgh Evening Courant* printed 22 November 1788, Burns, or least in the personae of his letter ("A. BRITON"), displays sympathy with American revolutionary Republicanism by describing it as "enlightened" and "honest":

> I will not, I cannot, enter into the merits of the cause; but I dare say, the American Congress, in 1776, will be allowed to have been as able and as enlightened, and, a whole empire will say, as honest, as the English Convention in 1688; and that the fourth of July will be as sacred to their posterity as the fifth of November is to us.[7]

This letter was a reaction to an anti-Jacobite sermon (to celebrate the centenary of the 1688 "Glorious Revolution") Burns had attended by the Reverend Joseph Kirkpatrick in the local church of Dunscore parish.[8] In the full letter, Burns attacks Kirkpatrick for describing the Stuarts as "bloody and tyrannical" and insists that his sermon was bent on "raking up the ashes" of a misfortunate dynasty.[9] Burns's ability to subtly balance political sentiments (delicately supporting the "Glorious Revolution" while mounting a public defence of the Stuarts) to the point of ambiguity is, unsurprisingly, also prevalent throughout his three main American works. In the same month that the *Edinburgh Evening Courant* letter appeared, Burns also wrote to his trusted correspondent Mrs. Dunlop (in a letter dated 13 November 1788) expressing similar sentiments. Evidently frustrated by the tyrannical and "bloody" depiction of the Stuarts, Burns again turns to the American Revolution to reflect:

> Is it not remarkable, odiously remarkable, that tho' manners are more civilized, & the rights of mankind better understood, by an Augustan's Century's improvement [...] an empire beyond the Atlantic has had its REVOLUTION too, & for the very same maladministration & legislative misdemeanors in the illustrious & sapientipotent Family of H—as was complained in the "tyranical & bloody house of STUART."[10]

In defending the "illustrious" House of Stuart, Burns suggests that it is not always tyrannical regimes (as implied by Kirkpatrick) that cause rupture, dissent and warfare. Here, the subtle implication is that the recent American Revolution was justified and partly a consequence of Hanoverian "misdemeanors" and legislative errors. That the American Revolution was an intriguing topic for Burns is further evidenced in a letter written to Robert Graham, dated 13 May 1789. Burns, who would have known to exercise epistolary caution given Graham's position as

Commissioner of The Scottish Board of Excise, describes his sincere admiration for Adam Smith's *Wealth of Nations* ("I could not have given any mere *man*, credit for half the intelligence Mr Smith discovers in his book") before stating:

> I would covet much to have his ideas respecting the present state of some quarters of the world that are or have been the scenes of considerable revolutions since his book was written.[11]

Here, Burns clearly alludes to the American Revolution as well as events in France ("are or have been"). In *Wealth of Nations*, Smith displayed some sympathy for American independence movements and predicted an inevitable change in the political and economic relationship between Britain and America.[12] Thus, Burns would have had a fair estimation, through his reading of the book, what Smith's ideas on the American Revolution might have been like. Of course, the full fervour of the French Revolution in the 1790s had reignited debates over the outcome of the American Revolution, with the young Republic being appropriated into both Jacobin and anti-Jacobin arguments. Wil Verhoven calls this "the American front of the French Revolution debate"; an assertion justified by his tracing of the upsurge in printed documents relating to America in Britain between 1792 and 1795. While the general publication rate of British novels fell in the period following the radicalisation of the French Revolution, the number of novels dealing with American content, as Verhoven notes, "rose in those years by over 60 percent".[13] Written in 1794, Burns's "Ode for General Washington's Birthday" should be considered within the context of this "American front" of the French debate.

Another letter to George Thomson, dated 28 August 1793, once again reveals Burns's engagement with revolutionary debates. Reflecting on his recent composition of "Robert Bruce's March to Bannockburn" (or "Scots, wha hae"), Burns states:

> …I had no idea of giving myself any trouble on the Subject, till the accidental recollection of that glorious struggle for Freedom, associated with the glowing ideas of some other struggles of the same nature, *not quite so ancient.*[14]

With a final verse that famously commands to "Lay the proud usurp-ers low!" in the cause of liberty, the "not quite so ancient" struggles he had in mind were clearly revolutionary in nature. By writing about the medieval Scottish Wars of Independence, however, Burns slyly escapes culpability in the same year that had seen the likes of Thomas Muir (1765–1799) and James "Balloon" Tytler face the consequences of per-ceived sedition and Republicanism.[15] What is perhaps most remarkable about juxtaposing Burns's epistolary reflections on America is the extent to which the American Revolution and its aftermath remained of pro-found importance to Scotland in the late-eighteenth century on a vari-ety of levels; whether commercial, political, intellectual, geographical or otherwise.[16]

"WHEN GUILFORD GOOD": THE FOLLY OF BRITISH POLITICS

"When Guilford Good" or "Ballad on the American War" first appeared titled as "A Fragment" in the Edinburgh edition of *Poems, Chiefly in The Scottish Dialect* (1787). A highly nuanced political song known, rather confusingly, by three different titles, it became most commonly referred to as "When Guilford Good our Pilot stood" after appearing under that name in James Johnson's 1788 *Scots Musical Museum* (Volume II) and George Thomson's 1793 publication of *A Select Collection of Original Scottish Airs for the Voice*. Composed much earlier than Burns's other American works (written in 1784), it was also the only one that was made available to the public in his own lifetime.[17] "Address of Beelzebub" was written in 1786 and "Ode For General Washington's Birthday" in 1794, yet neither was actually published, quite remarka-bly, until the mid-nineteenth century. That Burns's later American works did not surface is telling of the hostile environment in which Burns was writing, where challenges to the political hegemony (even in the form of poetry) would not go unpunished.[18] In line with this, the publication of "When Guilford Good" was not without wary hesitation, as demon-strated by Burns's letter to Henry Erskine, in December 1786:

> I showed the enclosed political ballad to my Lord Glencairn, to have his opinion whether I should publish it; as I suspect my political tenets, such as they are, may be rather heretical in the opinion of my best Friends[…]
> His Lordship seems to think the piece may appear in print, but desired me to send you a copy for your suffrage.[19]

In asking for advice from both Lord Glencairn and Henry Erskine, it seems Burns was well aware of the inflammatory political charge running through the song. In the first verse, Burns alludes to *"Guilford"* (1)[20] better known as Frederick, Lord North (1732–1792), who served as prime minister from 1770 and was in power during the period leading up to the American War. In the years that followed the American War, Peter D. G. Thomas notes that there was a historical condemnation of Lord North as "the minister who lost America",[21] thus, the term "pilot" (1) was employed by Burns with a strong hint of irony. The following lines in which the Americans "did nae less, in full congress/Than quite refuse our law, man" (7–8) not only suggests American resistance, but also alludes to the Declaration of Independence which begins with the words "IN CONGRESS".[22] However, there is no real sense of the song being overtly pro-American in the first verse. On the contrary, *"Guilford"* is portrayed as *our* pilot (though perhaps with noted irony) and the Americans reject *our* laws, almost suggesting a unity between Britain and the speaker.

Following America's rejection of British rule in the first verse, Burns goes on to depict the ambitious attempts of Richard Montgomery (1738–1775) to invade Canada under the orders of George Washington (1731–1799) in 1775. Burns conveys the building momentum of a resistant and ambitious America, by describing Montgomery as "na slaw, man" (10). The image is enhanced by the repetitive and warlike alternate line repetition of "man" that beats throughout the song, creating a crescendo of events. Montgomery is further described in an ambitious, honourable and courageous manner, ultimately meeting his demise "Wi' sword in hand, before his band" (15). An Irishman who mixed with "men of liberal views who were friends of the Americans",[23] the speaker's admiration for Montgomery is telling and also the first sign of a pro-American view in the song. The description of Sir Guy Carleton (1724–1808), the Governor of Quebec, who was instrumental in capturing many Americans, is far less admiring.

The third verse refers to, "Tammy Gage", or British commander General Thomas Gage (1718–1787) who, despite being Governor of Massachusetts, was allegedly kept under constant siege by the Continental Army in his Boston mansion and is thus depicted as a coward ("Was kept at Boston-ha, man") (18). Gage was succeeded by Sir William Howe (1729–1814) who became commander in chief of land forces in North America. Burns firstly alludes to Howe's pious apprehensions towards violence ("Wi' sword an' gun he thought a sin") (21), but then goes on to describe his subsequent brutal attacks in New York, where 3000 Americans were killed and many cattle seized on the Hudson in November 1776. The ruthless language ("bluid", "knife", "fork" and "hacked sma") (23) not only refers to the literal seizure and consumption of cattle, but also to the bloody slaughter of American lives. Once again, it seems, the British Commanders are portrayed in less than heroic terms. Thomas Gage is depicted as passive, useless and confined to a "cage", while William Howe ignores his religious convictions and proceeds into acts of brutality; with the colloquial, subsidiary titles of "Tammy" (17) and "Willie" (19) stripping them of conviction and integrity.

The following verse continues to hail the triumph of American arms as the speaker alludes to Sir John Burgoyne's (1722–1792) surrender to the American army at Saratoga, where he "lost his way, ae misty day" (27) on the 17 October 1777. It is, however, notable that Burns portrays *"Fraser"* as "brave" (26), which is the only point where a British military figure is described in an honourable light. Brigaider Simon Fraser (1729–1777), killed by American rifle shot on 7 October 1777, was the son of Hugh Fraser of Balnain, and thus descended from a brave and noble Jacobite family.[24] That Burns portrays the bravery of Fraser is perhaps revealing of his own patriotic empathy with past Scottish heroes and Jacobite clans, rather than an admiration for the British army in America. The last four lines of the verse further glorify American victory, as Marquess Cornwallis' (1738–1805) surrender at Yorktown is alluded to while revolutionaries seize every opportunity and courageously "claw" (30) their way to freedom. The reference to *"Clinton"* (31) refers to Sir Henry Clinton (1730–1795) who, as the war drew to a close, was forced to retreat to New York after American victories in the North and South, hence the reason Burns describes him as hanging up his sword. This is a powerful and resonating image to end the verse with. Sir Henry Clinton was "widely seen to share the blame for the defeat"[25] in the American War, and he thus symbolises the failure of the whole campaign. With the image of Clinton hanging up his sword ("He hung it to the wa' man") (32), Burns concludes his condensed summary of the American War, by highlighting British failure and American triumph.

While the first four verses of "When Guilford Good" selectively deal with key events from the beginning of the American War to its eventual conclusion, the remaining verses go turn to British politics. In verses five and six, Burns depicts several bumbling British politicians in caricature form, as they are thrown into chaos after the war:

> Then *Montague*, an' *Guilford* too,
>   Began to fear a fa', man;
> And *Sackville* doure, wha stood the stoure
>   The German Chief to thraw, man:
> For Paddy *Burke*, like ony Turk.
>   Nae mercy had at a', man;
> An' *Charlie Fox* threw by the box,
>   An' lows'd his tinkler jaw, man.
>
> Then *Rockingham* took up the game;
>   Till Death did on him ca', man;
> When *Shelburne* meek held up his cheek,
>   Conform to Gospel law, man:
> Saint Stephen's boys, wi' jarring noise,
>   They did his measures thaw, man;
> For *North* an' *Fox* united stocks,
>   An' bore him to the wa,' man.

(33–48)

None of the politicians here are described in terms of strength or conviction and, on the contrary, are subtly ridiculed. By drawing these figures together in two compressed verses and highlighting their shortcomings, Burns makes a complete mockery of British politics; "*Guilford*" contributed towards causing the war; "*Montague*" (John Montague, Earl of Sandwich 1718–1792) was regarded by many as a poor "strategist and wartime minister"[26]; and the "doure" (35) "*Sackville*" (Lord George Sackville 1716–1785) was regularly used as a "scapegoat for the loss of America".[27]

Burns's subsequent references to Edmund Burke (1729–1797) and Charles James Fox (1749–1806), both of whom opposed the American War and led a cunning campaign to topple the North administration, further portrays the increasing factionalism of British politics in the aftermath of the war. Burke had "Nae mercy" in turning on political opponents, while Fox, rather comically, "lows'd his tinkler jaw", possibly alluding to the idea that North's failure in America was "a great cause of amusement to Charles",[28] although it could also refer to his increasingly "loose" political beliefs, as he would, ás the song later depicts, go on to form a surprising alliance with Lord North. Burns is notably anti-Fox here which adds further complexity to his epistolary exchanges with Henry Erskine prior to the song's publication (given Erskine adhered to Fox and the Rockingham Whigs).[29] That Erskine was known for his "universal requisition" and "reasoned wit"[30] might be one reason Burns would rely on his advice, regardless of which party he was aligned with. More importantly, however, was the fact that Burns's patron at this time was the Earl of Glencairn who was also a notable Whig. Burns was likely concerned about offending Glencairn and other Edinburgh Whigs, which would explain why he needed permission, as it were, from Erskine before publishing the poem.

Here, Burns cautiously straddles the delicate line between not offending the Whigs (to the point where he could risk losing patronage) yet still managing to portray Fox in rather mocking fashion. The folly and instability of British politicians is further emphasised as "*Rockingham*" (Charles Watson Wentworth 1730–1782) does not last long as he takes up the "game" of being prime minister, while *Shelburne* (William Petty 1737–1805) is "meek" and faces stiff opposition from both the House of Commons and also from the coalition between North and Fox. The quarrelling between Fox and Shelburne was famously advantageous to William Pitt (1759–1806), who resisted both Shelburne and the North-Fox coalition, eventually becoming prime minister at the age of twenty-four.

In referring to the complex relationship between Burns's politics and his bids for patronage, Nigel Leask has stated that the poet was often able to solicit patronage from upper-class sponsors while at the same time "insisting on his 'independence'".[31] Of course, there were limits to how "independent" Burns could be when it came to the volatile issue of political reform in the decade following the American Revolution. To illustrate the point further, it might be useful, before continuing with the analysis of "When Guilford Good", to take the fate of Paisley poet Alexander Wilson (1766–1813) as a point of comparison. Wilson faced a series of fines, imprisonments and cautions after the publication of his poem "The Shark; or Lang Mills Detected", which openly criticised the government and the processes of the Industrial Revolution:

> A higher aim gars Willy think,
>   And deeper schemes he's brewin';
> Ten thoussan' fouk at ance to sink

> To poverty and ruin!
> Hail mighty patriot! Noble soul!
>   Sae generous, and sae civil,
>   Sic vast designs deserve the whole
>   Applauses of the devil
>   On ony day.
>
>   (19–27)[32]

Particularly against the backdrop of revolutionary events, it is understandable why Wilson's poem was seen as inflammatory, and—along with his controversial letter to William Sharp—it led to a series of court appearances and prosecutions.[33] Eventually, Wilson was forced to flee across the Atlantic, knowing there was little safety or future for him as a poet in Scotland. While Wilson did not so much engage with America in his poetry, it is telling that the Republic was his chosen geographical refuge when he was oppressed for holding certain political views. The example of Wilson's exile also further illustrates the caution Burns had to exercise in regard to rebellious political subject matter. Burns's ability to delicately straddle sensitive political boundaries in "When Guilford Good" is, in many ways, an admirable feat in itself.

Burns further mocks Fox's ministry in comparing political moves to "Clubs" (49), "Hearts" (49) and "Diamonds" (51), as if suggesting both a lack of sincerity and concern from those playing "the game". The card game imagery might also have been a clever allusion to the fact that Fox was a known gambler whose "losses were on a heroic scale"[34] with Burns implying that he was as careless a gambler as he was a leader. The song then describes how the English ("Saxon lads") (53) called on "*Chatham's boy*" (54) William Pitt, at which point Scotland "drew her pipe an' blew" (55). This line, which precedes the final two verses in the song, is significant in that it draws Scotland into the realm of British politics for the first time. This is an incredibly astute and timely insertion by Burns, given that Scotland's involvement in British party politics greatly increased in the period that followed the American Revolution. As Colin Kidd has noted, before 1782 "party politics scarcely impinged on Scottish affairs" and it was not until competing factions formed in the late-eighteenth century (namely the Fox-Northites and Pittites) that "party began to take a firmer hold in Scottish politics".[35]

While the infamous "Reign of Terror" in the 1790s unsurprisingly caused Burns to have a less favourable view of Pitt the Younger,

"When Guilford Good" clearly unveils positive ideas about the young politician.[36] At least in his early career, Pitt did champion various liberal and reformist causes (as did his father Lord Chatham "the Great Commoner") such as the American Revolution and Catholic emancipation. Two of the most striking images in the final two verses are indeed the "kindling eyes" of William Pitt's encouraging father, and the cunningness of the North-Fox alliance to have "Gowff'd *Willie* like a ba" (66), once again evoking the image of a careless "game". The preceding reference to "slee Dundas" (59) also encapsulates the ambiguity surrounding the legacy of Henry Dundas (1742–1811). While Dundas was unquestionably the political strongman of Scotland after the American War, his rule was often considered despotic, despite some of the benefits he conferred on the country. Burns's use of "slee" might initially seem, particularly to the modern reader, to suggest a negative and manipulative description of Dundas.

However, the *Historical Thesaurus of English* reveals that in the late-eighteenth century, "slee" usually connoted "skilfulness" and "proficiency"[37] while the *Dictionary of the Scots Language* has it defined as "smooth-spoken, oily, wily and persuasive in speech".[38] Therefore, the depiction of "slee Dundas" is not necessarily a negative one, but does emphasise his persuasive powers over the Scottish people ("north the Roman wa', man;") (60). Dundas was, after all, the most influential Scottish statesman in the London parliament for many decades, and despite many political controversies, nobody could question his longevity and persuasiveness. The final four lines of the song are packed with patriotic, warlike imagery:

> An' *Caledon* threw by the drone,
>   An' did her whittle draw, man;
> An' swoor fu' rude, thro' dirt an' bluid,
>   To mak it guid in law, man.
>
>   (69–72)

The "drone" (69) of bagpipes is dramatically interspersed with the beating repetition of "man" as *Caledon* draws out her "whittle", and swears "To make it guid in law" (70–72). While one reading of this might be that "*Caledon*" should, along with the "*Suthron*" (English), help Pitt to remain and prosper in power, the evocation of Scotland rising up, "whittle" in hand has broader resonances in that Scotland is urged to emulate America's successful democratic model ("mak it guid"). This stirring sense of Scottish empowerment is subtly bolstered by the song being set to the tune of "Gillecrankie" in the Edinburgh edition of 1787. The tune (better known as "Killiecrankie") had a long association with several Jacobite songs and was also later used for Mrs Grant of Laggan's (1755–1838) song "When Willy Pitt", in George Thomson's *A Select Collection of Original Scottish Airs for the Voice*; an appropriate choice given Burns's previous waxing lyrical on the former prime minister to the same tune. In James Johnson's *Scots Musical Museum*, however, "When Guilford Good" was set to the tune "M. freicedan", also known as "The Black Watch" or, as in James Kinsley's edition, "The Earl of Glencairn's", which derived from McGlashan's *Strathspey Reels* (1780). Accordingly, this tune also held strong Highland connotations.[39]

Despite these formal and thematic evocations of rebellion, it would be a stretch to suggest that the song suggests Scotland's secession from a unionist government. The depiction of Pitt, after all, is an overwhelmingly positive one and "*Caledon*" and "*Suthron*" are urged to get behind him as one. Though internal divisions are duly noted in the song, there is a sense that both the "saxon lads" and those "north the Roman wa" must unite and rally behind Pitt's opposition to the Fox-North coalition. To overemphasise a Scottish nationalist reading, then, would be limiting, particularly given the song reflects on the complexity of multiple transnational relationships: Scotland must negotiate its (potentially) reinvigorated prospects within the Union ("mak it guid in law, man") (72); Britain must reassess its imperial future after the loss of America ("quite refuse our law, man") (8); and Scotland and England must find common reformist hope in Pitt The Younger ("Up, Willie, waur them a', man!") (56).[40]

Arguably more so than any other of his poems or songs from the period, then, "When Guilford Good" reveals the extent of Burns's engagement with international affairs and politics. Evidently, Burns had access to several newspapers and pamphlets that detailed revolutionary events and provided commentary on their consequences for Britain and, more specifically, Scotland. Recent studies on late-eighteenth-century print culture, with particular reference to the American Revolution, have revealed the influence of both pamphleteering and the periodical press on shaping public opinion and we can clearly see the effects of this on Burns.[41] In addition to pamphlets, it is fairly certain that Burns was an avid reader of periodicals such as *The Edinburgh Evening Courant, The Gazetteer, Edinburgh Herald, The Mirror, The Observer* and the *Morning Chronicle*.[42]

More speculatively, considering the caricature-like representations of politicians in "When Guilford Good", another possible source of information for Burns might have been the political cartoons of the period.[43] The portrayal of Fox, for example, with his "tinkler jaw" playing the "Diamond's Ace, of *Indian* race" is resonant with several contemporary caricatures of the politician, and work remains to be done to uncover Burns's familiarity with these satirical illustrations.

From the satirical portrayal of political figures to the very tune the lyrics were written for, Burns makes his political points, but does so with a guarded sense of awareness through several subtle inflections. That he manages to strike this delicate balance is surely one of his main strengths as a political poet; controversial enough to provoke debate, yet equally cautious not to personally endanger his livelihood and escape prosecution.

"ADDRESS OF BEELZEBUB": THE "DEIL" SPEAKS

If "When Guilford Good" reveals subtle pro-American inflections, then Burns's later poem, "Address of Beelzebub", is a far more intense and scathing reprise of the American War and the turbulent state of British politics in the post-revolutionary period. Written in 1786, just two years after Burns penned "When Guilford Good", the poem did not appear in print until 1818 and it is easily seen why it would have proved controversial given the heated anti-aristocratic resentment that resonates throughout. Had the song been printed in Burns's lifetime, his patronage might also have been at risk due to its satirical attack on the Earl of Breadalbane, as made explicit in the poem's introductory dedication:

> To the Rt. Honble John, Earl of Breadalbane, President of the Rt Honble the Highland Society, which met, on the 23rd of May last, at the Shakespeare, Covent Garden, to concert ways and means frustrate the designs of FIVE HUNDRED HIGHLANDERS who, as the society were informed by Mr McKenzie of Applecross, were so audacious as to attempt an escape from their lawful lords and masters whose property they are emigrating from the lands of Mr McDonald of Glengary to the wilds of CANADA, in search of that fantastic thing –LIBERTY-[44]

As James Kinsley has previously noted, Burns was clearly unimpressed by "aristocratic (and patriotic) anxiety" and the "belated attempts to prevent emigration", particularly among Scotland's Highland population.[45] This opposes the popular notion of Highlanders being cleared and forced to flee later in the nineteenth century; thus serving as a useful reminder of the complex historiography of Highland emigration. Burns explicitly pairs the prospect of emigration with "LIBERTY", further demonstrating a vision of North America as being a promised land of freedom and democracy. Though considered here under the umbrella of Burns's American works, it is worth mentioning that the Highland Society meeting in question was a reaction, as Burns noted in his introduction, to proposed emigration to "CANADA". However, while Canada was a particularly popular destination for post-Culloden Scottish Catholics (the Quebec Act of 1774 extended statutory protection to the Roman Catholic church), the remainder of the poem deals predominantly with the American War and the same military figures that appeared in "When Guilford Good".

Taking on the Devil's persona to espouse venomous political ideas, the speaker strongly derides underprivileged Highlanders in the opening two stanzas. By adopting the voice of evil itself and having him side with the aristocratic Highland Society, Burns ironically exposes their brutal, repressive and ultimately sinful attitude. The Devil toasts the Earl of Breadalbane, president of the Highland Society and ironically exposes his selfish disregard for starving Highlanders ("hunger'd HIGHLAN BOORS!") (2). The subsequent language is equally scathing, as the Devil dismisses "nae duddie" (3), "desp'rate beggar" (3) and the "highlan hounds" (8), with connotations of them being little else but hungry wild animals. While the crude actions of the Earl of Breadalbane and other Lairds are exposed, it is worth noting that Burns did write a complimentary verse to Breadalbane in "Admiring Nature in her Wildest Grace", which he wrote in pencil over the chimney piece at the Kenmore Inn during his Highland tour of 1787, just a year after the "Address" was written.[46]

This is yet another example of how fluidly Burns could adapt his poetic personae and assume ambiguity, albeit in the name of patronage. This further qualifies Manning's assertion that Burns was a master of evoking what it is like "*to believe something at a particular moment*"[47] and reminds us of the artistic fluidity of the poet's "beliefs", or rather, "poetic views". The final lines of the second stanza echo the language of

"When Guilford Good". In Burns's earlier song, the speaker describes Richard Montgomery as going "thro' the lakes", while here the Devil also depicts the Highlanders as going "amang thae lakes an' seas" (11) in search of liberty. Similarly, the speaker in "When Guilford Good" describes how the Americans "quite refuse our law, man", which mirrors the Devil's assertion that the Highlanders will also "mak what rules an' laws they please" (12). The American forces are thus depicted as inspirational for the Highlanders, who continue to seek liberty, and free themselves from oppressive British rule. The bold American figures of John Hancock, first signatory of the Declaration of Independence (1737–1793), Benjamin Franklin, author of the constitution of Pennsylvania (1706–1790) and George Washington, the first president (1732–1799) are deemed to have set "Highlan bluid a ranklin" (14), which is ironic given that several Highland regiments fought against the Americans in the Revolutionary War.[48]

Yet Burns selectively chooses to focus on the inspirational power of these leading revolutionaries. The "fearless" (16) description of Montgomery once again echoes "When Guilford Good" (where he is described as bravely falling "wi sword in hand") and the Devil makes clear that these men have big "HEADS" and "HEARTS" (18); suggesting they might even inspire the degenerate Highlanders ("dunghill sons of dirt an' mire") to "PATRICIAN RIGHTS ASPIRE" (19–20). Nigel Leask has suggested that the Devil persona in "Address of Beelzebub" is quite different to the "folk trickster" of popular tradition in Scotland (as appears in Burns's "Address to the Deil", for example).[49] Indeed, there is a vindictive streak in Burns's "Beelzebub" in that he, if one is to take his narration quite literally, wants to see Highlanders suffer and kept in their "lowly" stations. The rhetorical brilliance lies in the fact that in siding with the aristocracy, Burns's speaker (the Devil) simultaneously exposes their discriminatory attitude.

As the third stanza continues, the bumbling British political figures of "When Guilford Good" are revisited. In Burns's earlier song, Lord North, George Sackville, Sir William Howe and Sir Henry Clinton were depicted in less than heroic terms, and thus the Devil's assertion that they should "watch an' premier owre the pack vile!" (22) and "bring them to a right repentance" (24) takes on added irony. Even without prior knowledge of Burns's song, it was well known that these men had failed to "save the honor o' the nation" (26) and were used as scapegoats for the loss of America. That *they*, of all people, should curb the aspirations of the Highlanders consequently seems ludicrous. In the lines that follow, the Devil proclaims that the Highlanders should never be granted universal rights or freedom:

> THEY! an' be d-mn'd ! what right hae they
> To Meat, or Sleep, or light o' day,
> Far less to riches, pow'r, or freedom,
> But what your lordships PLEASE TO GIE THEM?
>   (27–30)

As P. J. Marshall has noted, "Britain's rulers felt that they needed to assert their legitimacy against the universal rights of humanity which the Americans claimed to be championing" and thus "strenuous efforts" were made to reduce the claims of American democracy as "the tyranny of the mob".[50] The lines above allude to the contemporary idea that Britain's "lordships" must maintain a sense of justified superiority over the rowdy pack of "vile" Highlanders. In one of the most powerful stanzas of the poem, worth quoting in fell here, the Devil then suggests that the empowered aristocrats are in fact too soft on the Highlanders:

> But, hear me, my Lord! Glengary, hear!
> Your HAND'S OWRE LIGHT ON THEM, I fear:
> Your FACTORS, GREIVES, TRUSTEES an' BAILIES,
> I CANNA SAY BUT THEY DO GAILIES;
> They lay aside a' tender mercies
> An' tirl the HALLIONS to the BIRSIES;
> Yet, while they're only poin'd, and herriet,
> They'll keep their stubborn Highlan spirit.
> But smash them! Crush them a' to spails!
> An' rot the DYVORS I' the JAILS!
> The young dogs, swinge them to labour,
> Let WARK an' HUNGER mak them sober!
> The HIZZIES, if they're oughtlins fuasont,
> Let them in DRURY LANE be lesson'd!
> An' if the wives, an' dirty brats,
> Come thigganat your doors an' yets,
> Flaffan wi' duds, an' grey wi' beese,
> Frightam awa your deucks an' geese;
> Get out a HORSE-WHIP, or a JOWLER
> The langest thong, the fiercest growler,
> An' gar the tatter'd gipseys pack
> Wi a' their bastarts on their back!
>   (31–52)

The Devil's claim that the Lords "HAND'S OWRE LIGHT ON THEM" is deeply satirical. As Kinsley has noted, Highland proprietors were renowned for their increasingly harsh actions in the late-eighteenth century, consequently meaning "the ancient confidence and affection subsisting between chiefs and their clans" was "greatly weakened" and sometimes "totally annihilated".[51] Here, the Devil unleashes an array of derogatory insults aimed at the Highlanders. He describes their insolent attitude ("stubborn Highlan spirit"); portrays them as untamed animals ("The young dogs"); hints at their drunken idleness ("Let WARK an' HUNGER mak them sober!"); before asserting that the only solution is to "Crush them a' to spails!" and beat them with a "HORSE-WHIP", or a "JOWLER". While the Highland men are depicted as wild, unkempt animals, the Devil, in one of the most degrading lines of the poem, also suggests confining Highland girls to a life of prostitution ("Let them in DRURY LANE be lesson'd!").

By using the Devil's scathing rhetoric to expose underlying prejudices in eighteenth-century Britain, Burns evokes sympathy for the apparently victimised Highlanders rather than portray them as fearsome or uncouth. Though Burns clearly sympathises with Highlanders in the poem, there are instances elsewhere where he makes references to such negative Highland stereotypes himself, such as his 1787 "Inveraray Epigram" which he wrote on his 1787 West Highland Tour:

> There's naething here but Highland pride,
> And Highland scab and hunger,
> If Providence has sent me here,
> 'Twas surely in Anger.FFK
>
> (6–9)[52]

In addition to highlighting how rife the stereotyped Highlander was (in this case proud but hungry), we might view this as yet another example of Burns's extremely adaptable poetic voice and "opinions". However, given Burns wrote this when he found "himself and his companion entirely neglected by the Inn-keeper"[53] at Inverary, the derogatory sentiments were perhaps more a product of (thirsty) circumstance rather than any deep-rooted disdain or ingrained Lowland prejudice.

In the "Address", however, there is no question where the poet's sympathies lie. The final stanza depicts the lairds meeting once again, only instead of the setting being the Shakespeare in Covent Garden, they are now in Hell with the Devil. Rather tellingly, the Earl of Breadalbane is promised the "benmost newk" (56) beside the fireplace. The satirical power of the poem peaks with the evocation that the lairds' actions have guaranteed them a place in hell, not only alongside the Devil but with various other tyrants and oppressive rulers. The Highland chiefs are joined by "HEROD" (58) (who executed John The Baptist and mocked Jesus); "POLYCRATE" (58) (the ruthless and oppressive "tyrant of Samos"); and "ALMAGRO and PIZARRO" (60) (colonial oppressors who selfishly quarrelled over Peruvian territory, eventually resulting in Diego D'Almargo's death).[54] In a final smack of malevolent irony, the Devil asserts that the Highland Lords are "weel deservin't" (61) to be among such murderous and oppressive figures. In "Address of Beelzebub", then, America is depicted as the hallowed land where liberty is attainable regardless of rank or position.

The focal point of the poem—emigration—perfectly encapsulates both the metaphorical and geographical significance of America in that it figures as both an ideological concept and real-life choice (or lack of). That the Highlanders are prevented from departing for the more socially just American continent not only highlights political oppression but also, on a physical level, their very lack of individual freedom to move or migrate. While, historically, most emigrant Gaels in America were loyal to Britain (most notably in the revolutionary years), Burns dismisses nuanced historical fact in favour of purposeful metaphorical power.[55] Accordingly, the positive flourishes of hope in the poem remain attached to *ideas* about America and its political heroes. There is ultimately a suggestion that, just as John Hancock and Benjamin Franklin did before them, the Highlanders might still "to PATRICIAN RIGHTS ASPIRE" (20) and strive for justice and equality.

"ODE FOR GENERAL WASHINGTON'S BIRTHDAY": SONS OF LIBERTY

Written almost a decade after "When Guilford Good" and eight years after "Address of Beelzebub", "Ode for General Washington's Birthday" demonstrates Burns's continuing engagement with American politics over the course of a decade. Composed in 1794, the poem, quite remarkably, did not appear in its entirety until 1873 when American bookseller Robert Clarke purchased a manuscript in London and subsequently transported it to Ohio.[56] That it first appeared across the Atlantic might seem like a fitting twist of fate given the poem extols the first US president; however, the delayed publication in Britain was more likely due to the careful censorship of Burns himself and the subsequent editors of his work. Even in his private correspondence with Frances Anna Dunlop in 1794, Burns chose to omit the first three stanzas that evoke British tyranny in America and the consequential revolution. Instead, he sent only the last nineteen lines that deal with the Scottish Wars of Independence. That Burns self-censored his revolutionary sentiments is not entirely surprising, given Dunlop was previously displeased about him expressing provocative politics "even to an intimate".[57] Considered next to Burns's similar letter to George Thomson (discussed above) where he drew a parallel between "Scots wha hae" and "not quite so ancient" struggles, it seems the poet was adept at cloaking commentary on recent events in historical Scottish imagery.

In his book *Transatlantic Radicals and the Early American Republic*, Michael Durey has outlined how George Washington was often idealised by men of radical, dissenting beliefs, particularly in Scotland and Ireland, where to some he was a "living legend, whose lengthy shadow blanketed national politics".[58] One such individual was Irish Presbyterian minister Thomas Ledlie Birch (1754–1828) who declared in a 1784 speech that Washington's political efforts had "shed their benign influence over the distressed kingdom of Ireland".[59] Significantly, Birch's full address and Washington's reply were published in the *Belfast Mercury*, before the dissenter was subsequently arrested and put on board a "prison ship on Belfast Lough, in company with a number of other arrested United Irishmen".[60] He was eventually exiled to America, arriving in New York in September 1798. While this was a fate that Burns was trying to avoid, Birch's emphasis on Washington's influence over Ireland is not without some relevance to "Ode for General Washington's Birthday.". A sales catalogue for the London auction house of Puttock and Simpson for May 1861 reveals a description of an "Ode" manuscript where "Hibernia" is substituted for "Columbia",[61] suggesting that Burns may have written an earlier draft of the poem that lauded the endeavours of Irish reformers. However, that this appears to be a cancelled text is evidence, as Gerard Carruthers suggests, that "Burns was simply more interested, or at least thought his material worked better, in the context of American revolutionary republicanism".[62]

Furthermore, it may well be that Burns, as in his works that dealt with the Scottish Wars of Independence, chose to focus on a past revolutionary conflict (as a means of stealthily provoking thought on current affairs) rather than directly reflect on pressing struggles closer to home. Either way, Burns would have been well aware that events in France had "reactivated Britain's unresolved collective trauma over the loss of the American colonies".[63] While "Jay's Treaty" of 1794 averted further conflict between the USA and Britain, allowing for largely peaceful trade in the midst of the French Revolutionary War, the earlier friction between the two nations combined with the continuing metaphorical power of America in the 1790s meant that writing about the American Revolution was no less of a risk.

As demonstrated by the case of Thomas Ledlie Birch, Burns was by no means the only figure to draw on the symbolic power of Washington during this period. One other early supporter of the French Revolution that also heralded Washington was the poet and physician Dr John Aikin (1747–1822); a figure who Burns incidentally admired for his "use of natural history in poetry".[64] In his own "Ode" to Washington, Aikin espoused bold Republican sentiments, depicting Washington as being "greater far" than those who are merely born into power and Royalty:

> Elected chief of freemen! – greater far
>   Than Kings, whose glittering parts are fix'd by birth;
>   Nam'd by thy country's voice for long try'd worth,
> Her crown in peace, as once her shield in war!
>
> Deign, WASHINGTON, to hear a British lyre,
>   That ardent greets thee with applausive lays,
>   And to the patriot hero homage pays.
> O, would the muse immortal strains inspire,
> That high beyond all Greek and Roman fame,
> Might soar to times unborn, thy purer, nobler name!
>   (5–14)[65]

The rejection of grandiose classical tradition in favour of a more "noble", democratic "hero" is a trope that, as we shall see, is also present in Burns's depiction of the American president. However, Aikin's poem is far more explicit in its heralding of Republicanism and criticism of the extant monarchy. Unsurprisingly, this led to "the virtual ruin of his professional prospects",[66] and he was dismissed from his position as a physician at Yarmouth and forced to move to London.

Burns's poem, also written in a lofty "standard English", adopts the Pindaric ode, established in English by Milton, Cowley and Dryden. On one hand, this could be perceived as his succumbing to the likes of the Earl of Buchan, David Stewart Erskine (1742–1829); one of many genteel figures who urged Burns to swap his "provincial dialect" for English in order to compose works of "greater magnitude, variety and importance".[67] It is highly unlikely that this is the true reason Burns adopted English for the poem, with the more obvious answer lying in the poet's intent on subverting the Pindaric ode. Nigel Leask has recently noted that Burns's "Ode", along with his earlier poem "A Dream", parody Thomas Warton's "Birthday Odes" through the adoption of the Pindaric stanza and the "sublime" idiom of the originals.[68] Given Warton popularly used the form to celebrate monarchs (most notably George III), Burns's deliberate subversion of the form to toast a Republican president smacks of purposeful irony.

The negation of classical tradition in the first verse reinforces the point. The speaker is not inspired by the grandiosity and might of a "Spartan tube", "Attic shell" (1) (an Athenian lyre made by stringing tortoise shells) and "lyre Eolian" (3), but instead seeks the "bold note" of "Liberty" (3). Rather than epic Greek tradition, it is Columbia's "harp" (4) that inspires the speaker to sing about resistance to tyranny. Katie Trumpener has discussed how, in the eighteenth and nineteenth centuries, the harp was variously used as both an "emblem of a nationalist republicanism" (in Scotland, Ireland and England) and as a symbol of the relationship between "a land, their people' and their culture". Burns's adoption of "Columbia's harp", then, appears all the more purposeful and laced with ideological intent.[69]

From the beginning, the reader is aware that the "tyrant" (7) is Britain, and that "Columbia", the name favoured by those anxious to assert American independence from Britain, must heroically brave insults before winning its freedom and liberation. The culminative suggestion that America is an "Empire saved" (12) seemingly negates the idea of an independent Republic being free from a monarch or any form of oligarchy (due to the imperial inflections). However, that America is later portrayed as maintaining the "Royalty of Man" (28) suggests that the "Empire" in question has been saved due to the democratic inclusion of the people, rather than referring to one ruling power as might be also be connoted.

Where the opening stanzas of Burns's "Ode" depict America's heroic resistance to tyranny and successful liberation, the latter half of the poem deals with both England and Scotland's degeneration and failure to live up to their democratic origins. Burns harnesses the metaphorical power of America to embark on an enquiry into the complex and multifaceted origins of British democratic values. Two heroic figures (one Scottish, one English) are, like Washington, used as symbols of "liberty"; yet they are mournfully lamented as being dead and buried. The penultimate stanza, which deals with England, begins with the speaker recalling Alfred, King of Wessex from 871 to 899:

> Alfred, on thy starry throne,
>   Surrounded by the tuneful choir
> The Bards that erst have struck the patriot lyre,
> And roused the freeborn Briton's soul of fire,
>   No more thy England own.
>
> (29–33)

By the eighteenth century, King Alfred (c.848–899) had been eulogised as the founder of English law and the freedom and liberalism associated with it.[70] However, Burns's speaker laments how these democratic founding principles no longer hold sway over England. In contrast to "Columbia" maintaining "The Royalty of Man", England has lost "the freeborn Briton's soul of fire". Once again, musical imagery is used to convey freedom and liberation (the "tuneful choir" and the "patriot lyre"), resonating with the earlier depiction of Columbia's "harp" and "bold note". The speaker further describes England's degeneration into tyranny and "deeds of everlasting shame":

> England in thunder calls — 'The Tyrant's cause is mine!'
>   That hour accurst, how did the fiends rejoice,
> And hell thro' all her confines raise th' exulting voice,
>   That hour which saw the generous English name
> Linkt with such damned deeds of everlasting shame!
>
> (39–43)

Rather than being anti-English, what essentially prevails is the sense that the country has failed to live up to its potential; a sentiment that would have resonated strongly with some of the more radical factions of the Whig party who called for a "backward-looking" form of reconstitution inspired by historical, specifically English incarnations of liberty. One early proponent of this type of retrospective reform was Catherine Macaulay (1731–1791) who published the radically Whig *History of England from the Revolution to the Present Time* in 1788; a book that set out to highlight the "grand areas in our history"[71] and was considered a revisionist counterpart to David Hume'e "Tory" *History of England* (1754–1761). Often dismissed as a scandalous woman infringing upon male affairs, Macaulay's polemical pamphlets, books and direct links with reformist movements (which eventually led to her being received by George Washington for ten days at Mount Vernon in 1784) certainly deserve further scholarly attention, particularly in regard to radical Whig movements of the late-eighteenth century.

Having used King Alfred to symbolise England's democratic past, Burns's speaker evokes Wallace to convey Scotland's loss of freedom. With a sense of despair, the speaker turns to Scotland with "swimming eyes" (46) and declares that the country's "soul of freedom" (47) is gone, dead and buried in the past. Caledonia's "heaven-taught song" (45) has been reduced to "babbling winds in silence" (51); a dramatic and Ossianic metaphor that suggests Scotland's political values have been lost and can only be lamented. Echoing "Scots Wha Hae" ("Lay the proud usurper's low"),[72] the speaker yearns for a time when Scotland "Braved Usurpation's boldest daring!" (59). Here, the purposeful dialectical parallels in the poem become clear. Scotland's weakened "eye" (56) is directly in contrast to Washington's "eye" (in the second stanza) that could behold "The wildest rage", with the slight sound parallels between "Columbia" and "Caledonia" reinforcing the comparative frame. The tragedy for Burns's speaker is that Scotland has not lived up to its democratic origins and failed to embrace its own liberty. The closing lines of the poem reinforce this tone of disappointment, with the repetition of "no more" emphasising a lack of future hope:

> Dark-quenched as yonder sinking star,
> No more that glance lightens afar;
> That palsied arm no more whirls on the waste of war.
>
> (57–59)

Shrouded in metaphorical darkness, Scotland is described as being of a tottering, powerless age. The vibrant, musical and triumphant depiction of "Columbia" at the beginning of the poem is in stark contrast to the "babbling", "Dark-quenched" vision of Scotland at the end. For Burns's speaker, the message is clear: the people of both Scotland and England must take inspiration from America and reaffirm their democratic origins.

This chapter opened with a discussion of how America, and in particular the American Revolution, served to inform various political debates (both as a metaphor and geographical space) in late-eighteenth-century Britain. From the three main works discussed, it is evident that Burns, like several of his contemporaries, poetically engaged with the *idea* of what America stood for and used it as a point of inspiration for selected poems and songs. While the comic, satirical portrayal of British military figures in "When Guilford Good" (in opposition to successful American leaders) hinted at the idea that Britain might progress towards political reform (led by William Pitt The Younger), both "Address of Beelzebub" and "Ode For General Washington's Birthday" reflected on continuing democratic failure, while still framing America as a successful dialectical "other".

Equally important to bear in mind, however, is the contemporary ideological treatment of this subject by more radical poets and activists in the late-eighteenth century. Recent recovery work, symposiums and forthcoming edited collections on the likes of Thomas Muir and James "Balloon" Tytler will continue to serve as a pertinent reminder that Burns, through his reluctance to publish certain works and political ambiguity, was not among this group of pro-revolutionary transatlantic radicals who were forced to flee oppression in the period.[73] Though Burns certainly took risks, he was much more careful to (as he confided to Mrs Dunlop) "set a seal on my lips, as to these unlucky politics".[74]

This "seal" was further cemented in 1792 when the Board of Excise investigated Burns in the light of accusations of sedition; an incident that would have undoubtedly affected any further poetic treatments of America (and also influenced the much delayed posthumous appearance of his two later American Works). Such a cautious approach was not adopted, for example, by Tytler, whose 1795 poem "The Rising of the Sun in the West, or The Origin and Progress of Liberty" was prefaced by a stern "Argument" about how America had been appointed by God to "break this dreadful Enchantment" of British tyranny.[75] The Scottish radical was, of course, already exiled in Salem, Massachusetts by the time of its publication. Particularly when considered next to Tytler, then, we cannot lay claim to Burns's overtly radical support for American-inspired Republicanism.

Nonetheless, the American works provide concrete evidence that Burns was certainly inspired, at the very least in an artistic sense, by America and its relatively recent revolution; thus shedding further light on the layered transnational intricacies of his creative practice.

NOTES

1. John Locke, *Two Treatises of Government* [1689], ed. Peter Laslett (Cambridge: Cambridge University Press, 2005), 301.
2. It should be noted that the original title page was marked 1690 despite being published in December 1689.
3. *The Poems and Songs*, 1:239.
4. Andrew Noble, "Burns, Scotland, and the American Revolution", in *Robert Burns and Culture*, ed. Alker, Davis and Nelson, 31. For another analysis of Burns's poetry in relation to "American liberty" see Roger Fechner, "Burns and American Liberty", in *Love and Liberty: Robert Burns; A Bicentenary Celebration*, ed. Simpson (East Lothian: Tuckwell Press, 1997), 274–288.
5. *Letters*, 1:19.
6. *Glasgow and Evening Intelligencer*, 23 April 1792.
7. Nigel Leask, ed., *The Oxford Edition of the Works of Robert Burns, Volume I: Commonplace Books, Tour Journals, and Miscellaneous Prose* (Oxford: Oxford University Press, 2014), 288.
8. Ibid., 287.
9. *The Bard*, 307.
10. *Letters*, 1:337.
11. *Letters*, 1:410.
12. See Andrew S. Skinner, "Adam Smith and the American Revolution", *Presidential Studies Quarterly*, 7, nos. 2 and 3 (1977): 75–87.
13. Wil Verhoven, *Americomania and the French Revolution Debate in Britain, 1789–1802* (Cambridge: Cambridge University Press, 2013), 247.
14. *Letters*, 2:236.
15. Similar to the anniversary of Burns's birth in 2009, the 250th anniversary of Thomas Muir's birth in 2009 caused a wave of reinvigorated critical and popular attention.
16. See Bruce P. Lenman, "Aristocratic 'Country' Whiggery in Scotland and The American Revolution", in *Scotland and America in the Age of*

Enlightenment, ed., Richard B. Sher and Jeffrey R. Smitten (Edinburgh: Edinburgh University Press, 1990), 180–192.

17. Murray Pittock has recently called James Kinsley's attributed date of authorship (1784) into question, describing it as being "suppositiously dependent on the subject matter". See *The Oxford Edition of the Works of Robert Burns*, 3:28.

18. For a further discussion of this context see Emma Macleod, *British Visions of America, 1775–1820* (London: Pickering & Chatto, 2013).

19. *Letters*, 1:77.

20. *The Oxford Edition of the Works of Robert Burns*, 2:154.

21. Peter D. G. Thomas, "North, Frederick, Second Earl of Guilford [Lord North] (1732–1792)". Accessed 17 January 2013. http://www.oxforddnb.com/view/article/2034.

22. Bernard Bailyn, ed., *The Debate on the Constitution: Federalist and Antifederalist Speeches, Articles, and Letters During the Struggle Over Ratification, Part One: September 1787 to February 1788* (New York: The Library of America, 1993), 949.

23. H. M. Chichester, "Montgomery, Richard (1738–1775)". Accessed 18 January 2013. http://www.oxforddnb.com/view/article/19072.

24. *The Oxford Edition of the Works of Robert Burns*, 3: 28.

25. Ira D. Gruber, "Clinton, Sir Henry (1730–1795)". Accessed 19 January 2013. http://www.oxforddnb.com/view/article/5681.

26. N. A. M. Rodger, "Montagu, John, Fourth Earl of Sandwich (1718–1792)". Accessed 19 January 2013. http://www.oxforddnb.com/view/article/19026.

27. Piers Mackesy, "Germain, George Sackville, First Viscount Sackville (1716–1785)". Accessed 21 January 2013. http://www.oxforddnb.com/view/article/10566.

28. L. G. Mitchell, *Charles James Fox* (Oxford: Oxford University Press, 1992), 27.

29. Michael Fry, "Erskine, Henry (1746–1817)". Accessed 20 May 2013. http://www.oxforddnb.com/view/article/8858.

30. Ibid.

31. Nigel Leask, *Robert Burns and Pastoral: Poetry and Improvement in Late Eighteenth-Century Scotland* (Oxford: Oxford University Press, 2010), 188.

32. Clark Hunter, ed., *The Life and Letters of Alexander Wilson* (Philadelphia: The American Philosophical Society, 1983), 48.

33. Ibid., 47. Wilson sent a letter to William Sharp on Tuesday 22 May 1792, demanding money by threats and blackmail.

34. L. G. Mitchell, "Fox, Charles James (1749–1806)". Accessed 21 January 2013. http://www.oxforddnb.com/view/article/10024.

35. Colin Kidd, "Burns and Politics", in *The Edinburgh Companion to Robert Burns*, ed. Carruthers, 61.
36. *Robert Burns and Pastoral*, 142.
37. "Historical Thesaurus". Accessed 27 December 2015. http://historicalthesaurus.arts.gla.ac.uk/category-selection/?qsearch=slee.
38. "Dictionary of the Scots Language". Accessed 27 December 2015. http://www.dsl.ac.uk/entry/snd/slee.
39. James Kinsley gives the name of the tune as "The Earl of Glencairns's". See *The Poems and Songs*, 3:1026–1027. For a fuller discussion of Burns's association with the tune "Killiecrankie", see James Hogg, *The Forest Minstrel* [1810], ed., Peter Garside, Peter Horfsall, and Richard D. Jackson (Edinburgh: Edinburgh University Press, 2006), 338–339. See also *The Oxford Edition of the Works of Robert Burns*, 3:28–29.
40. This is also an allusion to the Jacobite song "Up and Warn A', Wullie". See *The Poems and Songs*, 3:1026–1027.
41. Harry T. Dickinson, ed., *British Pamphlets on the American Revolution, 1763–1785* (London: Pickering & Chatto, 2008).
42. John Robotham, "The Reading of Robert Burns", *Bulletin of the New York Public Library* 74, no. 9 (1970): 561–576.
43. For a selection of political cartoons featuring Fox, North and other notable politicians of the period, see Darper Hill, ed., *The Satirical Etchings of James Gillray* (Mineola: Dover, 1976).
44. *The Poems and Songs*, 1:254.
45. *The Poems and Songs*, 3:1184.
46. For a full account of the episode see *The Oxford Edition of the Works of Robert Burns*, 1:142, 358n.
47. Susan Manning, *Poetics of Character: Transatlantic Encounters 1700–1900* (Cambridge: Cambridge University Press, 2013), 240.
48. See, for example, J. P. Maclean, *An Historical Account of the Settlements of Scotch Highlanders in America Prior to the Peace of Paris in 1783 Together with Notices of Highland Regiments and Biographical Sketches* (Glasgow: John Mackay, 1900).
49. *Robert Burns and Pastoral*, 197–198.
50. P. J. Marshall, *Remaking the British Atlantic: The United States and the British Empire After American Independence* (Oxford: Oxford University Press, 2012), 137.
51. *The Poems and Songs*, 3:1185.
52. *The Oxford Edition of the Works of Robert Burns*, 1:136.
53. Ibid.
54. *The Poems and Songs*, 1:1185–1186.
55. See Matthew P. Dziennik, *The Fatal Land: War, Empire and the Highland Soldier in British America* (New Haven: Yale University Press, 2015).

56. Carruthers, "Burns's Political Reputation in North America", 91.

57. J. DeLancey Ferguson, "New Light on the Burns-Dunlop Estrangement", *Publication of the Modern Language Association (PMLA)* 44, no. 4 (1929), 1144. As Ferguson argues, Burns's political sentiments caused offence to Dunlop and would eventually lead to their epistolary "estrangement".

58. Michael Durey, *Transatlantic Radicals and the Early American Republic* (Lawrence: University Press of Kansas, 1997), 84–85.

59. Ibid., 85.

60. W. D. Bailie, "Birch, Thomas Ledlie (1754–1828)". Accessed 20 November 2015. http://www.oxforddnb.com/view/article/2437.

61. "First Day's Sale", in *Sales Catalogue for Puttock and Simpson* (1861), 24.

62. Gerard Carruthers, "Burns and Ireland", *International Journal of Scottish Literature* 6 (Spring/Summer, 2010), 4.

63. *Americomania*, 5.

64. *The Bard*, 233.

65. Francis Johnston and William Hamilton, eds., *The Washingtoniana: Containing a Sketch of the Life and Death of the Late Gen. George Washington, with a Collection of Elegant Eulogies, Orations, Poems, &c., Sacred to His Memory* (Lancaster: William Hamilton, 1802), 25.

66. Marilyn L. Brooks, "Aikin, John (1747–1822)". Accessed 15 November 2013. http://www.oxforddnb.com/view/article/230.

67. David Craig, *Scottish Literature and the Scottish People* (London: Chatto & Windus, 1961), 105.

68. *Robert Burns and Pastoral*, 137.

69. See Katie Trumpener, *Bardic Nationalism: The Romantic Novel and the British Empire* (Princeton: Princeton University Press, 1997), 19.

70. Patrick Wormald, "Alfred (848/9–899)". Accessed 27 December 2015. http://www.oxforddnb.com/view/article/183.

71. Catherine Macaulay, *History of England from the Revolution to the Present Time* (London: T. Cadell and J. Walter, 1778), 2.

72. *The Poems and Songs*, 2:708.

73. See "Thomas Muir at 250". Accessed 19 November 2015. http://www.thomasmuir.co.uk/thomasmuir250.html. On Friday 30 October 2015, a symposium was held at the University of Glasgow to honour the 250th anniversary of Muir's birth with an edited essay collection to follow. Incidentally, the event was co-organised by The Centre For Robert Burns Studies.

74. Burns wrote to Mrs Dunlop on 2 January 1793 though a large section of the manuscript was later cut away, presumably by someone fearful for Burns's political reputation. See *The Bard*, 361–362.

75. James Tytler, *The Rising of the Sun in the West, or the Origin and Progress of Liberty* (Salem: William Carlton, 1795), Preface.

PART II

American Print Culture and Poets

CHAPTER 3

"Tho' I to Foreign Lands": Burns's Poetry in America, c.1786–1801

> One Burns a Plowman near Kilmarnock has lately published a volume of Poems that draw much attention...[1]
>
> —William Richardson (1787)

While Robert Burns never actually made passage across the Atlantic "to foreign lands",[2] his poems and songs spread to America swiftly after the success of his first published volumes in Britain. The popularity and success of the 1786 Kilmarnock edition (*Poems, Chiefly in The Scottish Dialect)* provided further prospects for Burns at home, meaning that his tentative and indeed controversial emigration plans were to be put on hold. Within weeks of the publication of the Kilmarnock edition, Burns wrote to John Richmond with the intention "to try a second edition of my book" which would detain him "a little longer in the country".[3]

The second appearance of Burns's poetry "in guid black prent",[4] sold by William Creech in Edinburgh on 21 April 1787, famously catapulted the poet into the cultural sphere of Scotland's most eminent literati. In the same year, a third "London edition" was published and sold by Andrew Strahan and Thomas Cadell in collaboration with Creech.[5] While Burns entertained possible future patrons in Edinburgh, his volume, quite remarkably, was already being reprinted and sold in America as early as July 1788. In addition to Burns's poetry and songs arriving via "the lips and fiddles of immigrants",[6] several other transatlantic convergences, in print culture, trade and intellectual property laws, helped to facilitate the spread of his work and reputation.

© The Author(s) 2018
A. Sood, *Robert Burns and the United States of America*,
https://doi.org/10.1007/978-3-319-94445-6_3

Trading links in the late-eighteenth century meant that Scottish merchants were regularly in contact with North American seaports, particularly Philadelphia and New York, the main trading hubs on the Eastern seaboard. These links naturally extended beyond commerce in that news, books and political ideas were regularly exchanged back and forth across the Atlantic. As an article in the first *Glasgow Magazine and Review* suggested in 1783, without such a strong "connection between Commerce and the Liberal Arts" the "western part of the world" might not have emerged from "profound ignorance and barbarism"[7]; a statement that reveals as much about ideas of cultural superiority (discussed later in Chapter 5) as it does about Atlantic literary exchange.

Just six months after the publication of the Kilmarnock edition, William Richardson (1743–1814), then Professor of Humanity at The University of Glasgow, wrote a letter to his friend S. Rose revealing that Burns's volume had proved popular among travelling merchants, many of whom were trading in North America:

> One Burns a Plowman near Kilmarnock has lately published a volume of Poems that draw much attention. They are wonderful from a mere Plowman - and some of them pretty...For the members of the Caledonian Hunt & the Glasgow Manufacturers & Merchants, [illegible] who never read a verse before in their days are all furiously fond of them...[8]

That these merchants had "never read a verse before" yet were "furiously fond" of Burns is an early indicator of the poet's wide reach; his volume proving popular with individuals who were typically less concerned with the Arts and more focused on commercial pursuits. Yet it was not the travelling "manufacturers and merchants" who occasionally "read a verse" that facilitated the dissemination of Burns's work in the USA, but rather the entrepreneurial emigrant booksellers and printers who sold and reprinted *Poems* for profit.

The first record of *Poems* being available in America (though not an "American Edition" or reprint) can be found in an advertisement announcing the opening of a bookstore owned by John Reid, a Glasgow-born emigrant who had recently set up shop in New York.[9] The advertisement, placed in the New York-based *Independent Journal* of 7 July 1787, introduced the new bookseller before printing a considerable list of available titles among which *Poems* was included. Given the proximity of the advertisement to Creech's recently published Edinburgh edition, it is likely that Reid had purchased the volume in Scotland before transporting it to America along with a stock of other books.[10] The *Independent Journal* (in which Reid's advertisement was placed) was printed and edited by John and Archibald Mclean; also natives of Glasgow who moved to New York in 1783 and, as will subsequently be discussed, published the second (New York) American Edition of Burns's *Poems* in 1788. Here, we can already begin to see how a loosely connected network of Scots-born printers and booksellers—John Reid, Peter Stewart, John and Archibald Maclean—were to be influential on the spread and accessibility of Burns's work in America before the turn of the nineteenth century.

EARLY NEWSPAPER PRINTINGS, C.1787–1788

The same month that the New York-based *Independent Journal* printed John Reid's advertisement in New York, the *Pennsylvania Packet, and Daily Advertiser* printed the "The Rigs o Barley" on 24 July 1787.[11] The *Pennsylvania Packet* was founded in 1771 by John Dunlap (1747–1812). Born in Strabane, Northern Ireland, Dunlap emigrated to Philadelphia in 1757 to work as an apprentice bookseller and quickly progressed to become one the most eminent printers in late-eighteenth-century America. Under the orders of John Hancock (the same man praised by Burns in "Address of Beelzebub"), Dunlap produced the first copies of the "Declaration of Independence" while under contract to the Continental Congress in 1776. An Irishman turned American patriot, he also fought extensively in the Revolutionary War, seeing combat at the battles of Princeton and Trenton, and later rising to the rank of major in the First Troop Philadelphia City Cavalry. In his position as "Printer of The Journals of the Continental Congress", Dunlap was succeeded by David C. Claypoole (1757–1849) who later became his business partner at the *Pennsylvania Packet*.[12] During this period, Claypoole regularly exchanged letters with George Washington who requested that the Philadelphian newspaper be sent directly to his home in Mount Vernon.[13] That the paper's editors were inherently tied to America's political landscape (in both professional and personal capacities) is further demonstrated by the fact they also printed several of the Federalist and Anti-Federalist essays, letters and debates between 1787 and 1789.[14]

In spite of the newspaper's political tenor, Rhona Brown notes that when it came to printing Burns's work the editorial choices of the paper demonstrated an "appetite for the sentimental, pious Heaven-taught ploughman", suggesting that the poet's early appeal may have been human rather than political.[15] Indeed, the appearance of "The Rigs o' Barley" in July 1787 was attributed to "ROBERT BURNS, the celebrated Ayrshire Ploughman".[16] The subsequent printing of the "Banks of Ayr" and "Behind yon hills where Stinchar flows" the following November is consistent with the image of a rustic poet concerned with rural, nostalgic themes set in the Scottish countryside. Similarly, the appearances of "Prayer in the Prospect of Death", "A Prayer under the Pressure of violent anguish" and "The First Six verses of the nineteenth Psalm" provide further evidence of an "appetite" for Burns's (now relatively obscure) pious works and nostalgic constructions of pastoral Scotland.

However, the *Pennsylvania Packet* also printed some of Burns's more sociopolitically biting works such as "Man Was Made to Mourn" and, most notably, "When Guilford Good".[17] While no commentary or introduction to Burns's American political song was provided, the satirical portrayal of bumbling British figures and praise of revolutionary heroes would surely not have escaped the newspaper's readership nor its editors; particularly given Dunlap had fought in the war himself and later printed broadside copies of the Declaration of Independence. Moreover, the pastoral politics of both "Man Was Made to Mourn" and "The Cotter's Saturday Night" might well have taken on new resonances in the context of late-eighteenth-century Philadelphia, bringing to mind Colleen Glenney Boggs' assertion that texts and authors can often "take on different meanings in transatlantic contexts".[18]

In a recent study on the transatlantic circulation of Mary Shelley's *Frankenstein*, Elizabeth Young has suggested how the English novel could be variously reinterpreted in nineteenth-century America. For Young, *Frankenstein* spoke directly to "specific questions of national and racial formation in the nineteenth-century U.S. body politic"[19] and thus its arrival in America gave birth to several new frames of analysis and interpretation. Similarly, we might venture to speculate on how fresh sociopolitical contexts (namely late-eighteenth-century Philadelphia) might have impacted upon the initial printing and reception of some of Burns's poems in the *Pennsylvania Packet*.

Nigel Leask has recently outlined how the pastoral politics of "Man Was Made to Mourn" can be linked to the contemporary issue of "agricultural improvement" and its relation to commercial society in

Scotland, as theorised by philosophers such as Adam Fergusson (1723–1816) and Adam Smith (1723–1790).[20] Particularly in late-eighteenth-century Pennsylvania, where rapid urbanisation and the rise of commercial industries began to threaten traditional agrarianism, similar debates over the future of commerce, industry and agriculture emerged. These issues were raised in the Federalist and Anti-Federalist papers that appeared—primarily in New York and Philadelphian newspapers—between 1787 and 1789.[21] That Burns, with all his agricultural associations ("Ayrshire Ploughman"), began to be regularly printed in the same period that saw national divisions over, among other issues relating to the ratification of the Constitution, commerce and agriculture, is surely of some significance.

On the one hand, the speaker of Burns's "Man Was Made to Mourn" might be seen to align with the Anti-Federalists who, largely comprised of farmers and tradesmen, opposed centralised, hierarchal systems of governance that infringed upon the rights of landowning, self-sufficient agrarians. Resonantly, Burns's speaker has become entrapped (a "lordling's slave")[22] by the capitalisation of agriculture ("Where hundreds labour to support/A haughty lordling's pride") (19–20) and laments over losing both self-sufficiency and self-governance ("Man then is useful to his kind/Supported in his right") (35–36). However, it should be noted that the *Pennsylvania Packet* was considered a "Federalist newspaper" due to its printed calls for state delegates to ratify the constitution.[23] While this would seemingly be at odds with the above Anti-Federalist reading of Burns's poem, the paper did also— albeit more sporadically—publish Anti-Federalist sentiments.

Even after the Pennsylvania Convention ratified on 12 December 1787, a dissenting statement of Anti-Federalist objections titled "The Address and Reasons of Dissent of the Minority of the Convention of Pennsylvania to their Constituents" appeared just two weeks later.[24] Moreover, many of the Federalists (such as James Madison who would later become a member of Thomas Jefferson's Democratic Republican party) were also agrarians who advocated that democratic freedom was best achieved in an agricultural society.[25] Here, the complexity and scope of the Federalist and Anti-Federalist ideologies—particularly when it came to agriculture and commerce—increases rather than impedes the possibility that Burns's poems might have taken on added resonances in this new sociopolitical context.

Just a few months after "Man Was Made to Mourn" appeared, the *Pennsylvania Packet* printed "The Cotter's Saturday Night" in its entirety; a politicised, pastoral poem that also touches upon several themes pertinent to the context of agrarian debates in late-eighteenth-century Philadelphia. Burns's speaker, advocating agrarian self-sufficiency, envisions a virtuous population comprised of "thy hardy sons of *rustic toil*"[26] and dismisses "Princes and lords" (165) who have been tainted by "luxury's contagion" (177). For the speaker, the pastoral "*cottage*" is equal to, or even mightier than, the "*Palace*" while "An honest man's the noble work of GOD" (166–168). The former line is strikingly congruous with early nineteenth-century Jeffersonian ideals of "Agrarian Republicanism",[27] whereby a virtuous, moral superiority was inherently placed upon (in Jefferson's own words) "those who labor in the earth" since they are "the chosen people of God".[28]

A testament to the transnational "world of encounters" discussed previously, Jefferson had partly formed his ideas on agricultural virtue and improvement through his own engagement with Scottish philosophers such as Henry Home, Lord Kames (1696–1782), whose 1776 work *The Gentleman Farmer* suggested that agricultural improvement might bring man closer to a "natural", virtuous state.[29] We also know from both Jefferson's personal library and an 1813 letter to John Waldo that he was an admirer of Burns, with the president describing his as poetry "beautiful".[30] Whether or not he read and identified strains of Agrarian politics similar to his own in "The Cotter's Saturday Night" is a matter of conjecture. Regardless, on the basis of "Man Was Made to Mourn" and "The Cotter's Saturday Night" at least, it seems highly plausible that Burns's pastoral poetry would have been open to fresh frames of interpretation in the early USA.[31]

As noted, the *Pennsylvania Packet* also printed a succession of Burns's "religious" poems, and it is therefore worth considering the theological climate of Philadelphia during the period. As we shall see, there is much to suggest that these poems may have been chosen by the editors for reasons other than their apparent espousal of Presbyterian piety. By the eighteenth century, the old Quaker hegemony over most aspects of Philadelphia's political and social life had broken down and the Presbyterian element in the city had become increasingly powerful.[32] It was in Philadelphia that the first American Presbytery was assembled in 1706, and by 1789, just after the first appearances of Burns's poems, the Presbyterian Church in the USA was formed and led by

John Witherspoon (1723–1794). During the Revolutionary years, Philadelphia was a magnet for radical Irish Presbyterian ministers such as Thomas Ledlie Birch who, as discussed in Chapter 2, supported the American cause from its early stages and interpreted it as "the unfolding of Divine Destiny".[33] Birch, who had studied under the radical social philosopher John Millar at the University of Glasgow in 1770, embraced a complex form of revolutionary liberalism that conflated radical political thought with religious conservatism.

Despite being attached to a somewhat repressive theology, the radical spirit of Presbyterians such as Birch often manifested in sympathy for the American cause. As Liam McIlvanney has noted, radical Presbyterians often had a "hostile relationship with the crown"; pushed for a more "democratic system of government"; and strongly opposed "monarchical absolutism".[34] Reconsidering Burns's "To Ruin"[35] (which appeared in the *Pennsylvania Packet* in May 1788) we might easily draw out such liberal, political inflections amidst the sternly Calvinist rhetoric. The poem's message is at once religious and political; no government, monarchy or man is greater than the "Inexorable lord!" (1) whose "breathing word" (2) could destruct the "mightiest empire" (3). The humbling tone is most certainly God-fearing, yet the rejection of "empire" would surely strike a reverberating political chord in the context of an early Republic that had recently won independence from a ruling monarch. After all, there was a long established, if complex, interrelationship between Christianity and the American revolutionary spirit.[36]

Swift Reprints: The New York and Philadelphia Editions, c.1787–1788

As interest in Burns increased through the circulation of his poems in the New York and Philadelphian press, proposals began to appear for an American reprinting of *Poems*. These proposals marked the beginning of longer critical reviews and short biographical anecdotes about the "Ayrshire Ploughman". On 29 August 1787, the *Independent Journal* called on readers to subscribe for copies of a forthcoming American edition, stating that the "fame of this Author is spreading rapidly" and "the Merit of his Works is acknowledged by all who have had an opportunity of seeing them".[37] In line with the political ties of fellow emigrant editors John Dunlap and David C. Claypoole, J. and A. Maclean's

Independent Journal had serially published the Federalist Papers between October 1787 and 1788. The *Independent Journal* proposal is a fine example of entrepreneurial book advertising from the period, having promised potential subscribers that the "work will be printed on a new Type and good paper, in one handsome Volume Octavo" and that "Those who subscribe for twelve Copies, will have a thirteenth gratis".[38]

Unauthorised reprints of popular books were common in late-eighteenth-century America where, as Colleen Glenney Boggs notes, "publishers were not required to pay royalties to foreign authors, making it very attractive for American publishers to republish British works".[39] This vibrant reprint culture continued right up until the later nineteenth century when laws began to be tightened. It is only relatively recently, however, that scholars have come to recognise the magnitude of its impact on the transatlantic dissemination of literature in the eighteenth and nineteenth centuries, leading to a constellation of scholarly work on the processes by which texts, and indeed publishers, circulated around the Atlantic.[40] Thanks to the work of Richard Sher, Meredith McGill and Joseph Rezek among others, it is now more widely known that British emigrants with professional backgrounds swiftly capitalised on both copyright loopholes and the advent of a burgeoning American periodical press; demonstrated by the fact that eighteen individuals of British or Irish descent edited no fewer than forty-nine newspapers and magazines in America between 1783 and 1800.[41]

Transatlantic reprints also had wider implications that may have impacted upon readership demographics. William St. Clair has outlined how the price of reprinted British books were considerably lower than locally produced texts, meaning that Americans, in opting for cheaper reprinted books, had easier access to the literature being written in Great Britain than most of their contemporaries across the Ocean. St. Clair goes as far to call the late-eighteenth-century American copyright regime as "the single most important structural determinant of American reading for nearly a century".[42] These assertions ring true when mapping Burns's early American publication history (See Appendix A). Moreover, these editions were arguably more affordable (comparatively speaking) than in Britain and thus more accessible to a wider range of potential American readers.[43]

Included in J. and A. Maclean's advertisement were selected extracts from Henry Mackenzie's 1786 unsigned essay in the Edinburgh-based *Lounger,* which became "the most influential contemporary account of

Burns's poetry".[44] The editors, undoubtedly with good commerce in mind, selected the parts of Mackenzie's review, evidently circulating in America, that seemed most appropriate for their book proposal. There is an emphasis on Burns's "Genius"[45] followed by a flattering description of poems including "The Vision", "Invocation to Ruin" and his "Dialogue of the Dogs", most obviously a reference to "The Twa Dogs". Burns's poetic abilities, though praised, were underlined by the now-famous remark that he was a "Heaven-taught Ploughman" from a "humble and unlettered station". Here, J. and A. Maclean appropriate Mackenzie's expression (which caused lasting confusion through its suggestion that Burns was untutored) into their intriguing call for proposals, providing them with a USP, or "unique selling proposition", for their latest book proposal.

Though the proposal appeared as early as August 1787, the actual reprinting was delayed for over a year, most likely due to a lack of subscribers. This does not necessarily correlate with a lack of interest since matters may have been complicated by the increasing availability of the original London and Edinburgh editions that continued to be imported from Britain to America. Undeterred, the editors continued to attract interest by reprinting the same advertisement in the New York-based *Daily Advertiser* and *Morning Post* between August and October 1787, with the publication finally appearing in December 1788. However, while J. and A. Maclean were busy gathering subscriptions over the course of a year in New York, Peter Stewart and George Hyde had already started printing an edition of Burns's *Poems* in Philadelphia.

The Philadelphian partners, also Scots emigrants, produced a small-scale printing in July 1788 (thus recognised as the first ever American Edition of Burns's poetry). Incidentally, the first advertisement for the edition came in the *Pennsylvania Packet* and made references to the poems that had previously appeared in the newspaper including "Man was made to mourn", "The Cotter's Saturday Night" and "Invocation to Ruin".[46] While J. and A. Maclean's proposals contained extracts from Mackenzie's unsigned review in *The Lounger*, the advertisement for the Philadelphia edition quoted from James Anderson's appraisal, originally published in London's *Monthly Review* in December 1786. The Anderson excerpt largely corresponded with Mackenzie's image of Burns as an untutored ploughman through its description of the poet's "simple" and "artless" strains, although Anderson did obscure a completely rustic view of the poet by commenting on his "delicacy".[47]

There were, however, some significant differences between the first two American editions. Such differences would become a recurring trend in the decades that followed as non-standardised American editions differed greatly in style, content and presentation. Perhaps the most striking textual variation in the New York edition was its inclusion of the full names of satirised politicians in Burns's "A Fragment", or "When Guilford Good". Burns had initially omitted the full names of political figures (with both the Edinburgh and Philadelphia editions obscuring letters from their full titles as he had seemingly intended). However, in the New York edition, the sixteen names of prominent political figures from the American War were printed in full.[48] While the idea that J. and A. Maclean did this—bearing in mind the political inflection of the *Independent Journal*—with purposeful intent might be feasible, it is more likely that the full names appeared due to careless editorial adherence.

Another addition to the New York printing was the inclusion of "Scots poems, selected from the works of Robert Ferguson [sic]" (including "The Farmer's Ingle", "Braid Claith", "Hallow Fair", "Ode to the Bee", "On Seeing a Butterfly in the Street", "Ode to Gowdspink", "Caller Water" and "Epilogue Spoken by Mr. Wilson"). Though haphazardly tacked on to the final pages of the book, an advertisement in the *Independent Journal* of 12 July 1788 stated that the addition of Fergusson's poems "without any additional Expence [sic]" made the "Work more worthy of public patronage".[49] This was, perhaps, J. and A. Maclean's attempt at compensating subscribers who were still waiting for their copy after some months (blaming the "extream scarcity" [sic] of fine printing paper)[50] and assuring them that it would surpass the earlier Philadelphia volume. While the advertisement's description of Fergusson as "celebrated" connotes some sense of local familiarity, it is also notable that there were no American reprints of *Poems on Various Subjects* or any other collected edition.

However, given Fergusson's work was a fixture in the Scottish periodical press (particularly in Walter Ruddiman's *Weekly Magazine*), it is likely that pamphlets and periodicals containing his poems were circulating in America on some small scale. Moreover, enthusiasm for Burns's poetry also caused a rejuvenated interest in his "elder brother in Misfortune",[51] with Rhona Brown noting that "the construction of Robert Fergusson grew and mutated with the advent of Burns".[52] Susan Manning states that the bibliographic conflation of the two poets was evident in Scotland from 1787 onwards when booksellers, riding on the current vogue for Burns, began to re-advertise Fergusson's works.[53] However, little further commentary on Fergusson can be found in American periodicals from the period, not to mention that his poems appeared back to back with Burns's, without any indication of a change of authorship, in the edition.

With both the Philadelphia and New York editions in circulation by the end of 1788, the two volumes gradually became available in other states. Between 1789 and 1796, advertisement for *Poems* had appeared in Virginia, North Carolina, Massachusetts, Maryland and Rhode Island, primarily in daily newspapers such as the *Herald of Freedom* (Boston), *New York Daily Gazette, Salem Gazette* and *State Gazette of North Carolina*. Though both editions were widely available, there would not be another reprinting of *Poems* until after the poet's death when Philadelphia printers Patterson and Cochran reprinted the volume in 1798. One other notable Burns-related reprint that occurred in the period was an American edition of James Johnson's *Scots Musical Museum,* edited by John Aitken and printed in Philadelphia, 1797. Of course, the popularity of Scots songs in America had preceded Burns.

One year before the first American editions of *Poems* appeared, for example, a work by Alexander Reinagle (1756–1809) titled *A Select Collection of the most favourite Scots Tunes. With variations for the piano forte or harpsichord* was being printed and sold in Philadelphia.[54] As Serge Hovey has noted, by the late-eighteenth century Scottish ballads had long travelled to America anonymously, transforming and assimilating into American culture through oral and musical means. In the first volume of *The Robert Burns Song Book*, Hovey notes that Scots songs often "settled and evolved new variants" particularly "in the Appalachians", further citing the example of the "Soldier's Joy" which came to be regarded as a classic of the American fiddle canon, but was previously used by Burns for his cantata "The Jolly Beggars".[55]

As such, a portion of Burns's songs, particularly those he collected rather than authored, would have had slightly different processes of transmission and influence (oral and musical).[56] Yet even if some of the songs (or melodies) in Aitken's volume were already familiar to Scots emigrants, its publication would have surely increased awareness of Burns's hand in writing, collecting and reworking Scottish ballads. Aitken prefaced his edition with William Tytler's essay "On the Origins of Scottish Music", first published in Hugo Arnot's *The History of Edinburgh* (1779), which was perhaps deemed an appropriate

inclusion for transnational American audiences. He also added fully realised accompaniments instead of figured basses.[57] However, given there
are few surviving copies of the edition, it probably had a relatively small
print run and, unlike the New York and Philadelphia editions of *Poems*,
it does not appear to have been advertised or sold in other states beyond
Philadelphia.[58] The timely piracy of the Philadelphia *Scots Musical
Museum* might also be attributed to the upsurge of attention that the
poet's life and work received (on both sides of the Atlantic) in the immediate period following his death.

BIOGRAPHICAL INTEREST

In 1793, *The New York Magazine, or Literary Repository*, a publication
that counted William Dunlap (1766–1839), Charles Brockden Brown
(1771–1810) and Joel Barlow (1754–1812) among its regular con-
tributors, printed an article reflecting on the increasing fame of Burns
("The Poems of Robert Burns[…]are in every person's hands") and
quoted passages from Robert Heron's *Observations made in a journey
through the Western Counties of Scotland*. Heron's *Observations* reads, in
parts, like an initial draft of his later biography of the poet, published
in 1797. Notably, his reflections on Burns's education and honed poetic
craft veered away from a wholly rustic image of the "Heaven-taught
ploughman"; with the poet being praised for his "prudence and propriety" and ability to write "elevated" pastoral poetry.[59] However, in
the year following Burns's death, the same publication (*The New York
Magazine*) printed an article titled "Some of Account of Robert Burns"
which was to significantly taint and complicate Burn's reputation. The
article contained extracts from an obituary that had originally appeared
in the *The London Chronicle* of July 1796, apparently written by George
Thomson.[60]

   With an emphasis on the "failings" of Burns's genius, Thomson
reflects on how the poet wasted his time "in those haunts of village fes-
tivity" to which he "was but too immoderately attached", before declaring that he "was not qualified to fill a superior station to that which was
assigned him" due to his "distempered imagination".[61] Juxtaposed with
(selected extracts of) Heron's depiction of Burns conducting himself
with "wonderful prudence and propriety", the poet's biographical image
had evidently become malleable, with different accounts reflecting the
interests and prejudices of those writing and re-writing his life story.[62]

Further complicating these variable accounts in America, however, was the fact that newspaper editors (and subsequently book publishers) had the power to select which reviews, obituaries or biographical accounts to clip and draw upon, adding yet another layer of complexity to competing representations of Burns.

In his recent book *The Genius of Scotland* (2015), Corey Andrews has mapped the mechanisms of "cultural production" that shaped, altered and continually revised Burns's posthumous reputation. Andrews draws on theory by Pierre Bourdieu to establish how "artistic mediators"[63] (publishers, critics, biographers and so forth) reworked and commodified Burns's life story by crafting the image of a "brilliant but deeply flawed genius of Scotland".[64] Andrews describes Thomson's obituary as a "thinly-veiled disapproval" of the poet's lifestyle that focused on his moral "failings", further suggesting that the prickly (epistolary) relationship between the two might have affected Thomson's portrayal of Burns ("the two never met and frequently did not see eye to eye").[65] Regardless of Thomson's personal agenda, the swift publication of the obituary in New York, just months after appearing in London, is a testament to how rapidly these processes of "cultural production" had begun to transform the posthumous reputation of Burns in America as well as in Britain. After its initial American appearance in *The New York Magazine*, the obituary was subsequently reprinted in *The American Universal Magazine* and *The Philadelphia Magazine* the same year.[66]

In addition to the circulation of Thomson's obituary, excerpts from Heron's full biography *A Memoir of the Life of the Late Robert Burns* began to appear, initially in *The Philadelphia Magazine* in 1798. While the full *Memoir* also suggests that Burns was prey to "moral failings" and imbecility, the extracts printed in the Philadelphian publication were generally a positive overview of the poet's character and abilities. Heron's biography has been widely derided by critics for its misrepresentations and errors, yet the *Philadelphia Magazine* extract provides valuable insights into Burns's development as a poet. Eschewing the "Heaven-taught" myth, the *Philadelphia Magazine* article lavishes praise on the Scottish Parish School education system ("the most beneficial that have been ever instituted in any country") and attributes it for nurturing the "infant energies" of Burns before tracing his intellectual development from "labour to learning".

Furthermore, Burns is portrayed as an ardent scholar; having read the likes of Blair, Beattie and "the wild strains of *Ossian*".[67] Here, we can again see how American editors (as "artistic mediators") could prune source texts to fit their own agenda or interests.[68] Another notable aspect of the article is its implicit association of Burns with Freemasonary ("He eagerly sought admission into the brotherhood of *Free masons*"). Burns would famously become the toast of Masonic clubs on both sides of the Atlantic, and one of the largest Burns collections in North America remains in the Library of the Supreme Council, 33°, Washington, DC.[69] This early Masonic association was bolstered by a subsequent issue of *The Philadelphia Magazine* the same year where the opening verses of "Farewell to the Brethren of St James's Lodge, Tarbolton" were printed under the bold title "MASONIC SONG".[70]

Unlike his earlier *Observations*, Heron's full *Memoir* does not appear to have been reprinted in America. Consequently, these selective and shortened extracts suggest that the early biographer's influence may have been minimal. Rather than his songs and poetry, then, it was Burns's life that became the staple of interest in the American press towards the end of the eighteenth century. Even the poetic elegies that appeared reflected heavily on Burns's intriguing and contested life story. In 1797, a poetic tribute by Edward Rushton (1756–1814) appeared in the New York-based *Time-Piece*. It was reprinted in several American newspapers and literary periodicals the same year including *The Medley* (20 October) and *New York Gazette* (2 October). The *American Daily Advertiser* later printed and attributed the song to William Roscoe (1753–1831) under the title of the "Helpless Swallow" in April 1803; thus causing several other newspapers to follow suit and reprint the mistake. Adding to the confusion, Rushton's early poetic tribute to Burns is not the same as his later, more expansive "To The Memory of Robert Burns", which appeared in his collected *Poems* (1806) alongside the initial tributary effort (though the former was slightly modified and titled "The Swallow"). Both poems, which were sporadically reprinted in the American press between 1797 and 1815, cast Burns as a tragic victim who had been failed by the Scottish gentry.

In "The Swallow", Rushton's speaker laments how "ye affluent!"[71] (13) could have transformed Burns's "anguish to delight" (12); while in "To The Memory of Robert Burns" the speaker ponders whether Burns might have found some shelter "on this side Tweed" (64).[72] This not only propagates the idea that the Scottish gentry were partially responsible for Burns's demise, but also pertains to Nigel Leask's assertion that the fate of Burns became something of a *cause célèbre* in Liberal English circles, particularly in Liverpool.[73] In a prophetic, often-neglected verse, Rushton's speaker later suggests that the Scots diaspora, whether in India or America, will continue to remember and recite Burns's "witching" verse with "pride":

> Where Ganges rolls his yellow tide,
> Where blest Columbia's waters glide,
> Old Scotia's sons, spread far and wide,
> Shall oft rehearse,
> With sorrow some, but all with pride,
> Thy witching verse.

(85–90)

It is notable that Rushton, a supporter of the American Revolution, though heavily critical of the transatlantic slave trade, evokes "blest Columbia", alluding to an idyllic vision of the country, which might partly explain why his poem was repeatedly reprinted in New York and Philadelphia. Rushton's sentiments provided an alternative to Thomson's damning obituary by deflecting blame on to hierarchical British structures:

> While darkness reigns, should bigotry,
> With boiling blood and bended knee,
> Scatter the weeds of infamy
> O'er thy cold clay
> Those weeds, at light's first blush, shall be
> Soon swept away.

(97–102)

Rushton's depiction of Britain as hierarchal and corrupt was in line with several contemporary accounts in the American press. An article on the front page of the *Republican Journal* also printed in 1797, for example, described "the horrible scenes of misery" in Britain in comparison with the "inestimable blessings of liberty and independence" that Americans enjoyed.[74] This was a highly selective appraisal of political circumstances given that just one year later the "Alien and Sedition Acts" were passed by the Federalists in the 5th US Congress. As the popular song "Jefferson and Liberty" would famously suggest at the turn of the nineteenth century, many felt the Acts were indicative of America's very own "reign of terror".[75] Nonetheless, that Rushton depicted Burns as a tragic victim provided a compelling counter-argument to Thomson's biographical claims, which continued to be repeatedly "scattered" over the poet's "cold clay" through the American periodical press.

However, it is vital to remember that the chronological excavation of print sources does not necessarily suggest a linear trajectory of the poet's reputational development in the USA. It would be an oversimplification to suggest that Burns arrived as the "Ayrshire Ploughman" (in the *Pennsylvania Packet*) and subsequently evolved into the parish-educated poet (Heron), flawed debauchee (Thomson) or victim of a tyrannical society (Rushton). These varying representations would have functioned simultaneously; often dependent upon what sources or periodicals were available to readers. Prior to James Currie's 1800 edition, which was to become the most influential factor in narrating Burns's life and work, it is therefore difficult to fully ascertain a dominant biographical narrative or "cultural production" of the poet before the turn of the nineteenth century.

JAMES CURRIE: A TRANSNATIONAL AGENDA

James Currie's *The Works of Robert Burns* was hugely popular in Britain, going through approximately five editions and ten-thousand copies by 1805 and an estimated twenty editions by 1820.[76] Thomas Dobson of Philadelphia produced the first American edition in 1801, just over one year after it had first appeared in Britain. Three years later, a second edition was printed by William Fairbairn and by 1815 there were four available editions of the *Works* in Philadelphia alone.[77] In addition to American reprints, the frequency with which Currie's edition was being printed in Britain meant that originals also regularly made their way into the hands of American booksellers and readers.

Nigel Leask has stated that the Currie edition was "the main portal through which Burns's life and poetry reached the Romantic and nineteenth century reader",[78] and it seems this was not exclusive to Britain, with the checklist of American editions up to 1866 (see Appendix A) revealing the widespread availability of the edition on the American side of the Atlantic. Consequently, most nineteenth-century American critical reviews and biographies of Burns, for better or worse, reveal some influence of Currie's moralising edition. A divisive and highly selective biographical text, much criticism has been directed towards both Currie and the edition.[79] Rather than further highlight editorial flaws, inaccuracies and ideological shortcomings, however, it is hoped that a brief overview of previous criticism combined with a reinterpretation of Currie's "prefatory remarks" will offer up fresh perspectives on how *The Works* was partially crafted with a transnational (at times specifically American) readership in mind.

In 1831, William Wallace Currie, son of James Currie, published a biography of his father's life, work and achievements. In a chapter outlining Currie's involvement with the Burns edition, Wallace states:

> ...various admirers and biographers of Burns (and amongst others, Gilbert Burns himself) have appeared before the public, whose declared object has been to vindicate his memory from the exaggerations and misrepresentations affecting his character, which Dr. Currie is charged by them with having admitted into his Life.[80]

As early as 1831, then, Currie was already being accused of "exaggerations and misrepresentations" causing his son to go on the defensive. Though Gilbert Burns had corresponded extensively with Currie during the edition's inception, he eventually took issue with the way his brother's character was portrayed in "Life of Burns". In 1820, an eighth edition published by Cadell and Davies (London) even contained "Some further particulars of the Poet's Family" by Gilbert Burns (later reprinted in Philadelphia as discussed below). Despite widespread sales and popularity, fierce criticism has continued to plague Currie's edition, with critics quick to point out the editor's habit of "inventing tragic motifs"[81] and highlighting the "rhetoric of moral blame"[82] attached to the narrative. Even Robert Donald Thornton's 1963 biography *James Currie The Entire Stranger*, which depicts Currie in a predominantly positive light, strikes a conciliatory tone when discussing his editorial approach:

> Currie's understanding of the responsibilities and the privileges of the biographer was that of his time [...] Short of distortion, any second person must be protected in good name and his wishes for use of material bearing upon his good name must be respected [...] the biographer might refine or correct until, for example, his subject shone like the Queen Anne letter-writer he aspired to be.[83]

In keeping with Thronton's defence, it is perhaps unfortunate that Currie has become the scapegoat for such prolonged criticism. After all, Currie agreed to undertake the edition in order to create sympathy (and raise funds) for Burns's surviving wife and children, who reaped the financial benefits of widespread sales. Currie's initial motivations for the edition can be found in a series of letters sent to publishers Cadell and Davies between 1797 and 1799.[84] Reflecting on the "circumstances that led me to take a share in it", Currie explains his "original connections" to Dumfriesshire—"The County in which Burns died, is that in which I was born"—before turning to the more pressing concern of providing "immediate subsistence" for Burns's family.[85] This gesture was seemingly typical of an individual who was known for his charitable nature, medical prowess, progressive politics and deep abhorrence of slavery.

Yet even in these early epistolary exchanges, Currie's misjudged pre-occupation with Burns's "excentricities, wanderings & errors" is prevalent. In Leask's view, Currie's biography was partly motivated by "a desire to exonerate his country from blame in precipitating Burns's (highly publicised) premature sickness and death".[86] It seems that Currie, anxious to defend his proud, enlightened heritage, needed to somehow blame Burns in order to exonerate Scotland. In doing so, he not only produced an inaccurate account of Burns's life but also tarnished his own reputation in that the edition has long been remembered for its inaccuracies and agenda of moral blame.

However, there are important aspects of Currie's edition that remain relatively overlooked. Due to his own extensive transatlantic travels, Currie was in a better position than most to fully understand the potential reach of Burns beyond the borders of Scotland, and within a "world of encounters" that he had personally experienced. It is, therefore, logical to reconsider Currie under a transnational critical microscope. Moreover, as Gerard Carruthers and Pauline Mackay have pointed out, "the history of Burns editing has not been properly narrated"[87] and thus it makes sense to return to the first and, arguably, most influential editor of the poet.

Born in Dumfriesshire, Currie later spent a considerable amount of time in America during the revolutionary years, moving to Virginia in 1771 to begin an apprenticeship for Glasgow tobacco merchants William Cunninghame and Company. There is little in Currie's correspondence to suggest he strongly opposed the American Revolution, yet with tensions turning increasingly violent he became aware that it was difficult to remain in the country while maintaining any sympathy for Britain. In a letter to his aunt, Miss Christian Duncan dated 14 September 1774,

Currie expressed his admiration for the "spirit of enthusiasm" shown by the revolutionaries, but was more concerned about how events might "distress the merchants with you greatly, particularly the Glasgow merchants".[88] A year later in Pinckney's *Virginia Gazette* of 23 March 1775, Currie published a letter defending the Scottish tobacco merchants in Colonial Virginia (who were accused of unfair business practice) while remaining diplomatic in regard to American independence.[89] Wallace seems to provide an apt summary of his father's delicate position:

> Although he regarded the noble spectacle of an infant nation starting forth into independence with that strong interest which is congenial to every generous breast, the youthful attachments and prejudices of Mr. Currie, as he writes, were entirely British.[90]

While Currie might have admired the "noble spectacle" of independence on some level, he ultimately saw little future for himself in America on a long-term basis. It seems any political enthusiasm (for the revolutionaries) was overshadowed by patriotic "attachments". His commercial, rather than political, mind worried more for the catastrophic impact that widespread conflict might have on transatlantic commerce. After two failed attempts to leave America, a short (forced) stint in the colonial army and a volatile period trading between Antigua and St Eustatius, Currie eventually fulfilled his ambition of enrolling in medical school: obtaining his degree from Glasgow University (after training at Edinburgh) on 30 March 1780, before moving to Liverpool where he would establish his reputation as a physician.

Though living in England and maintaining Unionist sympathies, Currie was fiercely proud of his Scottish heritage. More significantly, he understood, first-hand, what it was to be part of the global Scots diaspora; an important point that has been too overlooked in Burns Studies. When it came to editing and repackaging the work of Scotland's most renowned contemporary poet, then, the editor would have surely known that his audience was not confined within British national borders. Leith Davis has touched upon this in her essay "Negotiating Cultural Memory: James Currie's *Works of Robert Burns*", in which she identifies Currie's positioning of Burns as "a symbol who unites Scots around the globe".[91]

Elsewhere, Davis has outlined how much of Currie's writings are concerned with the damaging effects of "national prejudice, first in America and then in Britain". Across several letters and other correspondence,

Davis highlights the "motif of national prejudice as a disease" and the evocation that "National Enmity" is a "passion gone to excess".[92] Part of Currie's concern, of course, was the anti-Scots prejudices he had experienced living in both America and England. Pertaining to a trans-national reading of *The Works*, the first passage in Currie's four-volume edition begins by highlighting the reach and potential of Burns's poetry outside of Scotland. Currie firmly establishes that Burns's poetry is read and admired "in every part of the sister islands", revealing that he was well aware that his edition too might well go "beyond the limits" of Scotland.[93] Reinforcing the point:

> It seems proper therefore to write the memoirs of his life, not with the view of their being read by Scotchmen only, but also by natives of England, and of other countries where the language is spoken or understood.[94]

A following footnote in Currie's "Life" follows suit. Describing "Their Groves of Sweet Myrtle" as a "beautiful strain", the editor claims that it may be "confidently predicted" that the song "will be sung with equal or superior interest on the banks of the Ganges or on the Mississippi, as on those of the Tay or the Tweed".[95] From the onset, then, Currie's edition has—what might be referred to as—a "transnational agenda". He even dedicated *The Works* to another wandering Scot in "a distant region of the world" by thanking Captain Graham Moore, a Royal Navy commander, who first recommended the poems of Burns to him.[96]

With a fuller recognition of Currie's transnational agenda, we might consider the edition as being partially framed to the suit the needs of a wider readership that were less acquainted with the daily realities of Scottish life. Currie's further "Prefatory remarks" support the idea, with much of the content reading like a guide to Scotland's civic education system for transnational audiences. In praising the egalitarian aspects of Scotland's parish schools, Currie seems to exonerate Scotland in conveying how civic structures played a large part in the poet's growth:

> In the very humblest condition of the Scottish peasants every one can read, and most persons are more or less skilled in writing and arithmetic; and under the disguise of their uncouth appearance, and of their peculiar manner and dialect, a stranger will discover that they possess a curiosity,

and have obtained a degree of information corresponding to these require-
ments. These advantages they owe to the legal provisions made by the parliament of Scotland in 1646[...]It is common for the established schools
even in the country parishes of Scotland, to enjoy the means of classical
instruction, and many of the farmers, and some even of the cottagers, sub-
mit to much privation, that they may obtain for one of their sons at least,
the precarious advantage of a learned education.[97]

By 1800, extracts of Heron's *Memoirs* had already—through highlighting Burns's formative education—offered an alternative to the myth of
the "Heaven-taught ploughman". Yet Currie, with his extended explanation, respectable endorsement and much larger print outreach, expands
greatly on the idea and in doing so extols the civic virtues of Scotland,
portraying the education system as a successful model:

> That it is on the whole favourable to industry [...] seems to be proved by
> the most striking and decisive experience; and it is equally clear, that it is
> the cause of that spirit of emigration and of adventure so prevalent among
> the Scotch.[98]

Here Currie portrays Scotland as developing, through its education
system, into an industrial nation in a manner akin to a stadial theory of sociocultural evolution. The extent to which Currie was infused
in Enlightenment debate becomes apparent as he seemingly subscribes
to a fruitful interrelationship between commercial and moral progress.
Currie's assertion that civic education is "favourable to industry", of
course, opposes the associations of Burns (and his works) with "virtuous
agrarianism" as discussed in the previous chapter. Currie also attributes
education as being a catalyst for emigration and "adventure", suggesting
that educated Scots have had to seek new frontiers in order to fulfil their
potential. In Currie's view, "knowledge and poverty poured the adven-
turous natives of the north over the fertile plains of England, and more
especially, over the colonies which she had settled in the east and west".[99]
Currie, a proud Scot but also a Unionist, alludes to prosperous opportunities in England ("fertile plains"), which might have reflected his own
position as a Scots physician in Liverpool, before suggesting that the most
ample opportunities were to be found in "the colonies". In a slightly
curious passage, Currie then turns to reflect on national patriotism:

> In free governments it is found more active than in despotic ones, because, as the individual becomes of more consequence in the community, the community becomes of more consequence to him.[100]

Currie's reference here to "free governments" is ambiguous. The description of the individual being of "more consequence" certainly chimes with the liberty-seeking revolutionary rhetoric of the late-eighteenth century. However, despite his opposition to the war in France; sympathetic treatment of French prisoners; and co-founding of the socially progressive "Liverpool Literary Society", Currie insisted to "the very end of his life" that he was always a "loyal monarchist".[101]

Regardless, the evocation of "free governments" would have surely stoked glowing embers in post-revolutionary America, while the discussion of civic education responded to ongoing contemporary debates. Most famously, Thomas Jefferson argued, in his *Bill for the More General Diffusion of Knowledge* (1779), that accessible, civic education would result in a more prosperous future. Yet for all these transnational inflections, imposing these contextual "American" readings of Currie's "prefatory remarks" is redundant without actually discussing contemporary critical responses. Thus, we must turn to how the edition was received in prominent American literary journals, periodicals and newspapers of the period.

THE WORKS: AMERICAN CRITICAL RESPONSES

Just months after Currie's edition was published in Britain, the New Hampshire-based *Farmer's Museum* reprinted the beginning of Currie's "Life of Burns". Despite the agricultural title of the weekly tabloid, the paper's primary focus was literature. It was also renowned for being "friendly to Great Britain", which its editors deemed the "bulwark of civilization", and "hostile to France, which was considered the center of disorder". Nonetheless, a specifically *American* strain of revolutionary sensibilities could still be discerned from the paper's two masthead epigrams: "Where Liberty is, there is my country" and "The Liberty of the Press is essential to THE RIGHTS OF MAN".[102] Introducing Currie's *Works*, the *Farmer's Museum* article reflected on the "small part" of the poet's biography that readers might be familiar with, before describing how the new edition was a "more complete dress". An excerpt from

Currie's "Life" was then printed with an editorial note that it would be "novel to most of our readers".[103]

One of the most nuanced early American assessments of Currie's edition appeared one year later in *The American Review and Literary Journal* (the short-lived successor to the *Monthly Magazine and American Review*). Though unsigned, the article was likely written by America's "first professional writer"[104] Charles Brockden Brown (1771–1810). Having previously co-founded the *Monthly Magazine and American Review* with fellow "Friendly Club" members (Charles Adams, Timothy Dwight and Samuel Miller), Brown subsequently became primary editor and contributor to *The American Review and Literary Journal* and later *The Literary Magazine and American Register* (in which appeared another 1803 article on Burns as discussed later). That these publications provided strikingly similar commentaries on Burns—combined with the fact that journal editors usually multitasked as chief writers—further suggests Brown as the author. Though Burns scholars are quick to cite later nineteenth-century commentators such as John Greenleaf Whittier, Walt Whitman and Ralph Waldo Emerson (all to be discussed in Chapter 5), it seems Brown may have been the first major American literary figure to engage with Burns in any great detail. Before exploring the 1801 *American Review*'s article however, it is worth considering the magazine's introductory preface. Emphasising the importance of periodicals for cultivating literature, it states:

> When, now, that our population is increased, our national independence secure, and our governments established, and we are relieved from the necessities of colonists [...] Nothing, it is thought, will tend more to excite this attention, and to render the pursuits of knowledge more compatible with those of business, than those periodical publications which impart information in small portions; by which, men engaged in active occupations, may gradually acquire a degree of intellectual cultivation and improvement, without any infringement of the time allotted to their customary and necessary concerns.[105]

Chapter 2 touched upon the profound importance of periodical literature for Burns's own educational development and awareness of transnational affairs. Similarly, the above statement directly links America's intellectual and cultural "improvement" to the periodical press. It is telling that the editor chose to include an extensive article on Burns in a publication devoted to the "cultivation" of *American* literature. Here marks a transition from the advertisements placed by Scots emigrant printers and editors such as Peter Stewart, George Hyde and J. and A. Maclean.

The inclusion of Burns in such a focused, literary-specific journal is the first instance of the Scottish poet being written about in relation to his significance for American literature, rather than as a commodity being sold to the reading public by emigrant printers. The rhetorical concern with America's literary-cultural development also supports the idea that Brown authored the preface given his early novels, in particular *Wieland*, deal extensively with issues of representation, sociocultural development and voice in the early American Republic. There are even echoes of Currie's "prefatory remarks" (in regard to a literate "Scottish peasantry") in Brown's own writing. In his lesser-known novel *Clara Howard* (also appearing in 1801), the protagonist Philip Stanley regards himself as "American Peasantry" since "our notions are more the off-springs of the books we read than of external circumstances".[106] Brown's use of the phrase "American Peasantry"—chronologically congruent with Currie's reflections on the "Scottish Peasantry"—was uncommon during the period, suggesting a possible influence.

The beginning of the review first heralds the "neatness and accuracy" of Philadelphia publisher Thomas Dobson, who had chosen to print Currie's work from a "mass of British publications". Dobson's choice is commended and described as "deserving" since it will afford not just "amusement" but also "instruction to his countrymen". After lavishing praise on the "distinguished" Dr Currie for his "elegant piece of biography and criticism", the reviewer turns to why the work might be of particular interest to "the American reader":

> The *prefatory remarks*, concerning the character and conduct of the Scottish peasantry, which in some respects, may be applied to the people of *New England*, will be interesting to the American reader, and throw light on those circumstances which contributed to form the early character of Burns.[107]

Responding to Currie's transnational agenda, the reviewer goes as far as to suggest a commonality between the "Scottish peasantry" and the "people of New England". After quoting Currie's passage on Scotland's legal provisions for "educating the poor", similar "provisions made in New England" are described:

> It is with pleasure and pride that we can cite the laws of a considerable portion of our country, which may vie with those of Scotland, so justly applauded by Dr Currie. But we cannot, at the same time, but express our surprise and regret, that the legal provisions made in New England, for the education of children, and the establishment of parish schools, so universally approved and admired, have never been adopted with any effect in other states of America.[108]

Indeed, early settlers in New England modified laws from Britain to develop one of the first systems of accessible education in the American colonies. In an early twentieth-century essay titled "Compulsory Education in the American Colonies", Marcus W. Jernegan states that by 1771, "all of the territory of New England, with the exception of Rhode Island, was under a system of compulsory education", which he attributes to the avoidance of conflicting legislations between "state, county and district" by the implementation of a uniform "general compulsory law".[109]

As was the case in Scotland, eighteenth-century education was directly linked to religion, with a Puritan moral code at the root of an early New England emphasis on enlightening the wider populace. Consequently, by the turn of the nineteenth century access to higher education was widely available in New England, with David F. Allmendinger pointing out that "a flood of students from poor families" and "rural and hill communities" populated New England Colleges from 1800 onwards ("never before had these families sent sons to college").[110] It is pertinent that Currie's narrative of Burns, outlining both his rural origins and education, was appearing in the same period that rural "sons were abandoning farms" in favour of educational institutions in New England.[111] This certainly qualifies the reviewer's comparison of "legal provisions made in New England" with civic structures in Scotland. Reaching a conclusion, the reviewer reaffirms the importance of the edition in America:

> We shall conclude our brief account of these volumes, by wishing that our readers may feel as much satisfaction in their perusal, and derive as much and as various pleasure and instruction from them, as we have done.[112]

The ultimate hope here is that readers do not just derive "pleasure", but also "instruction" from Currie's *Works*, providing an insight into the edition's warm reception in an influential American literary magazine. In 1804, responses to the second Philadelphia edition of Currie's *Works* appeared in *The Literary Magazine, and American Register*. Modelled on British literary journals and subsequently becoming "the most imposing" American literary review of the period, Brown was sole editor and main contributor along with publishers C and A Conrad.[113] Perhaps unsurprisingly, given the earlier 1801 review, Burns featured regularly within the magazine. In the pages preceding Brown's article, the "Banks of Cree" and "Address to The Wood-Lark" were printed as individual poems with the following notice:

> Some of the most beautiful poems of Burns are to be found among his lyrics, contained in the fourth volume of Currie's edition of his works. He wrote the most of these after he had been to Edinburgh, after his taste had been more cultivated, and his reputation established. The two following pieces, extracted from these, cannot fail of meeting with a cordial reception from our readers.[114]

The "two beautiful" pastoral poems concerned are attributed to a more "cultivated" period of Burns's life; a sentiment that echoes Currie's account of poet's time in Edinburgh. A further reference to the Currie edition appears in the journal's "List of new publications in November", where W. Fairbairn's 1804 Philadelphia edition (the second American edition of the *Works*) is advertised for "3 dollars".[115] Finally, Brown's most extensive appraisal appears in a later section of the journal titled "Adversaria". Simply titled "Burns", Brown begins with a brief overview of the poet's humble beginnings and a sweeping commentary on how his "ardent sensibility" swelled to "an overflowing height by the first books put into his hands". As in the 1801 review, Brown emphasises the poet's education before focusing the rest of his article on language:

> His versification, no less than his thoughts, is sometimes rude even to coarseness[…]with a taste which is not the least circumstance of wonder of his life, he not only avoids the coarser part of the phraseology of his country, and selects the better, but attains to an elegance of the English language, which can be rivalled by few of our modern poets.[116]

Here, the treatment of Burns's language is not entirely definitive. Scots language is described as "rude to coarseness" yet it still manages to attain "an elegance of the English language"; allowing Burns to produce poetry "which can be rivalled by few of our modern poets". The further emphasis on poetic language appears, to use a term from the 1801 essay, to be "instructive" to the American reader:

> He has nothing of that extravagance which we may justly call the *chivalry of poets*; he never labours to celebrate a Chloe or a Phyllis [...] His scene of action is never the "Velvet Green of Idalia", the "impurpled margin of Helycon" or the "clouded summit of Parnassus"; his lovers never converse but by the "*burn side*"; they never wander but through "*corn riggs*" nor make their mutual confessions but on "*the braes of Ballochmyle*", The Tweed or Yarrow.[117]

Brown praises Burns's use of locale and linguistic register, suggesting that poetry can concern locality, employ elements of dialect yet still be equal in merit to works written in "standard English" concerning classical subject matter. Accordingly, in his biography of Charles Brockden Brown, David Lee Clark notes that Brown regularly questioned the merits of ancient Classics in his literary criticism:

> A natural result of his insistence on "moral tendency" was Brown's reaction against the sensuality characterizing many of the ancient Classics [...] Although, like all educated young men of his time, Brown had received thorough training in the classics, he shared the moralistic view that they were as a whole unfit for fastidious tastes.[118]

Ernest Marchand, in an early twentieth-century article on Brown, went further to suggest that Brown was characteristic of the "rise of a middle class morality" that questioned the moral rhetoric of Classics that had hitherto been "accepted in their entirety by an aristocratic society".[119] This provides further reasoning as to why Brown might have deeply valued Burns's use of language, and perhaps even viewed it as being potentially influential on contemporary American poets, as discussed later in Chapter 5. *The Literary Magazine and American Register* was not only consistent in its praise for Burns, but also for repeatedly asserting the editorial merit of James Currie. In 1806, for example, the magazine printed a "Biographical sketch of the Late Dr Currie", which appears to have been a reprint of an obituary written by fellow physician, writer and associate Dr John Aikin. The article praises Currie for his editorial approach in the *Works*, rendering the edition successful in both philanthropic ("Repeated editions produced a small balance for profit") and literary ("a rich treat to the lovers of poetry and elegant literature") capacities.[120]

That Brown and his editorial collaborators reprinted the full obituary reveals the relative familiarity that readers must have had with Currie through the widely available reprinted American editions. When compared with any subsequent editor or biographer of Burns, then, it remains clear who garnered the highest amount of exposure in early to mid-nineteenth-century America.

NOTES

1. "Letter from W. Richardson to S. Rose, 1 Jan, 1787" cited at University of Glasgow Special Collections, MS Gen 520/2. Thanks to Stephen Mullen for this reference.
2. *The Poems and Songs*, 1:271.
3. *Letters*, 1:54–55.
4. Ibid., 96.
5. It should be noted that Creech did not inform Burns about the "third edition" nor his arrangement with Strahan and Cadell. See *The Critical Heritage*, 11.
6. Esther Hovey, "Burns' Songs American Connection", *The Burns Chronicle* (2001), 17.
7. *The Glasgow Magazine and Review* 1 (1783): 1–2.
8. "Letter from W. Richardson to S. Rose".
9. Painter, "American Editions", 435.
10. Ibid., 436. Painter speculates that Reid may have sailed on the ship *George* which arrived in New York on June 26.
11. As Rhona Brown has documented, the Philadelphian daily continued to print individual poems and songs by Burns in the months that followed. The "Rigs o' Barley" also appeared in the Philadelphia-based *Independent Gazetteer* in the same month. See Rhona Brown, "'Guid Black Prent': Robert Burns and the Contemporary Scottish and American Periodical Press" in *Robert Burns and Transatlantic Culture*, ed. Alker, Davis, and Nelson, 71–87. In addition to Brown's illuminating essay, the National Library of Scotland has recently collected and catalogued issues of the *Pennsylvania Packet* that contain poems

or songs by Robert Burns from 24 July 1787 through 27 November 1788.

12. Dunlap lost his contract after printing a letter that leaked information about French aid to the Americans during the War. The letter was authored by Thomas Paine and signed off as "Common Sense".

13. See "George Washington to Davic C. Claypoole". Accessed 25 January 2015. http://founders.archives.gov/documents/Washington/99-01-02-09057.

14. In a series of eighty-five essays, Alexander Hamilton, James Madison and John Jay (publishing anonymously under the name "Publius") argued for the creation of a strong federal government in order to unite and preserve the liberties of individual States. These essays formed an integral part of the debate between the Federalists and Anti-Federalists, who were strongly divided over the ratification of the Constitution.

15. Brown, "Guid Black Prent", 83.

16. *Pennsylvania Packet*, 24 July (1787).

17. *Pennsylvania Packet*, 14 March (1788).

18. Colleen Glenney Boggs, "Transatlantic Romanticisms", in *Transatlantic Literary Studies 1660–1830*, ed. Eve Tavor Bannet and Susan Manning (Cambridge: Cambridge University Press, 2011), 232.

19. Elizabeth Young, *Black Frankenstein: The Making of an American Metaphor* (New York: New York University Press, 2008), 250.

20. *Robert Burns & Pastoral*, 23–24.

21. For a recently edited collection of all the "Federalist Papers" complete with "Anti-Federalist" responses see Terence Ball, ed., *The Federalist: With Letters of Brutus* (Cambridge: Cambridge University Press, 2003).

22. *The Poems and Songs*, 1:116–19.

23. Craig R. Smith and David M. Hunsaker, *The Four Freedoms of the First Amendment* (Longrove: Waveland Press, 2003), 23.

24. See also *The Pennsylvania Packet* of Friday, October 26 (1787) that printed both the first of the Anti-Federalist Papers written by "Brutus" and also a public call for state delegates to come forward to join the state's ratifying convention.

25. For example, in "Federalist Paper No. 12" Alexander Hamilton argues that agriculture and commerce need not be opposed.

26. *The Poems and Songs*, 1:174.

27. For a recent discussion of the "republic-democracy-agriculture correlation" on both sides of the Atlantic see Manuela Albertone, *National Identity and the Agrarian Republic: The Transatlantic Commerce of Ideas Between America and France (1750–1830)* (Surrey and Burlington: Ashgate, 2014), 7.

28. Thomas Jefferson, *Notes on the State of Virginia*, ed. Frank Shuffelton (New York: Penguin, 1998), 170.

29. See Richard B. Sher, *The Enlightenment and the Book: Scottish Authors and Their Publishers in Eighteenth-Century Britain, Ireland and America* (Chicago: University of Chicago Press, 2008), 504; and Christopher Alan Bayly, *Imperial Meridian: The British Empire and the World, 1780–1830* (London: Longman, 1989), 84–85.

30. Merrill D. Peterson, ed., *Thomas Jefferson: Writings* (New York: Library of America, 1984), 1296.

31. A further point of comparison might be George Crabbe's 1783 "Anti-Pastoral" poem "The Village", which was widely reprinted and sold in America some seven years before "The Cotter's Saturday Night" first appeared. An advertisement in the *New York Daily Gazette* of 11 November (1791) advertised the "fourth" American edition of the poem.

32. Andrew Hook, "Philadelphia, Edinburgh and the Scottish Enlightenment", in Sher and Smitten, *Scotland and America in the Age of the Enlightenment*, 233.

33. David A. Wilson, *United Irishmen, Unites States: Immigrant Radicals in the Early Republic* (Ithaca: Cornell University Press, 1998), 123.

34. Liam Mcllvanney, *Burns the Radical: Poetry and Politics in Late Eighteenth-Century Scotland* (Edinburgh: Tuckwell Press, 2002), 18.

35. *The Poems and Songs*, 1:19.

36. See Robert M. Calhoun, "Religion, Moderation and Regime Building in Post-Revolutionary America", in *Empire and Nation: The American Revolution in the Atlantic World*, ed. Eliga H. Gould and Peter S. Onuf (Baltimore: John Hopkin University Press, 2005), 217–239.

37. *The Independent Journal*, 29 August (1787).

38. Ibid.

39. Boggs, "Transatlantic Romanticisms", 230.

40. See, for example, Richard B. Sher, *The Enlightenment and the Book* (Chicago: University of Chicago Press, 2006); Meredith McGill, *American Literature and the Culture of Reprinting* (Philadelphia: University of Pennsylvania Press, 2003); and Joseph Rezek, *London and the Making of Provincial Literature: Aesthetics and the Transatlantic Book Trade, 1800–1850* (Philadelphia: University of Pennsylvania Press, 2015).

41. Nigel Leask, "Irish Republicans and Gothic Eleutherarchs: Pacific Utopias in the Writings of Theobald Wolfe Tone and Charles Brocken Brown", *The Huntington Library Quarterly* 63, no. 3 (2000): 366.

42. William St. Clair, "Publishing, Authorship and Reading", in *The Cambridge Companion to Fiction in the Romantic Period*, ed. Richard

Maxwell and Katie Trumpener (Cambridge: Cambridge University Press, 2008), 44–45.

43. The advertised prices of American editions of Burns's *Poems* fluctuated and were often advertised as lower priced than other "English books". In the *Virginia Independent Chronicle*, for example, the price of the same volume fluctuated between 4 and 6 shillings. See the *Virginia Independent Chronicle*, 11 February (1789) and 11 October (1789).

44. *The Critical Heritage*, 67.

45. I will return to critical descriptions of Burns as "Genius" in Chapter 4. For further discussion of Burns in relation to evolving theories of "genius" see Corey Andrews, *The Genius of Scotland: The Cultural Production of Robert Burns, 1785–1834* (Leiden and Boston: Brill and Rodopi, 2015) 11–35; Tim Burke, "Labour, Education and Genius" in Rodger and Carruthers, *Fickle Man*, 13–24; Ronnie Young, "Genius, Men, and Manners: Burns and Eighteenth-Century Scottish Criticism", *Scottish Studies Review* 9 (2008): 129–147; and Thomas Crawford, "Burns, Genius, and Major Poetry" in Simpson, *Love and Liberty*, 341–353.

46. *Pennsylvania Packet*, 16 July (1788).

47. Ibid.

48. See Robert Burns, *Poems Chiefly in the Scottish Dialect, to Which Are Added Scots Poems Selected from the Works of Robert Fergusson* (New York: J & A Maclean, 1788), 225.

49. Painter, "American Editions", 447.

50. Ibid.

51. *The Poems and Songs*, 1:323.

52. See Rhona Brown, *Robert Fergusson and The Scottish Periodical Press* (Farnham: Ashgate, 2012), 257.

53. Susan Manning, "Robert Burns's Transatlantic Afterlives", in *Robert Burns and Transatlantic Culture*, ed. Alker, Davis, and Nelson, 149–169.

54. Advertised in *The Pennsylvania Packet* of 28 August (1787).

55. Serge Hovey, "The Retrieval and Performance of The Songs of Robert Burns", 15. Thanks to Kirsteen McCue for this reference. This is an undated typewritten document retrieved from The University of Mississippi. See also Kirsteen McCue, "'Magnetic Attraction': The Transatlantic Songs of Robert Burns and Serge Hovey", in *Robert Burns and Transatlantic Culture*, ed. Alker, Davis, and Nelson, 233–247.

56. For example Carol McGuirk notes: "In a survey conducted between 1938 and 1942, the Writer's Project of Roosevelt's Works Progress Administration collected texts of "American" songs for deposit in the archives of the University of Virginia: among these songs, folk-collected

as "Virginian", are "Banks o' Doon", "Banks of Allan Water", "Bonnie jean", etc." See Carol McGuirk, "Haunted By Authority: Nineteenth-Century American Constructions of Robert Burns and Scotland" in *Robert Burns and Cultural Authority*, ed. Robert Crawford (Iowa City: University of Iowa Press, 1997), 147.

57. G. Ross Roy, "Robert Burns", in *The Edinburgh History of the Book in Scotland Volume 2: Enlightenment and Expansion 1707–1800*, ed. Stephen Brown and Warren McDougall (Edinburgh: Edinburgh University Press, 2007), 2:592.

58. Though few surviving copies of Aitken's edition remain, it has been recently uploaded to the online database *America's Historical Imprints*.

59. *The New York Magazine, or Literary Repository* 4 (1793): 680.

60. Though the obituary was published anonymously, critics have generally concurred with J. De Lancey Ferguson who first claimed Thomson as author. However, the editors of the forthcoming OUP edition of Burns's *Songs For George Thomson*, led by Kirsteen McCue, continue to seek concrete evidence. In the interest of consistency, the remainder of my discussion refers to Thomson as the author. See J. DeLancey Ferguson, "The Earliest Obituary of Burns: Its Authorship and Influence", *Modern Philology* 32, no. 2 (1934): 179–184.

61. *The New York Magazine, or Literary Repository* (1796), 118–119.

62. The ideological nature of Burns biographies will be returned to in Chapters 3 and 4 of this book.

63. See Pierre Bourdieu, *The Field of Cultural Production: Essays on Art and Literature*, ed. Randal Johnson (New York: Columbia University Press, 1993).

64. *The Genius of Scotland*, 149.

65. Ibid. For a further discussion of Thomson's relationship to Burns, see Carol McGuirk, "George Thomson and Robert Burns: With Friends Like These", *Eighteenth Century Scotland* 9 (1995): 16–20.

66. Lucyle Werkmeister has highlighted how Thomson's obituary was selectively edited in the London press to reflect Opposition and Ministerial positions. There appears to be no consistent pattern that suggests a political bias in the American press. See Lucyle Werkmesiter, "Robert Burns and the Daily Press", *Modern Philology* 63, no. 4 (1966): 322–335.

67. *The Philadelphia Monthly Magazine; or, Universal Repository of Knowledge and Entertainment* 1, no. 2 (1798): 83.

68. This "ideological clipping" would be a frequently occurring pattern in nineteenth-century American editions and will be discussed further in the following chapter.

69. See my article "An American Trove of Burnsiana: The William R. Smith Collection", *The Burns Chronicle* (2015): 39–47.

70. *The Philadelphia Monthly Magazine; or, Universal Repository of Knowledge and Entertainment* 2, no. 7 (1798): 47.

71. Edward Rushton, *Poems* (London: J. M'creery, 1806), 83.

72. Rushton, *Poems*, 58.

73. Rushton's poem was part of a larger collection of tributes by William Roscoe and other Liverpool poets, originally published individually in the *Liverpool Phoenix*, but later collected into one volume in 1800 titled *Liverpool Testimonials to the departed Genius of Robert Burns*. See *Robert Burns and Pastoral*, 279.

74. *The Republican Journal*, August 14 (1797).

75. The song was first published the Philadelphia-based *Aurora* of January 24 (1801). It is regularly cited as one of the first Presidential "Campaign Anthems". See "Songs Along The Campaign Trail". Accessed 14 March 2017. http://www.npr.org/templates/story/story.php?storyId=95408459.

76. *Robert Burns and Pastoral*, 266.

77. See Appendix A.

78. *Robert Burns and Pastoral*, 266.

79. For a recent account of the exaggerations and moral fabrications of the Currie edition see Gerard Carruthers and Pauline Mackay, "Re-reading James Currie; Robert Burns's First Editor", *John Clare Society Journal* 32 (2013): 73–84.

80. William Wallace, ed., *Memoir of The Life and Writings, and Correspondence of James Currie, M.D. F.R.S. of Liverpool*, 2 Vols (London: Longman, Rees, Orme, Brown, and Green, 1831) 1;308.

81. McGuirk, "Haunted By Authority", 144.

82. *Robert Burns and Pastoral*, 281.

83. Robert Donald Thornton, *James Currie The Entire Stranger & Robert Burns* (Edinburgh and London: Oliver & Boyd, 1963), 390–391.

84. See "James Currie". Accessed 15 March 2017. http://jamescurrie.gla.ac.uk/search.php.

85. "James Currie to Cadell and Davies, 7 Dec, 1797". Accessed 15 March 2017. http://jamescurrie.gla.ac.uk/details.php?id=55.

86. Ibid.

87. Carruthers and Mackay, "Re-reading James Currie; Robert Burns's First Editor", 83.

88. *Memoir of The Life and Writings*, 17–18.

89. During this period, Scots were often depicted as villainous traders and enthusiastic British Army recruits in the American press.

See, for example, *The Connecticut Gazette*, April 28 (1775) and *The Pennsylvania Packet*, September 25 (1775).

90. *Memoir of The Life and Writings*, 26–27.

91. Leith Davis, "Negotiating Cultural Memory: James Currie's *Works of Robert Burns*", *International Journal of Scottish Literature* 6 (Spring/Summer 2010). Accessed 1 May 2016. http://www.ijsl.stir.ac.uk/issue6/davis.htm.

92. Leith Davis, "James Currie's *Works of Robert Burns*: The Politics of Hypochondriasis", *Studies in Romanticism* 36, no. 1 (Spring, 1997): 46.

93. *The Works*, 1:1.

94. Ibid., 2.

95. Ibid., 333–334.

96. Ibid., "Dedication".

97. Ibid., 3–4.

98. Ibid., 6.

99. Ibid., 7.

100. Ibid., 29.

101. Margaret DeLacy, "Currie, James (1756–1805)". Accessed 28 December 2015. http://www.oxforddnb.com/view/article/6954.

102. Ronald Lora and William Henry, eds., *The Conservative Press in Eighteenth-and-Nineteenth-Century America* (Connecticut: Greenwood Publishing Group, 1999), 103–111.

103. *Farmer's Museum, or, Literary Gazette* 8, no. 400 (1800). Accessed 8 December 2015. http://www.sc.edu/library/digital/collections/cbook0.html.

104. "Our Founding Novelist". Accessed 8 December 2015. http://www.neh.gov/humanities/2010/januaryfebruary/feature/our-founding-novelist.

105. *The American Review and Literary Journal* 1 (1801), Preface.

106. Charles Brockden Brown, *Memoirs of Charles Brockden Brown, the American Novelist, Author of Weiland*, ed. William Dunlap (London: Henry Colburn, 1822), 147.

107. *The American Review and Literary Journal*, 255.

108. Ibid., 256.

109. Marcus W. Jernegan, "Compulsory Education in the American Colonies: I. New England", *The School Review* 26, no. 10 (1918): 749.

110. David F. Allmendinger Jr., "New England Students and the Revolution in Higher Education, 1800–1900", *History of Education Quarterly* 11, no. 4 (1971): 382.

111. Ibid.

112. *The American Review and Literary Journal*, 259.

113. David Lee Clark, *Charles Brockden Brown: Pioneer Voice of America* (Durham: Duke University Press, 1952), 218.
114. *The Literary Magazine, and American Register* 2 (1804), 20.
115. Ibid., 648.
116. Ibid., 594.
117. Ibid., 595.
118. *Charles Brockden Brown*, 252.
119. Ernest Marchand, "Literary Opinions of Charles Brockden Brown", *Studies in Philology* 31, no. 4 (1934): 541–566.
120. *The Literary Magazine, and American Register* 5 (1806), 84.

CHAPTER 4

"On Western Ground": American Reprints, c.1801–1859

It seems proper therefore to write the memoirs of his life, not with the view of their being read by Scotchmen only...[1]

—James Currie (1800)

While James Currie's *Works* was the most influential edition of Burns's poetry in nineteenth-century America, it was no by means the exclusive biographical portal through which Americans had access to information about the poet's life. Though differing by minor deviations in their subtitles, several books titled *The Poetical Works of Robert Burns* began to be published from 1804 onwards at an almost annual rate across several states (see Appendix A). With the legal freedom to print, edit and repackage British books, American publishers constructed their own idiosyncratic editions, often with new subtitles that offered up some original epithet or fresh piece of information about Burns (such as Benjamin Johnson's "With the Author's Life Written by Himself"[2] (in Philadelphia 1804) or Peter Stewart's "Together with a new Appendix, and a Concise History of his Life"[3] (also in Philadelphia, 1807).

Though Currie's narrative continued to pervade these editions, they were not always direct reprints of the *Works*, suggesting that new editions from London were continuing to be carried, and subsequently reprinted, across the Atlantic. For example, Benjamin Johnson's *Poetical Works* appeared in the same year that Cadell and Davies printed their London edition of the same name. Differing in content and layout, both contained extensive excerpts from Currie's "Life" as acknowledged in Cadell

© The Author(s) 2018
A. Sood, *Robert Burns and the United States of America*,
https://doi.org/10.1007/978-3-319-94445-6_4

and Davies's preface ("all who hereafter write or think of Burns, must necessarily consult").[4]

By 1808, there were ten separately printed and distributed American editions of Burns's poetry (and "songs" if we include John Aitken's 1797 *Scots Musical Museum*). This number would increase at a rapid rate as new materials—in the form of letters, poems and songs—continued to surface in Britain. In 1808, R. H. Cromek's *Reliques of Robert Burns; Consisting Chiefly of Original Letters, Poems, and Critical Observations on Scottish Songs* was published in London, also by Cadell and Davies. As with the Currie edition, it took just a year for it to be reprinted in America. In a joint publishing venture, the American edition was simultaneously printed in Philadelphia and New York by Bradford and Inskeep; Coale and Thomas in Baltimore; and Oliver C. Greenleaf in Boston. Though critics have lambasted Cromek's claims of originality as entirely fraudulent, his edition did in fact contain some genuine materials that were absent in Currie's edition, specifically in the form of new letters and information gathered directly from Burns's family.[5] Having seemingly gone to great lengths to collect and publish this new information, Cromek's legacy has nevertheless been that of a fraudster which is largely due to his bowdlerised version of certain texts (such as the first "Commonplace Book");[6] his later associations with "Honest" Allan Cunningham[7]; and his habit of introducing poems with overly elaborate descriptions ("he threw himself on the side of a corn stack, and there conceived his sublime and tender elegy").[8] Yet by 1809, Cromek had added a considerable amount of new biographical information—whether reliable or not—about Burns which subsequently became available in several states. Significantly, *Reliques* was the first edition to reveal details about Burns's "Ode" to the first president of the USA through the inclusion of his 1794 letter to Frances Anna Dunlop ("I design it as an irregular Ode for General Washington's birthday"). However, as noted in Chapter 2, Burns's letter (and thus Cromek's *Reliques*) omitted the first three stanzas that focused on the American Revolution and British tyranny in the Atlantic world.

Cromek's edition did also attract attention in American periodicals and literary journals, though it was not always positive. The same year that *Reliques* was first reprinted in America, a small reference to it appeared in a list of new publications in *The American Register: Or General Repository of History, Politics and Science*:

Some reliques of Burns have come to light this year, but their title to ven-
eration is small. Cumberland, without regret be it spoken, will write no
more epic poems. Wolcott, who will not be sorry to say, is probably forever
silent.[9]

The magazine, co-edited by Charles Brockden Brown, pays comparatively little attention to the edition despite its new materials. In juxtaposing Cromek's *Reliques* with Wolcott who is "forever silent" and
Cumberland who will "write no more epic poems", the edition is rendered obsolete. This sentiment probably owed more to the sheer success,
dissemination and level of literary engagement that Currie's edition had
attracted, rather than reflecting on the credibility of Cromek's editorial
efforts and additions.

Moreover, the nonchalance with which *The American Register* treated
Cromek's *Reliques* is not necessarily a fair and widespread summation
of how the edition was received. The same year, Francis Jeffrey's influential review of *Reliques*, originally published in the *Edinburgh Review*,
was reprinted in several Philadelphian newspapers including an 1809 edition of *Select Reviews, and Spirit of the Foreign Magazines*. Jeffrey begins
by dismissing the comparisons between Burns and dialect poets such as
the Wiltshire-born Stephen Duck (1705–1756) and Irish poet-prod-
igy Thomas Dermody (1772–1802). According to Jeffrey, Burns could
never "rightly be estimated as a poet, till that vulgar wonder be entirely
repressed which was raised on his having been a ploughman".[10] Jeffrey's
disavowal both expands and alters an image of Burns that had been
depicted in the American press. Though both Currie and Heron had
highlighted Burns's early education, Jeffrey's statement is considerably
more bold and conclusive regarding the myth of Burns being an uned-
ucated "Heaven-Taught Ploughman". In line with Brown's commentary
on Burns's language, Jeffrey also describes Scots as an effective literary
language and, crucially, chosen aesthetic device:

Scotch is, in reality, a highly poetical language; and that it is an ignorant,
as well as an illiberal prejudice, which would seek to confound it with
the barbarous dialects of Yorkshire or Devon. In composing his Scottish
poems, therefore, Burns did not make an instinctive and necessary use
of the only dialect he could employ […] he could write in the dialect of
England with far greater purity and propriety than nine tenths of those
who are educated in that country.[11]

While Cromek's *Reliques* was never reprinted on the same scale as Currie's edition, certain aspects of it remained influential in America. The *Salem Gazette* of 25 February 1823 rightly drew attention to Cromek's recovery of Burns's "Elegy to Highland Mary", which the editor credits as being the most "moving" and "tender" works "of all the productions of his great and original genius".[12] Despite the hyperbolic introduction, the writer is correct to highlight Cromek's "discovery"[13] of "Highland" Mary Campbell (c.1766–1786) who, as will later be discussed in Chapter 6, garnered a cult-like fascination in the USA. Regardless of this influential editorial addition, it seems the shadow of Currie's edition was long cast by the time that Cromek's *Reliques* appeared in America.

ROMANTIC APPETITES: LETTERS & CORRESPONDENCE

Further demonstrating the fascination for Burns's personal life was the publication of Burns's correspondence with Mrs. Agnes M'Lehose, disguised by the *noms d'amour* "Sylvander" and "Clarinda".[14] In July 1809, the Philadelphia-based *Select Reviews, and Spirit of the Foreign Magazines* not only contained a review of Cromek's *Reliques*, but also advertised the first American edition of *Letters Addressed to Clarinda, &c*, which was printed by John B. Austin in Philadelphia. With the addition of the bold subtitle "Never before published in America", the edition was a copy of the first publication of the letters by Thomas Stewart in Glasgow, 1802; an endeavour he controversially undertook without Mrs. M'Lehose's permission.[15] That the letters were printed twice in Philadelphia and subsequently reproduced again in Washington (1818) gives some indication of the romantic appetite for what would become the poet's most famous love letters.

Various copies of both *The Works of Robert Burns* and *The Poetical Works of Robert Burns* continued to be published at a steady annual rate in the early nineteenth century. Some publishers, such as F. Lucas and J. Cushing of Baltimore, reproduced the exact same edition in consecutive years (the same version of the *Works* was reprinted in 1814, 1815 and 1816) suggesting that publishing Burns was a profitable venture due to consistent demand. In 1818, Philadelphia publisher Benjamin Warner produced a version of *The Poetical Works of Robert Burns*[16] that highlighted, in its subtitle, Burns's "Correspondence with Mr. Thomson". While the Burns-Thomson correspondence had, albeit doctored by

Thomson, originally appeared in the Currie edition, it took until some years later that a publisher highlighted it as a title specifically.

One possibility is that, as knowledge about Burns continued to spread, his reputation as a songwriter and collector was coming to light. The same year, Warner separately printed and sold a book titled *The Scottish Minstrel: Being a Complete Collection of Burns' Songs*. Warner's volume is not to be confused with Robert Archibald Smith's (1780–1829) collection of the same name, which was published in six volumes in Scotland between 1821 and 1824. Rather, the American printing was solely focused on Burns's songwriting pursuits and correspondence with Thomson rather than a broad, sweeping collection of Scottish song, thus further testifying to the contemporary vogue for the poet.

The book featured songs from "the beautiful work projected and executed" by George Thomson (*A Select Collection of Original Scottish Airs for the Voice*) and also included the Burns-Thomson correspondence which promised to exhibit Burns's "notion of song-writing, and his opinions on various subjects of taste and criticism".[17] While James Johnson's *Scots Musical Museum* was reprinted in Philadelphia in 1797, George Thomson's *A Select Collection of Original Scottish Airs for the Voice* does not appear to have been reprinted—individually or in multivolume format—in its entirety in nineteenth-century America.[18] However, many subsequent editions of *The Poetical Works of Robert Burns* feature and advertise, usually in their subtitles, the "Correspondence of Mr. Thomson".

In 1820, Wells and Lily of Boston printed *The Letters of Robert Burns*; a collection of letters that had been extracted from the Currie edition, chronologically arranged and repackaged into one volume. Notably, Burns's poetry was completely absent from the book, suggesting that the letters alone were worthy of public interest. However, the 1820 Boston printing of *The Letters* appears to have been a one-off and another publication of Burns's epistolary correspondence (as a stand-alone work) did not occur again until 1843, when Robert P. Bixby of New York reprinted W. C. M'Lehose's *Correspondence Between Burns and Clarinda* (an edition that corrected and improved upon Thomas Stewart's 1802 collection). That Burns's letters and correspondence were usually attached to all-encompassing editions of his poetry might explain the absence of such exclusively edited letter collections.

A notable Philadelphia reprint occurred in 1823 when publisher B. Chapman reproduced a copy of the eighth edition of Currie's *Works*, originally published by Cadell and Davies in London (1820) and containing "Some further particulars of the Poet's Family" written by Gilbert Burns. Particularly pertinent to a New England readership were Gilbert's remarks on "the effects of refinement of taste on the laboring classes of men". Attached as Appendix "No. III" and "No. IV", Gilbert's epistolary exchanges with Currie regarding "labouring class education" were reprinted as well as his "additional remarks on the causes which contributed to the formation of the peculiar Character of the Peasantry of Scotland".

Where Currie was sceptical that literature was appropriate for "Scottish Peasants" who (he felt) might benefit more from commercial training, Gilbert, in a partial defence of his brother, argued that literature and "delicacy of sentiment" were the "surest foundation of morality and virtue".[19] Viewed through a transnational, specifically American lens, these printed philosophical exchanges were of high relevance at a time when the New England rural poor were "abandoning farms" in favour of college and consequently igniting similar debates over whether or not civic education would be economically beneficial and contribute to the advancement of "liberty" in America.[20] Gilbert's editorial additions and reflections on education were included in several subsequent American editions, perhaps most notably in William Pearson's frequently reprinted 1832 New York edition, discussed later in this chapter.

"ALAS, HIS SUN SHONE!": LOCKHART & CARLYLE

The fragmentary processes by which Burns's reputation and work were materially unfolding in America took a significant turn in 1828, when the *New York American* of 27 June 1828 reprinted extracts from J. G. Lockhart's "Life of Burns" (originally written as a contribution to Volume XXIII of the series *Constable's Miscellany*). A year later in 1829, the same magazine reprinted Thomas Carlyle's unsigned review of Lockhart's "Life", originally printed in the *Edinburgh Review* (December, 1828) and later considered by some as "the most influential critical essay on Burns of its period".[21] As much of a stand-alone biographical piece as it is a review, Carlyle's essay offers a highly contextual, "Romantic" revision of Currie's "Enlightenment"-infused account of the poet. Where Currie emphasised the benefits of education and civic structures on Burns's intellectual development, Carlyle describes the poet as a natural "prodigy" who rose from the "deepest obscurity, without help, without instruction, without model".[22] Replacing Currie's empirical bio-graphical approach with a flamboyant, visionary narrative, Carlyle does not so much prescribe to Mackenzie's "Heaven-Taught" myth but rather revises it for the Romantic-era by depicting Burns as a transcendental "genius":

> Alas, his Sun shone as through a tropical tornado; and the pale Shadow of Death eclipsed it at noon! Shrouded in such baleful vapours, the genius of Burns was never seen in clear azure splendour [sic], enlightening the world: but some beams from it did, by fits, pierce through; and it tinted those clouds with rainbow and orient colours, into a glory and stern gran-deur, which men silently gazed on with wonder and tears![23]

Carlyle's account is far less concerned with empirical priorities (unlike Currie's previous emphasis on civic education and the supposed "conditions" of the "Scottish Peasantry"), instead depicting Burns as a seer to his generation ("enlightening the world") whose life and work was intertwined in transcendental unity. Excerpts from both Carlyle's review and Lockhart's "Life" were, unsurprisingly, swiftly inserted into American editions of Burns's poetry. As we shall see, Carlyle's Romantic revision of Burns's life was to be influential on subsequent American biographers and intellectuals (namely Samuel Tyler and Ralph Waldo Emerson).

In 1831 New York publisher W. Stodart printed, on its own and entirely separate from Burns's poetry, Lockhart's "Life". The biography is arguably more interesting for its preface, "An Essay on The Writings of Burns For The American Edition",[24] than anything else. Making reference to "Gilbert Burns, Thomson, Dr. Currie, Cromek, Walker, Peterkin, Heron, Scott, Jeffrey, Wordsworth, Campbell, and Wilson" (the list in itself reveals the array of Burns sources widely available to American readers), the preface initially suggests that "hitherto, almost to a man, his biographers, critics, and reviewers, have been either his rela-tions, personal friends, or Scotsmen" who were negatively affected by "consanguinity, intimacy or nativity".[25] The preface goes on to suggest that American readers bear the advantage of impartiality:

> Perhaps there could not exist a more fit place to discuss the nature and extent of the poetical claims of Burns, than on western ground, standing here, as we do, uninfluenced by the strong biases so well known to exist, on behalf of illustrious names, in all large and old societies.[26]

Revealing a nuanced awareness of the transatlantic dissemination of literature, the writer further suggests that:

> A cause, argued in the same manner, sometimes issues in a different result when carried into another court. A change of air sometimes effects in the constitution of a patient, and *pari passu* in a creed, what no
> > "poppies, mandragoras,
> > > Or drowsy syrups,"
>
> could [...] prepare the mind of the reader for the *discussion* of the *con* as well as the *pro* on the subject of the poetical merits of Robert Burns, which has at least the promise of novelty.[27]

This relatively equivocal introduction quickly turns into an attack on the "pretensions" surrounding the merit of Burns as both a poet and man. The writer, whose identity remains unclear, asserts that while Burns might be a "a good Scottish poet" he is "disqualified from arriving at the same felicity and skill in the use of English, and more especially when it is considered that the *copia verborum* is one of the essential qualities of a great poet".[28] Refusing to bow to Burns's "admirers and eulogists", the preface highlights that, unlike the works of Scott and Byron, "foreign translations of his works have not yet appeared" and that they are generally "not pleasing to the English reader without a glossary".[29]

Continuing in this tone, the writer reflects on Burns's fame being a product of "patriotic tendencies", scathingly suggesting that "one must have been born a Scotsman to relish with *goût* the writings of Burns".[30] Despite being written on "western ground" and thus apparently uninfluenced by "strong biases", undertones of Lockhart's "Life" are present throughout, particularly in the assertion that "the public voice of Scotland had unanimously been raised on behalf of the poet".[31] Thomas C. Richardson has made a credible case for "national enthusiasm" being "central to Lockhart's writing about Burns", situating his "Life" as being a factor in the development of Burns and Scottish nationalism.[32] Indeed, this preface seems to react to Lockhart's pairing of Burns with "national enthusiasm", particularly in its criticism of the "unequivocal eulogy" expressed by Scottish Burns critics and publishers. It also seems to be informed by the way Lockhart—as Sir Walter Scott described it—"judiciously slurred over" Burns's "vices and follies".[33] Reflecting on the hypothetical longevity of Burns's poetry had he lived longer, the reviewer rhetorically remarks:

But who can truly desire that the poet of nature should have continued to write until he had no readers for his last production? [...] Would it have been desirable to have found him throwing crude, diluted water-gruel stuff of poetry, generated by the lees of Port, Burgundy, Champagne, late hours, and the carbon of sea coal, by the side of that balsamic nectar-like menstrum, which the green fields, the genial warmth of the blessed sun, and the pure air, teeming form the fresh earth, concocted in a genial brain, in the kail-yard, or behind the plough at Mossgiel?[34]

Aside from showcasing the writer's cathartic flair, the image of Burns "generated by the lees of Port, Burgundy, Champagne" in the "late hours" smacks of Lockhart's narrative expansion of Heron's suggestion that too many of Burns's hours "were spent at the tables of persons who delighted to urge in conviviality to drunkness—in the tavern—and in the brothel".[35] Lavishing flamboyant praise on Milton ("His personages are nothing less than the Godhead, the Savior, archangels, burning seraphims, myriads of angels")[36] and Shakespeare (who "fills the mind of man with sage aphorisms drawn from the conduct of airy nothings"),[37] the reviewer sets them apart from Burns in their ability to "intensely *elevate* what we see around us"; declaring that the Scottish poet must be "content to be established" in the "second" rank of poets.[38]

Unlike Walt Whitman's much later declaration of Burns as a "third, perhaps fourth class"[39] poet which, as Robert Crawford and I have argued elsewhere, might be attributed to a "persistent anxiety of influence", the writer here unabashedly derides Burns's poetic ignorance of lofty literary convention.[40] Where Charles Brockden Brown praised Burns for straying from the classical "chivalry of poets", the reviewer above—perhaps influenced by Lockhart's more conservative narrative—derides the poet's versification and character. In a preface that is fiercely critical in tone, it is remarkable how positive the writer remains towards Lockhart ("in the advanced pages, the freshness and excellent quality of the *materiel* are every where discernible").[41] Carruthers and Mackay have suggested that Lockhart was "a key player in Britain's powerfully conservative Romantic culture" which is why he portrayed Burns as "impulsive and ungentlemanly"; in stark contrast to the way the same author depicted Scott as "the great Romantic gentleman" (celebrated in five biographical volumes in 1838).[42]

It is clearly Lockhart's "impulsive and ungentlemanly" account of Burns that the reviewer seems to react to, with the scathing preface serving as a pertinent reminder of how crucial editors, biographers and repackaged editions were on the frequent (re)shaping of Burns's image and reputation.

RADICAL CELEBRITY: WILLIAM PEARSON AND ALLAN CUNNINGHAM

In 1832, New York printer William Pearson published a comprehensive edition of *The Works of Robert Burns* that was advertised as not only the "Truest Exhibition of the Man and the Poet" but the "Fullest Edition of His Poetry and Prose Hitherto Published".[43] The edition included Lockhart's recently printed "Life"; "Correspondence from Dr. Currie's Edition; Sketches of the poet by Himself, Gilbert Burns, Professor Stewart and Others"; as well as songs from both James Johnson's *Scots Musical Museum* and George Thomson's *A Select Collection of Original Scottish Airs for the Voice*. Essentially a comprehensive amalgamation of all available materials, Pearson's edition was reprinted more frequently than any other edition in the decade that followed, often by different publishers (Judd Loomis and Co. in Hartford 1836 and Robinson and Franklin in New York, 1839).

A telling reactionary response to the Pearson edition can be found in the New York-based *Knickerbocker* of August 1833. It should be noted that the magazine's cultural milieu, known as the "Knickerbocker Group", included William Cullen Bryant, Henry Wadsworth Longfellow, Oliver Wendell Holmes Sr. and James Russell Lowell; all of whom, as we shall see in Chapter 5, either wrote about or were partly influenced by Burns. The *Knickerbocker* review portrays a far more "revolutionary" account of Burns than previously described. The anonymous reviewer begins by declaring that "Burns was emphatically the poet of the people" before describing an alleged meeting between Burns's eldest son and George IV:

> Did bold uncowering independence ever burst forth in more elevated strains, t han in those glowing lines, "A man's a man for a' that?" That they were highly esteemed by the poet himself, may be ascertained from the fact, that Fourth, when introduced to the royal presence. And how did the heartless despot treat the orphan-boy of the immortal bard, who left these manly lines as a precious deposit [...] dismissed him from his presence![44]

Given Robert Burns II (1786–1857) had worked in the London Stamp Office under the invitation of the British Prime Minister while his younger brother, Colonel James Glencairn (1794–1865), was an imperial loyalist working for the East India Company, the newspaper's emphasis on a despotic British monarch is clearly laced with ideological bias. One notable inclusion in the edition (that might well have bolstered this "revolutionary" image) was the last few stanzas of "Ode For General Washington's Birthday", which was reprinted under the bold new title: "ODE TO LIBERTY".[45] Such textual nuances might well have partially framed the *The Knickerbocker* reviewer's empowered, anti-aristocratic tone:

> But Burns has had his revenge. The more he is known the better his sterling merit is appreciated; the more deeply we dive into his character, the richer mines do we discover; and he has long since taken his niche among the great and glorious names that will descend to the end of time, as the best benefactors of the humans race: while the memory of "the finest gentleman in Europe," is, like that of a Sardanapalus, "damned to everlasting fame."[46]

The language here suggests an evolving fascination and understanding of Burns's life and revolutionary poetry. The classical allusion to the destructive decadence of the Greek king "Sardanapalus" further derides hierarchial structures and places Burns as the antithesis to them; the truly democratic "poet of the people". Ultimately, however, the review concludes with a sentimental depiction of the poet that overrides any political associations:

> We are confident, that no true son of "Auld Caledonia;" no lover of the plaid and the tartan, who loves to think on days "of auld lang syne," will neglect to procure a copy of this imperishable monument of his country's fame.[47]

The reference to the "plaid and the tartan", far from promoting Burns as a beacon of revolutionary fervour and global appeal, adheres to a twee and nostalgic association of the poet with Scotland, the "Land of Romance".[48] Echoing the sentiments in the preface to W. Stodart's *Life of Robert Burns* ("one must have been born a Scotsman to relish with goût the writings of Burns"),[49] the review ends by suggesting that it is the sons and admirers of "Auld Caledonia" that will find enjoyment in Pearson's edition (the "imperishable monument"). While the political and revolutionary traits of Burns might be hinted at, it would be a stretch to suggest that this was a widely recognised association or perception of the poet. Rather, the Pearson edition, with its comprehensive, patchwork-like inclusion of various sources, provided an amalgamated version of Burns for American readers and critics who would subsequently adopt and perceive the poet to their own, often conflicting, ends.

One important, if highly questionable, biographical insertion that the Pearson edition did not include was Allan Cunningham's "Life", which was published in London between January and December 1834. An American edition appeared swiftly on the heels of the original, when Hilliard, Gray and Company printed a version of *The Works* in Boston, complete "With His Life by Allan Cunningham".[50] The unreliable nature of "Honest" Allan Cunningham's account of Burns has been subject to, justifiably, much ridicule in Burns scholarship. Nonetheless, after the initial printing in Boston, Cunningham's "Life" was reprinted at a steady rate. By the 1860s there had been, at the very least, thirty separately printed and distributed editions that contained (variable) materials from Cunningham's frequently revised edition.

If the Pearson edition and its reviews had hinted towards depicting a more revolutionary and politically engaged Burns, then some elements of Cunningham's "Life" bolstered the idea of Burns as an ardent revolutionary. Lockhart's biography famously gave credence to the story of Burns sending carronades to French Revolutionaries, a purported incident that Carruthers and Mackay have described as a "conservative myth" that "would eventually become a favourite story for left-wing fans of the bard".[51] In an expanded version of his "Life of Burns", Cunningham alluded to the *Rosamund* incident in a typically dramatic account of the poet's final hours:

> To the poet himself, death, which he now knew was at hand, brought with it no fear […] He was poor – he gave his pistols, which he had used against the smugglers on the Solway, to his physician, adding with a smile, that he had tried them and found them an honour to their maker, which was more than he could say to the bulk of mankind![52]

In an 1841 New York edition titled *The Life and Land of Burns,* Cunningham's account of how he could "well remember" the poet's Republican ethos was also reprinted:

> That Burns was numbered among the republicans of Dumfries I well remember: but then those who held different sentiments from the men in power, were all, in that loyal town, stigmatized as democrats: that he either desired to see the constitution changed, or his country invaded by the liberal French, who proposed to set us free with the bayonet, and then admit us to the "fraternal embrace", no one ever believed. It is true that he spoke of premiers and peers with contempt; that he hesitated to take off his hat in the theatre, to the air of "God save the King"; that he refused to drink to the health of Pitt, saying he preferred that of Washington – a far greater man…[53]

Cunningham's assertion here is powerful. Burns is depicted as a democratic rebel in the face of British oppression and a symbolic martyr for repressed revolutionary politics. Another article by Cunningham that also featured in the American press was "Robert Burns and Lord Byron", originally printed in the *London Magazine* in August 1824. Just two months later, the article appeared in the Boston-based *New England Galaxy* and was later reprinted in *The New York Literary Gazette* and *Phi Betta Kappa Repository.*

Though Cunningham's "first hand" account ("I knew one, and I have seen both") is not to be taken as reliable, his juxtaposition of the poets' "fame" and "reputation" nevertheless highlights a mid-nineteenth-century fascination for "literary celebrities", as recently documented by scholars such as Eric Eisner and Tom Mole.[54] While Byron is usually the focal point of research into the culture of nineteenth-century "literary celebrity", Burns might equally be a worthy subject of enquiry given his own self-marketing and the magnitude of his posthumous fame. Ghislaine McDayter has suggested that Byron was the first poet "in the business of selling not just poetry but himself" and thus "his fame depended as much on his personal as on his poetic charms".[55] Through his rustic self-fashioning (as in the preface to the Kilmarnock edition), social cavorting and adept ability to switch between personae, it might be argued that Burns's fame also depended upon his "personal" charms and self-marketing abilities. As Corey Andrew summarises, critical enquiry has revealed Burns to be "well aware of the marketing value" of his various personae (in particular the "heaven-taught ploughman") and he almost certainly "manipulated the facts of his life to match the contours of his celebrity".[56] This made Burns, as Andrews further suggests, a "particularly modern writer" who had the ability, and shrewd awareness, to "inhabit various selves for specific purposes"—including self-commodification.

In this way, future critical investigations into the origins and trajectory of "literary celebrity" would do well to include Burns. On a more material (specifically bibliographic) level, McDayter suggests that competing nineteenth-century publishing houses continually produced a steady flow of Byron editions to satisfy the market's "voracious appetite" no matter whether the text was "Byron's, was about Byron, or was merely thought to be about him".[57] Even a quick glance of the chronological checklist of Burns print editions in America (see Appendix A) reveals a similarly intense appetite for the poet's work, life, songs, letters and anything else associated with him.[58]

Clearly, then, Burns was a literary commodity as well as a poet, as evidenced by the steady stream of American publications that not only contained his poetry, but also packed in as much "original" biographical material as possible. Here, we might again refer back to the idea that the legacy of Burns was both maintained and reinvented by mechanisms of "cultural production".[59] In the cases of both Burns and Byron, "artistic mediators"—namely publishers and editors—not only appeased a public appetite for materials about the poets, but also intensified it.

AN AMERICAN BIOGRAPHY

In 1848 Samuel Tyler, a Scottish-born Baltimore-based lawyer, wrote and published the first full-length American biography of Burns. In addition to his occupational commitments to the "Maryland Bar", Tyler considered himself an "amateur philosopher" and was a regular contributor to literary periodicals. His first publication was an 1844 book titled *Discourse of the Baconian Philosophy*, which, in the broadest terms, argued that Anglo-American periodicals were "teeming with expositions and commentaries of the Baconian philosophy".[60] His later biography of Burns similarly veers towards pseudo-philosophy. In his preface, Tyler whimsically attempts to describe "the spirit of Romance in the heart of man" before identifying that "love is the best preservative" for "all the affections". It is "love", according to Tyler, that is the best and least acknowledged aspect of Burns's poetry:

> If, therefore, I have succeeded in drawing attention to this peculiar feature of Burns's poetry, while I have given due consideration to others, I have done what I designed to do, and deem it sufficient apology for having written another work on Burns, when so many abler minds have done so, but have not given so much prominence to this peculiar feature, which is so characteristic of the poet. And I have further endeavoured to defend Burns, as a man, from false opinions of him.[61]

Tyler's mission to defend Burns from "false opinions" clearly outlines his objection to extant biographical portrayals. It is not clear whether his idea of "false portrayals" alludes to the politically subversive, temperamental poet or the overindulgent peasant Scot who met his demise due to "rank appetites". Either way, Tyler's attempted defence transpires into a thoroughly banal, even pious depiction of the poet. If Currie had attempted to make Burns more palatable to a wider reading public, then it seems Tyler, writing decades later, went a step further in attempting to present an almost angelic figure of both "Burns as a Poet" and "Burns as a man". Tyler's first chapter, titled the "Theory of the Beautiful", immediately links the beauty in Burns's poetry to the "Creator":

> For he was emphatically the poet of the Beautiful. The world was evidently designed as the dwelling place of a being who delights in scenes of beauty. For the Creator has taken as much care to make everything beautiful, as he has to make every thing useful.[62]

Though, as previously discussed, Burns's early access to education was documented by the turn of the nineteenth century, Tyler does his best to drive home the image of Burns as the divinely inspired bard, further stating that he was "educated in no school, trammelled by no master" and thus he "caught his inspiration on from nature herself".[63] Ultimately for Tyler, it was "God who made him the ennobling genius".[64] Despite the widespread reprinting of Currie's essay on the "Scotch Peasantry", Tyler does his best to describe the dreary "prosaic condition" from which Burns rose:

> For no man was ever born in a more prosaic condition of life. Everything near him, and everything around him, was as dull as human life ever furnishes [...] his condition seemed to be the very one where thought and feeling must languish and expire. But the irrepressible energies of genius can conquer even these difficulties.[65]

As noted, however, Carlyle's Romantic revision of Burns (as put forth in his review of Lockhart) was in wide circulation by this point and was evidently echoed, to base degree, in the fantastical claims of Tyler. Tyler's description of the poet's "irrepressible energies" despite his "dull" surroundings seems to derive from Carlyle's declaration that Burns's "genius" could "pierce" through and "tint clouds with rainbow and orient colours, into a glory and stern grandeur!"[66]

However, void of Carlyle's transcendental charisma, Tyler's account foreshadows the "stale appreciation" of Burns as an inconsequential love poet prominent in twentieth-century criticism, as outlined by Murray Pittock in *Robert Burns in Global Culture*.[67] Tyler's biography does not appear to have been reprinted beyond the initial 1848 edition. Thus, in comparison with the wider availability of Lockhart, Currie and Cunningham, we might render it as having minimal influence. Yet the first (and only) full-length American biography of Burns still serves to remind us that the myth of the "heaven-taught" ploughman was not only present in mid-nineteenth-century America, but also being expanded upon and promoted through print culture.

In the decade that followed Tyler's biography, American editions of Burns's poetry continued to be published at a rapid rate, each with their own version—or amalgamated version(s)—of Burns's "Life" attached. In some cases, the same publisher printed different editions in the same year. For example in 1852, publishers Leavitt & Allen, founded by George A. Leavitt, simultaneously printed *The Poetical Works of Robert Burns* which contained a "Sketch of his Life, by James Currie"[68] and *The Works of Robert Burns*, "Containing his "Life" by John Lockhart".[69] This not only suggests that printing Burns was a profitable enterprise, but also hints towards there being a collectors' market eager to obtain as many editions (or as much information about Burns) as possible.

As was the case with the early printers of *Poems*, connections can here be drawn between many of the publishers who were simultaneously printing Burns. Two years prior to Leavitt & Allen's editions in 1852, George A. Leavitt's father, Jonathan Leavitt, printed his own version of William Pearson's *The Works* via his renowned New York publishing house Leavitt, Trow & Co. A year later in 1851, George S. Appleton, who was Jonathan Leavitt's brother-in-law, printed an edition titled *The Complete Works of Robert Burns* in Philadelphia, which included Allan Cunningham's biography. That same year, his own brother Daniel Appleton printed the edition in New York under the company name D. Appleton & Co. All of the aforementioned publishers would go on reproducing, separately and in different States, editions of Burns's poetry throughout the remainder of the nineteenth century. While this might suggest there was, to some extent, an interconnected monopoly on publishing Burns in America, the evidence more importantly reveals the extent to which Burns was deemed a literary commodity; evidenced by the fact that over 160 different American editions of his "life" and works were available across different states by 1866 (see Appendix A and B).

Robert Chambers and "The Tree of Liberty"

It was not, however, any of the interconnected printers mentioned above that presented the first American edition of Robert Chambers's *The Life and Works of Robert Burns* in 1852, which was produced by Harper & Brothers of New York (another colossal nineteenth-century printing firm that eventually evolved into present-day Harper-Collins). Curiously, the Chambers edition was first printed in Britain in 1838; an anomaly in that the majority of American editions were usually reproduced within a year. While a portion of the original 1838 Chambers editions would likely have made their way to America, it is unclear why it took so long for an American reprinting to occur.

Similar to William Pearson's earlier New York edition, Chambers amalgamated a wide array of previous biographical sources. The preface acknowledges how Currie had previously gathered biographical materials "from the poet himself, his brother Gilbert, Professor Stewart, Mr. Syme, and others", yet Chambers hastens to add that Burns's first editor ultimately "tried to avoid provoking any loud demonstration from those who took unfavourable views of the life and conversation of Burns".[70]

Summarising "other biographies of the poet", Chambers notes that only "two deserve particular notice", pointing to Lockhart (who "adds little to the details previously known") and Cunningham (who "gives a greater amount of fresh anecdote"). While Chambers seems to praise Cunningham to a higher degree, he concludes that the editor still "failed to produce a work which could leave nothing to be desired".[71] All of the biographers and works that Chambers references, of course, were readily available and accessible in America at the time. Even in the same year that the Chambers edition appeared, for example, D. Appleton of New York offered *The Complete Poetical Works of Robert Burns* with a biography by Allan Cunningham, while Leavitt & Allen produced *The Works* containing Lockhart's "Life".

What the Chambers edition did offer American readers—to an even larger extent than Pearson—was the bolder image of a more politically subversive, revolutionary Burns. Later in his preface, Chambers depicts Burns as an "Undying Voice" for "mankind", who was dedicated to espousing the "equality of consideration due to all men".[72] Short of calling Burns a revolutionary Republican, Chambers depicts Burns as more radically democratic and egalitarian than ever before. One of the most significant inclusions in the edition, particularly in regard to its appearance on the American side of the Atlantic, was Chamber's introduction to "The Tree of Liberty"; a poem he obtained from a manuscript given to him by James Duncan of Mosesfield, Glasgow. However, as will be discussed shortly, the poem had already appeared in America in earlier American reprints (though it was Chambers who was first to highlight the significance of its revolutionary rhetoric).

Perhaps the most contested text associated with Burns, there remains a great deal of scepticism as to whether Burns actually wrote "The Tree of Liberty", and work continues to be carried out on the matter. Gerard Carruthers and Norman R. Paton have recently suggested Alexander Geddes (1737–1802) as being a possible alternative author, but with no affirmative evidence, the jury remains out.[73] Nonetheless, it is worth briefly comparing the previous formal analysis of "When Guilford Good" in Chapter 2 with "The Tree of Liberty". The similarity in metre and measure between the two poems is striking, with both poems conveying themes of liberation amidst the beating repetition of "man", set to the tune of Killiecrankie. Yet, as Carruthers and Paton have noted, there remains a great deal of other "unanswered questions" regarding its provenance and transmission, and this formal similarity alone is far from sufficient in declaring authorship.

In the years leading up to the Revolution, "people planted poplars to signify their growing demands to obtain freedom from the yoke of British rule", with a famous Elm tree near Boston Common becoming a symbolic rallying point for revolutionaries until it was felled by British soldiers in 1775. Just over a decade later, Thomas Jefferson, in a letter teeming with patriotic rhetoric, wrote to W. S. Smith referring back to the symbolic motif:

> And what country can preserve its liberties if their rulers are not warned from time to time that their people preserve the spirit of resistance? Let them take arms. The remedy is to set them right as to facts, pardon and pacify them. What signify a few lives lost in a century or two? The tree of liberty must be refreshed from time to time with the blood of patriots and tyrants. It is it's [sic] natural manure.[74]

During the French Revolution the symbolic power of "trees of liberty" hit new precedents as Jacobins adopted the motif, shortly followed by radical groups in Scotland and Ireland. Later on, the United Irishmen similarly adopted the Tree of Liberty as a populist cultural emblem. A quick reference to a "catechism" used by the United Irishmen articulates, albeit in simplified terms, the growing revolutionary fervour that was circulating around the Atlantic world:

> What is in your hand?
> It is a branch.
> Of what?
> Of the tree of liberty.
> Where did it first grow?
> In America.
> Where does it bloom?
> In France.
> Where did the seeds fall?
> In Ireland.[75]

The point here is to establish that, while the poem in Chambers's edition begins by referencing the "tree o France",[76] the very notion of the "Tree of Liberty" was rooted in revolutionary American Republicanism and reformist politics. Complicating matters even more is the fact that, by the time the poem appeared in Chambers's edition, "Liberty Trees" were being adopted by several other movements during the European Revolutions of 1848.

In Italy, for example, Republican Florentines "erected liberty trees and liberty poles" in a bid to encourage the city to "unite with the Republicans of Rome".[77] Regardless of these transatlantic complexities, the reprint of Chambers's edition depicted Burns as directly engaging with American revolutionary rhetoric. Even in his introduction to the poem, Chambers depicts Burns as the "poor bard" whose "democratic effusions" had been suppressed by others:

> It is far from likely that the whole of the democratic effusions of Burns have come down to us. For many years, that kind of authorship was attended with so much reproach, that men of humanity studied to conceal rather than to expose the evidence by which it could be proved against him. And even after the poor bard's death, the interests of his young family demanded of all the admirers of his name, that nothing should be brought forward which was calculated to excite a political jealousy regarding him.[78]

Chambers makes a valid point in that (as previously discussed) Burns's "Ode for General Washington's Birthday" and "Address of Beelzebub" were indeed concealed until long after the poet's death, and the "terror" of the revolutionary years had subsided. However, to state that this was the case for the even more radical "Tree of Liberty" further propagates the image of Burns as "repressed Republican". Once again, here lies the power and influence of Burns's editors and biographers in shaping his identity. With the inclusion of one new poem (not even proven to be his own) and an added editorial epithet, Burns is cast as an ardent friend to America's founding principles through staunch, Republican ethos.

While the Chambers edition was reprinted twice again the following year (Harper & Brothers in New York and Lippincott, Grambo & Co. in Philadelphia, 1854), the authorship of the "Tree of Liberty" had already been called into question by Chambers's editorial rival Allan Cunningham. This is where the intricate inconsistencies between printed editions on different sides of the Atlantic become complex. Cunningham initially included the poem in the 1840 London edition of *The Works*, published by T. Tegg, with the poem appearing in its entirety along with a footnote acknowledging that it had first "appeared in Chambers 1838 edition, having been taken from an MS in the poet's hand writing in the possession of Mr. James Duncan, Mosesfield, near Glasgow".[79] Crucially, though, the poem did not appear in the Cunningham edition reprinted by J. Crissy of Philadelphia in the same year.

Just two years after the 1840 London edition (in which Cunningham *did* include the poem), the editor had seemingly changed his mind, deciding to omit it and emphatically declare in his preface that "There are eleven stanzas in the *Tree of Liberty* of which the *best* compared with 'A man's a man for a' that' of Burns, sounds like a cracked pipkin, against the heroic clang of a Damascus blade".[80] However, the poem continued to be attributed to Burns in America, even before the Chambers reprint. It appears, for example, in the 1843 New York and Philadelphian printings of *The Complete Poetical Works of Robert Burns* (printed by D. Appleton in New York and G. Appleton in Philadelphia).

Thus, "The Tree of Liberty" in fact first appeared—in America but not Britain—in revised versions of Currie's *Works*, rather than editions attributed to Chambers. It was the Chambers edition, nonetheless, that added the editorial emphasis on its revolutionary importance. By 1855, the "Tree of Liberty" not only featured in American reprints of both Chambers and Cunningham but was simultaneously being derided and refuted in works *also* edited by Cunningham (as in the Boston edition of *The Complete Works of Robert Burns*).

The case of the "Tree of Liberty", then, provides a fitting microcosmic reminder of how the broader reputation of Burns in nineteenth-century America was continually reshaped and altered by inconsistent reprints (or unauthorised American editions) and contrasting biographical narratives.

NOTES

1. Robert Burns, *The Works of Robert Burns; with an Account of His Life, and a Criticism on His Writings. To Which Are Prefixed Some Observations on the Character and Condition of the Scottish Peasantry*, 4 vols., ed. James Currie (Liverpool: J. M'creery, 1800), 1:2.

2. *The Poetical Works of Robert Burns* (Philadelphia: Benjamin Johnson, Jacob Johnson, & Robert Johnson, 1804). This was a reprint of the "history of myself" letter written to Dr. Moore, dated 2 August 1787.

3. *The Poetical Works of Robert Burns* (Philadelphia: Peter Stewart, 1807).

4. *The Poetical Works of Robert Burns* (London: T. Cadell and W. Davies, 1804), Preface.

5. J. DeLancey Ferguson, "In Defense of R. H. Cromek", *Philological Quarterly* 9 (1930): 239.

6. *The Oxford Edition of the Works of Robert Burns*, 1:38.

7. Dennis M. Read, *R. H. Cromek, Engraver, Editor and Entrepreneur* (Farnham and Burlington: Ashgate Publishing, 2011), 4.

8. R. H. Cromek, ed., *Reliques of Robert Burns* (London: Cadell and Davies, 1808), 238.

9. *The American Register: Or General Repository of History, Politics and Science* 4 (1809): 117.

10. *Select Reviews, and Spirit of the Foreign Magazines* 2 (1809): 10.

11. Ibid., 17–18.

12. *The Salem Gazette* 1, no. 16 (1823): 1.

13. See Gerard Carruthers, "In Search of Highland Mary". Accessed 7 January 2016. http://www.electricscotland.com/familytree/frank/burns_lives128.htm.

14. In 2000, Donny O' Rourke edited a collection of the letters aimed at a broader readership titled *Ae Fond Kiss: The Love Letters of Robert Burns and Clarinda: Love Letters of Burns and Clarinda*, ed. Donny O' Rourke (Edinburgh: Mercat Press, 2000).

15. *Letters Addressed to Clarinda*, etc., *by Robert Burns, the Ayrshire Poet, Never Before Published* (Glasgow: Thomas Stewart, 1802). See also Pauline Anne Gray, "Prudes, Pirates and Bills of Suspension: The Correspondence of Burns and Clarinda", *The Burns Chronicle* (2005): 9–13.

16. *The Poetical Works of Robert Burns* (Philadelphia: Benjamin Warner, 1818).

17. *The Scottish Minstrel: Being a Complete Collection of Burns' Songs* (Philadelphia: Benjamin Warner, 1818), 3.

18. Though no full editions have been traced, it should be noted that Kirsteen McCue, chief editor of the forthcoming Oxford University Press edition *Burns's Songs for George Thomson*, is currently searching for Philadelphian reprints of Thomson. Moreover, there is some evidence to suggest that Thomson's early Scottish volumes were circulating in Philadelphia. See Anne McClenny Krauss, "James Bremner, Alexander Reinagle and the Influence of the Edinburgh Musical Society on Philadelphia", in *Scotland and America in the Age of Enlightenment*, eds. Sher and Smitten, 259–274.

19. See *The Works of Robert Burns, with an Account of His Life and a Criticism on His Writings, The Eighth Edition*, 4 vols. (T. Cadell and W. Davies, 1820), 1:381–402. For a fuller account of the exchanges, see *The Oxford Edition of the Works of Robert Burns*, 20–21.

20. See Carl F. Kaestle, "The History of Literacy and the History of Reading", in *Perspectives on Literacy: Civic Engagement and Service Learning Collection*, ed. Eugene R. Kintgen, Barry M. Kroll, and Mike Rose (Carbondale: Southern Illinois University Press, 1988), 110.
21. *The Critical Heritage*, 351.
22. *The New York American* 9, no. 857 (1829): 2.
23. Ibid.
24. *Life of Robert Burns, by J. G. Lockhart* (New York: W. Stodart, 1831), 3.
25. Ibid.
26. Ibid., 3–4.
27. Ibid., 4. Jeremy Smith has deconstructed such arguments against Burns's "limited" linguistic range and register. See Jeremy J. Smith, "Copia Verborum: The Linguistic Choices of Robert Burns", *Review of English Studies* 58, no. 233 (2007): 73–88.
28. Ibid., 4–5.
29. Ibid., 5.
30. Ibid.
31. Ibid., 8.
32. Thomas C. Richardson, "John Lockhart's Burns: Stirring 'National Enthusiasm'", *Studies in Scottish Literature* 30, no. 1 (1998), 159.
33. Walter Scott, *The Journal of Sir Walter Scott*, ed. David Douglas, 2 vols. (Edinburgh: David Douglas, 1890), 2:195.
34. *Life of Robert Burns*, 9.
35. Ibid., 144.
36. Ibid., 17.
37. Ibid.
38. Ibid., 18.
39. Gary Scharnhorst, "Whitman on Robert Burns: An Early Essay Recovered", *The Walt Whitman Quarterly Review* 13, no. 3 (1996): 218.
40. Robert Crawford, "America's Bard", in *Robert Burns and Transatlantic Culture*, eds. Alker, Davis, and Nelson, 110; and Arun Sood, "A Modern Poet on the Scotch Bard: Walt Whitman's 1875 Essay on Robert Burns", *The Walt Whitman Quarterly Review* 32, no. 4 (2015): 230–236.
41. *Life of Robert Burns*, 18.
42. Carruthers and Mackay, "Re-reading James Currie; Robert Burns's First Editor", 74.
43. *The Works of Robert Burns* (New York: William Pearson, 1832), Another edition which appeared the same year, printed by Leavitt and Allan, included much of the same content. See Appendix A.
44. *The Knickerbocker* 2 (1833): 148.
45. *The Works of Robert Burns* (New York: William Pearson, 1832): 77.
46. *The Knickerbocker*: 148–149.

47. Ibid., 149.
48. See Andrew Hook's discussion of nineteenth-century American perceptions of Scotland as a "Land of Romance", in *Scotland and America*, 116–174.
49. J. G Lockhart, ed., *Life of Robert Burns* (New York: W. Stodart, 1831).
50. *The Works of Robert Burns, by Allan Cunningham*, 4 Vols. (Boston: Hilliard, Gray & Co., 1834).
51. Carruthers and Mackay, "Re-reading James Currie; Robert Burns's First Editor", 74. For more on this "conservative myth" see also Gerard Carruthers and Jennifer Orr, "'The Diel's Awa Wi' the Exciseman': Robert Burns the Giver of Guns to Revolutionary France?", in *Fickle Man*, ed. Rodgers and Carruthers, 257–266.
52. Allan Cunningham, "Life of Burns", in *The Complete Works of Robert Burns, by Alan Cunningham* (Boston: Phillips, Sampson and Company, 1857), 54.
53. *The Life and Land of Burns by Allan Cunningham* (New York: J. & H. G. Langley, 1841), 147–148.
54. Tom Mole, ed., *Romanticism and Celebrity Culture* (Cambridge: Cambridge University Press, 2012) and Eric Eisner, *Nineteenth-Century Poetry and Literary Celebrity* (London: Palgrave Macmillan, 2009).
55. Ghislaine McDayter, "Conjuring Byron: Byromania, Literary Commodification and the Birth of Celebrity", in *Byromania: Portraits of the Artist in Nineteenth and Twentieth Century Culture*, ed. Frances Wilson (London: Macmillan Press, 1999), 46.
56. Corey Andrews, "'Far-fam'd RAB': Scottish Labouring-Class Poets Writing in the Shadow of Robert Burns, 1785–1792", *Studies in Hogg and His World* 23 (2013): 41.
57. Ibid., 53.
58. Correspondingly, Chapter 6 will outline a "material" fascination for Burns "beyond text".
59. *The Genius of Scotland*, 149.
60. Samuel Tyler, *Discourse of the Baconian Philosophy* [1844] (London: Forgotten Books, 2013), 16.
61. Samuel Tyler, *Robert Burns, as a Poet, and as a Man* (New York: Baker & Scribner, 1848), 5.
62. Ibid.
63. Ibid., 57.
64. Ibid.
65. Ibid., 34.
66. Ibid.

67. Murray Pittock, "'A Long Farewell to All My Greatness': The History of the Reputation of Robert Burns", in *Robert Burns in Global Culture*, ed. Pittock, 34.

68. *The Poetical Works of Robert Burns* (New York: Leavitt & Allen, 1852).

69. *The Works of Robert Burns* (New York: Leavitt & Allen, 1852).

70. *The Life and Works of Robert Burns, by Robert Chambers* (New York: Harper & Brothers, 1852), Preface.

71. Ibid.

72. Ibid., 8.

73. Carruthers and Paton, "Did Robert Burns Write the Tree of Liberty", in *Fickle Man*, eds. Rodger and Carruthers, 242–257.

74. "Thomas Jefferson to W. S. Smith". Accessed 13 November 1787. http://www.loc.gov/exhibits/jefferson/105.html.

75. Kevin Whelan, *The Tree of Liberty: Radicalism, Catholicism, and the Construction of Irish Identity 1760–1830* (Cork: Cork University Press, 1996), 57.

76. *The Life and Works*, 87.

77. Timothy Mason Roberts, *Distant Revolutions: 1848 and the Challenge to American Exceptionalism* (Charlottesville: University of Virginia Press, 2009), 100.

78. *The Life and Works*, 87.

79. *The Works of Robert Burns, with Life by Allan Cunningham, and Notes by Gilbert Burns* (London: T. Tegg, 1840), 292.

80. *The Works of Robert Burns*, ed., Allan Cunningham (London: George Virtue, 1842), Preface.

CHAPTER 5

"Bob'o'lincoms of Our Own": Burns and American Poets, c.1800–1859

We rejoice to meet with an author national enough to break away from the slavish deference, too common among us, to English grammar and orthography...[1]

—James Russell Lowell (1892)

In addition to, or beyond, a widespread biographical fascination for Burns, his poetics also had a considerable literary influence on nineteenth-century American poets. Charles Brockden Brown had hinted at this in his *Literary Magazine and American Register* as early as 1804, and Robert Walsh went a step further in 1811:

We have often been asked in the country of Mr. Scott, whether the people of the United States were generally acquainted with the poetry of Burns and Beattie. The answer, which we have given, and which we still give, to this query, is calculated to startle the credulity of those, who see us in a more tilling and shopkeeping race. We are quite satisfied that – proportionably [sic] to the difference of the population in the two countries – the works of the two poets we have cited and even of Mr Scott, are here more widely circulated, more generally read, and perhaps better understood than in England taken separately from Scotland. The dialect of the latter is more familiar and more grateful to us than to the inhabitants of her sister kingdom.[2]

Underlining the availability of Burns's works, Walsh also implies that they offered an alternative to the hegemony of a cultivated English

© The Author(s) 2018
A. Sood, *Robert Burns and the United States of America*,
https://doi.org/10.1007/978-3-319-94445-6_5

literary establishment. This brings to mind Joseph Rezek's idea of the first three decades of nineteenth-century American literature being informed by a "complex and influential provincial aesthetics" that emerged in concert with "wildly popular literatures of Ireland and Scotland".[3] Rezek posits that writers (and readers) in Ireland, Scotland and the USA shared a common "provincial" ground and thus rejected London's literary authority; channelling resentment into a reactionary, "anti-English nationalism"[4] that informed the print culture, literary composition, reception and aesthetics of the period. As we shall see, in resisting some of the elitist conventions of English literature, particularly in regard to poetic form, place and vernacular language, early American poets did indeed find a common ally, or indeed inspiration, in Burns.

Whether adhering to the idea that British, or specifically English, poetry stifled American thought, or adopting the more sanguine attitude that classical literary models had to be followed, literary imperialism plagued American poets long after the Revolution. In 1788 (incidentally the same year that Burns's first *Poems* appeared), American poet Philip Frenau (1752–1832) wrote the following verse under the title "Literary Importation"[5]:

> Can we never be thought to have learning or grace
> Unless it be brought from that damnable place
> Where tyranny reigns with her impudent face?
>
> (23–25)

Frenau's verse is an adequate summation of the ongoing struggle to assert American intellectual credibility and literary worth. Articles in the British periodical press continued to deride American literature well into the nineteenth century. Sydney Smith's (1771–1845) frequently quoted piece in the 1820 *Edinburgh Review* suggests the extremity of British attitudes, with its rhetorical sneering that questioned: "In four quarters of the globe, who reads an American book? Or goes to an American play?"[6] Smith was by no means a lone voice and such derision was evident in the British press from the Revolution right through the nineteenth century.[7] This naturally led to reactionary responses on the opposite side of the Atlantic.

In 1783, the American lexicographer Noah Webster (1758–1843) bellowed a literary battle cry that declared "America must be as independent in literature as she is in politics" and as "famous for arts as for arms". Webster's primary goal was to "have some influence in exciting a spirit of literary industry"[8] among young American writers. This incentive, however, was often hard to nurture. In an article titled "Essay on American Poetry" in the 1818 *North American Review*, pioneer-poet William Cullen Bryant (1794–1878) complained:

> With respect to the prevailing style of poetry, at the present day, in our country, we apprehend that it will be found, in too many instances, tinged with a sickly and affected imitation of the peculiar manner of some of the late popular poets of England.[9]

Several years later in 1869, Bryant praised Burns for succeeding "in an age of formalism in poetry, of cold and feeble imitation and parrot-like repetition".[10] Bryant does not clarify or further allude to which English poets he felt were being "sickly" imitated in America. Rather than contemporary British Romantics (Bryant publicly esteemed the poetics of Wordsworth, Coleridge and Southey),[11] his attack on "imitation" more likely referred to Augustan or neoclassical traditions; given the likes of Pope, Milton and Dryden continued to be emulated by Americans attempting to produce their own version of British *belles lettres*.[12]

Yet for Bryant, it seems Burns was considered within different parameters (having succeeded in "an age of formalism") to earlier eighteenth-century British poets and praised for his poetic innovation. Henry Wadsworth Longfellow (1807–1882) also called for a "new and delightful expression" that strayed from the imitation of "indifferent models" and offered an alternative to "the degenerate spirit" of "English poetry",[13] while Thomas Jefferson praised Burns for his "beautiful" dialect in an 1813 letter that Robert Crawford has described as a "manifesto for American language".[14]

In the preface to his 1848 *Biglow Papers*, James Russell Lowell (1819–1891), in a self-referential mock review, praised (himself as) an "author national enough to break away" from the "slavish deference" to "English grammar and orthography".[15] Here, it seems adopting a local, vernacular orthography was considered one way of asserting national American resistance to a standardised English hegemony; thus making explicit why Burns's Scots-language poetry might have been particularly well-received or inspirational. In juxtaposing the sentiments of Longfellow, Bryant, Webster and Lowell, the repeated emphasis on national credibility suggests that these early to mid-nineteenth-century poets were consciously engaged in a constructivist bid to contribute towards a burgeoning American national (at least literary) identity.

Whether or not the formation of an American poetic canon was integral to contemporary process of "nation-building" in the nineteenth century is a question that continues to divide.[16] Less debatable, however, is the fact that Burns, through his linguistic fluency and poetic form, was regularly looked upon more favourably than other eighteenth-century British poets and transatlantic literary imports.

POEMS, CHIEFLY IN THE SCOTS-AMERICAN DIALECT

Despite Bryant and Longfellow's simultaneous praise for Burns and derision of poetic imitators, "Scots mimicry" was the first manifestation of Burns having any poetic influence in America. Shortly after the first American editions of *Poems* appeared, a stream of Scots imitation poems began to be printed in the periodical press. Andrew Hook must be credited with excavating the majority of these poems in his excellent 1975 book *Scotland and America: A Study of Cultural Relations, 1750–1835*. However, very little appears to have been written about the poems since. This is surprising given the extent to which transatlantic literary studies has encouraged scholars to move beyond Anglophone frames of reference to consider more nuanced, transnational linguistic and literary intersections. Colleen Glenney Boggs, for example, suggests that the most interesting developments in the field "challenge the associations of nation and language as epistemological hegemons that structure literary studies".[17] The Burns "imitation poems" are a fine example of the complex processes by which vernacular traditions, originating within one nation, can form new offshoots and evolve in fresh geo-cultural contexts.

Though American literary historiography might reduce these "imitations poems" to a footnote, their regular appearance(s) still hints at the (albeit small-scale) acceptance and taste for Scots as a viable literary language in America. Up until the reprinting of Burns's poetry, it was extremely rare for Scots-language poems to feature in the American dailies or literary periodicals. From 1790 right through to the turn of the nineteenth century, however, a flurry of Scots poems appeared, primarily in the *New York Magazine* and *Port Folio*. The majority of unsigned poems adopted the Standard Habbie and functioned as elegiac tributes to Burns and, in some cases, his Scots-language predecessors:

> Fair fa' ye Robie, canty callan,
> Wha rhym'st amaist as weel as Allan,
> An pleasant highlan' lads an' lawlan,
>   Wi your auld gab,
> May never wae come near your dwallin,
>   Nor scaith nor scab.[18]   (1–6)

Though Allan Ramsay's poetry was not reproduced in America until later in the nineteenth century, his pastoral comedy *The Gentle Shepherd* was reprinted as early as 1750 and was reprinted well into the 1790s.[19] The appearance and popularity of Burns's vernacular effusions may well have, as was the case with Macpherson's *Ossian* and Robert Fergusson, maintained or reignited interest in his predecessors' literary works.[20] In addition to elegiac verses, several of the poems directly mimicked, to varying effect, Burns's own poetry, such as "To the Blackbird in Winter" which was printed in the *Port Folio* of 1806:

> Poor bird! My heart is truly wae,
> Forlorn to see thee, wand'rin sae,
>   E'en heav'n vicegerent –
> Unfeelin' man – he waits to slay
>   Thee like a tyrant.[21]   (1–5)

Minus the artful and deeply philosophical imagery of Burns's "To a Mouse" and "To a Mountain-Daisy", the remainder of the poem mirrors the two former compositions in tone and sentiment. The majority of these compositions were indeed either mediocre reproductions of Burns's best-known poems, panegyric verses or comic observations. However, a more politically subversive use of Scots can be found in the work of a poet who has, hitherto, largely ignored in Burns scholarship. Robert Dinsmoor (1757–1836) was an American-born poet of Ulster-Scots descent who, in his first published volume in 1828, declared himself the "Rustic Bard" of New Hampshire. As scholarship on Ulster-Scots language, culture and literature continues to flourish (the formation of the Ulster-Scots Language Society has been credited as the principal agent sparking the revival)[22] it seems a pertinent time to revisit the work of Dinsmoor.

In 2012, the Ulster Historical Foundation published *Robert Dinsmoor's Scotch-Irish Poems*, edited by Frank Ferguson and Alister

McReynolds. The recovery of Dinsmoor's work is, as Ferguson and McReynolds point out, important for the development of Ulster-Scots scholarship in that it ties together the language, culture and experiences of the torrent of Ulster-Scots who emigrated to America almost a century after leaving the Lowlands of Scotland.[23] Dinsmoor's great-grandfather had originally moved from the Tweed area of Scotland to the plantations of Ulster in the early eighteenth century, and a few decades later his own grandfather crossed the Atlantic, building a house in Fort George, Brunswick between 1718 and 1720. It is widely known that a large portion Ulster-Scots emigrants appeared in the forefront of the American Revolution,[24] and Robert Dinsmoor was no exception, having fought against the British during the Revolutionary War and notably being present during the surrender of Sir John Burgoyne at Saratoga; an episode that Burns himself wrote about in "When Guilford Good" ("Burgoyne gaed up, like spur an' whip").

In 1828, Massachusetts publisher A. W. Thayer published a collection by Dinsmoor titled *Incidental Poems: accompanied with letters...Together with a preface, and sketch of the author's life (written by himself)*. Even a quick glance at the title page bares resemblance to the editions of Burns's poetry that were simultaneously circulating in America. Not only was this a collection of poetry, but there was added emphasis on "letters" and "a sketch of the author's life". The title page also attributes the work to "Robert Dinsmoor, Rustic Bard"; a term that echoes Burns's own self-presentation as "a Bard of rustic song" in "The Bard's Epitaph". The book's preface might easily be mistaken for some of the early descriptions of Burns as the untutored, "heaven-taught" ploughman. The author is described as having composed his poems "from the untutored impulses of his own mind" due to the fact that "his right to poetry was derived from the God that made him".[25] Yet much like the emergence of Burns's schooling in the American press, Dinsmoor's "heaven-taught" talents are also qualified by "New England customs":

> Every one acquainted with New England customs, knows, that in a farmer's house, you commonly see, a Bible and Watt' Psalm-Book, his Lyric Poems, Pope's Essay on Man, Pilgrim's Progress, and an Almanac. This constitutes their library; and from sources like these, our author probably derived all his juvenile literature.[26]

After discussing the merits of Shakespeare's and Addison's treatment of "nature", the preface then extols the virtues of Dinsmoor's approach while acknowledging his literary limitations. While "there is no art, no refinement, no sublimity" in his lines, there is a "fresh importation of images from the living world"; and his "homely and rustic air" is described as "profoundly original".[27] The claims for Dinsmoor's "originality" are on the basis of him being the first "poet of domestic life as it is exhibited in New England".[28] The preface goes on to describe Dinsmoor's New England-based muse:

> She is a nymph, dressed not in the classic wreaths of Greece and Rome; nor does she wear the roses and lilies of Italy or England. Her garland is white-weed, a less fanciful plant, but the production of our own soil. We hear, not the nightingales of a foreign grove, but the Bob'o'lincoms of our own.[29]

Here, Dinsmoor rejects "nightingales" (used as a motif by Roman, Greek and English poets ranging from Sappho to Keats) in favour of "Bob'o' lincoms"; a loaded reference to both a species of bird unique to North America (the bobolink) and also William Cullen Bryant's corresponding poem "Robert of Lincoln".[30] Acknowledging the ambitious claims of originality, the writer of the preface comes to admit that: "It may be said that he writes in the Scotch dialect, and with manifest reference to Burns". A defence of Dinsmoor is then put forward, firstly on the basis of his emigrant heritage ("respecting his using the Scotch dialect, we would remark, that he is really of Scotch descent, though of American birth") and then on his adherence to scenes of locality ("whatever similitude there may be between them, he shews [sic] peculiar judgment in not transfusing, a single sample of foreign scenery into his native land").

In a more disputable statement, the writer then states that Dinsmoor "began to write poetry probably before he knew that Burns existed" and it was not until a friend gave him a copy of Burns's poetry that he realised that they "were congenial spirits".[31] There might well be some truth in Dinsmoor having experimented with poetry at a young age (he was two years older than Burns), yet it is hard to imagine that the Scots-language effusions included in *Incidental Poems* were written before the New England poet had read Burns (though Allan Ramsay's Scots pastoral comedy *The Gentle Shepherd* might have been another formative influence given its popularity in America).[32]

It is also curious that Dinsmoor's use of dialect is wholly attributed to his "Scotch-descent" rather than it being recognised as an aesthetic device. This was, perhaps, an attempt to answer the admittedly complex question of why Dinsmoor, born and bred in America, often chose to write in Scots as well as English. A useful comparison might here be drawn with contemporary "labouring-class poets" across the Atlantic such as John Clare (1793–1864) in England and Samuel Thomson (1766–1816) in Ulster. Despite not hailing from Scotland, both poets produced works that adopted a "heavily stylized, literary version of the Scots tongue" to various ends; whether political, regional or to express "labouring-class" experience.[33]

Pertinently, Corey Andrews has recently recovered the connections between Burns and contemporary "labouring-class" Scottish poets who were "writing in his shadow" such as John Lapraik (1727–1807), David Sillar (1760–1830) and Janet Little (1759–1813).[34] While these poets were "less admiring" (of Burns) than "it appears on the surface", Andrews highlights a perceived affinity based on a "shared nationality" and "shared class status". More explicitly, their "strong feelings of kinship" with Burns were "based upon the common experiences of living and working in rural Scotland".[35] While Dinsmoor could claim little kinship with Burns on the basis of "nationality" or "working in rural Scotland", his desire to write a communal poetics that articulated New England characters, places and local habitation seems to have derived, to some extent, from a "labouring-class" tradition that repelled the upper-class hegemony of English poetry. This might partly explain his decision to employ Scots. However, rather than acknowledging direct kinship with Burns as a "peasant" or "labouring-class" poet, Dinsmoor's preface is more concerned with distinguishing his own use of the locale:

> If he resembles Burns, it is with all the diversity of the two countries in which each were born. Burns is the bonny Doon flowing through the banks and braes of Scotland; and Dinsmoor, is the Merrimack, passing through our western soil and reflecting from its crystal bed the western scenery through which it passes.[36]

In addition to depicting "western scenery" such as the Merrimack River (which rises at the confluence of the Pemigewasset and Winnipesaukeer rivers in New Hampshire), many of Dinsmoor's poems specifically describe the Ulster-Scots emigrant experience in America. In "To Mrs. Agnes Park", Dinsmoor, writing in "standard English" yet still employing Burns's favoured Habbie stanza, remarks on the long journey made by Ulster-scots to America, "this bless'd land":

> Let us that Providence adore,
> Though loud Atlantic billows roar,
> Which took our sires from Albion's shore,
>   Or Scotia's strand,
> And brought their offspring safely o'er
>   To this bless'd land.[37]   (31–36)

The positive depiction of America in the final line is reminiscent of Burns's own frequent association of the country with liberty. Where Burns was both empathetic and proleptic to the emigrant experience ("Tho' I to foreign lands must hie") ("Farewell to the Brethren of St. James's Lodge, Tarbolton",)[38] (5), Dinsmoor's poems directly narrate not just the anticipation and process of emigration but also the experiences of life in a newly settled "bless'd land". In a poem titled "Thanksgiving Day", the speaker delights at a family celebration beside a "rousing fire" with "wholesome fare", before turning to the wider issues of national politics theology:

> Perhaps in leisure hours you choose
> To pass the time, and to amuse,
> The Unitarian scheme peruse;
>   But, sir, take heed,
> Their subtle reasoning may confuse,
>   And wreck your creed.
>
> Lowell and Channing may debate,
> As politicians, wise and great,
> Predict their country's future fate,
>   By reasoning clear;
> And shew blind rulers of the State,
>   What courses to steer[39];   (25–30)

Here, the use of Burns's poetic form to reflect on a national American holiday might be compared with Sophia Little's (1799–1893) 1828 poem "Thanksgiving". As David Hill Radcliffe notes, Little reworked Burns's "Cotter's Saturday Night" and effectively translated it "from Scotland to America and from a masculine to a feminine idiom" (addressing "New England's daughters and substituting "Kebbuck" for "Pumpkin Pie""). Radcliffe further speculates that Little's poem may well have been the model for Joseph Hulbert Nichol's 1830 poem "Connecticut Christmas Eve", which records New England folkways in ottava rima.[40]

In Dinsmoor's "Thanksgiving Day", the references to William Ellery Channing (1780–1842) and Reverend Charles Russell Lowell Sr. (1782–1861) are notable for their distinctly American theological concerns. Channing was a leading proponent of Unitarianism in America, arguing for the importance of human nature in discovering religious truths in his widely disseminated essays *The System of Exclusion and Denunciation in Religion* (1815) and *Objections to Unitarian Christianity Considered* (1819). His essays and sermons would come to be influential on the transcendentalist movement led by Ralph Waldo Emerson who, as will be discussed, recited a monumental tribute to Burns in Boston in 1859.

Reverend Charles Russell Lowell, also a prominent Unitarian pastor at the West Congregational church in Boston, was the father of poet James Russell Lowell. Lowell not only met and corresponded with Emerson, but also formed part of the influential New England "Fireside Poets"; many of whom cited Burns as an inspiring influence. While the oblique interconnectedness of American literary figures who read and admired Burns is mildly fascinating in itself, a more interesting point begins to emerge when reading the subsequent verses of Dinsmoor's poem:

> But shall they teach us to degrade
> Him, who is all creation's Head?
> The mighty God, who all things made,
>   Call him a creature?
> Say Godhead never was display'd
>   In human nature!   (31–36)

Ferociously renouncing the Unitarianism of Lowell and Channing, Dinsmoor, an elder at a Presbyterian church, upholds a strict Calvinist orthodoxy. For Dinsmoor, it is an insult that "The mighty God, who all things made" could ever be considered as being present "In human nature". The main point here is that—despite their widely conflicting religious and philosophical outlooks—Dinsmoor, Lowell and Emerson all either praised or, to some extent, copied Burns. This provides a telling example of how Burns's poetry was adopted and appropriated by divergent American theological groups and individuals, from conservative Calvinists or progressive transcendentalists.

If, as Susan Manning has suggested, Burns's musings on religion are particularly difficult to pigeonhole (for all "the poetic ridicule" he "remained a churchgoer all his life"),[41] the strict Calvinist currents running through Robert Dinsmoor's poems are far less ambiguous. Dinsmoor's English verses often hailed "The mighty God, who all things made", but equally his Scots verses depict a fearful, Calvinistic relationship with God, as in "Answer To The Rev. David M'Gregore":

> If we can trust what Scripture saith,
> Christ is our God, an' Saviour baith,
> Then let us fix our hope an' faith
>   On that foundation;
> Wha trusts aught else, maun sink in death
>   An' deep damnation![42]   (27–30)

There are other occasions where Dinsmoor's Scots verse achieves a typically Burnsian dramatic tone or comic effect. In "Spring's Lamentation and Confession",[43] for example, Dinsmoor begins his verses about a dog with familiar comic irony:

> Long hae I liv'd wi' kind Miss Bessy,
> Wha kept me cozie, warm an' fleshy;
> In lanely hours she would caress me,
>   An' mak' me fain,
> Baith e'en an' morn I gat a messy,
>   As though her wean.[44]   (7–12)

Dinsmoor similarly uses Scots to channel Burns's egalitarian vernacular energy. In a poetic response to a letter received from Silas Beton ("To Silas Beton"), who had complained of poverty and lack of corn, Dinsmoor wrote:

> I aye was free wi' a' my might,
> To help the poor dependant wight,
> Nor wad I drive him out at night,
>   Amang the snaw;
> To warm his bluid, I took delight
>   An' fill his maw.[45]   (13–18)

The language here takes on added resonance and associational power given the familiarity readers would have had with Burns's common poetic reverence for those "constantly on poortith's brink" ("The Twa Dogs", 104).[46] Dinsmoor's volume also included a small miscellaneous collection of poems written by other New Englanders who were writing in Scots. These poems are largely similar to the early imitation poems that appeared in the American dailies, and it is likely that many of them had in fact been collected and reprinted from the periodical press. While the majority remained unsigned, others are attributed to authors, with a Revd. David M'Gregore being the most frequent contributor (whose verses are largely similar to Dinsmoor's own) and most notably a Scots poem by a young "J.G. Whittier", which will be discussed later in this chapter.

However, one poet not included in the volume, whom Dinsmoor might be best compared with, is David Bruce (c.1760–1830). With no attempt at concealing where his inspiration lay, Bruce wrote his own *Poems Chiefly in The Scottish Dialect*, printed by John Colerick in the Pittsburgh town of Washington in 1801. Though preceding Dinsmoor, Bruce cannot be counted among the American-born poets who reveal the poetic influence of Burns given he emigrated from Caithness to Maryland in 1784. Nonetheless, his poems, arguably more so than Dinsmoor, reflected on distinctly local themes; with many referencing national and state politics such as his fervent satires on the Pennsylvania State officials. Bruce's poems originally appeared in the *Western Telegraphe* or *Washington Advertiser* signed under the pseudonym of the "The Scots-Irishman", and it was not until Colerick printed the full volume that the poet's true identity was revealed.

Hailing from Caithness, Scotland, Bruce's self-presentation as "The Scots Irishman" could, rather tentatively, be linked to the possibility he spent a portion of his formative years in County Londonderry.[47] Yet his "Scots-Irish" personae were more likely employed to comment on national topics while maintaining an egalitarian, "everyman" status in his Pittsburgh locale. As Anatol Lieven has commented, the Scots-Irish (or Ulster-Scots) were renowned for their critical attitudes towards "educated elites" and thus Bruce's persona and linguistic register might well have been fraught with subtle implications.[48] This would negate David Simpson's claim that early American dialect poetry avoided "confrontations or polemical positions" with "good humor"; citing the example of John Adams's "Ploughjogger" persona that was far from being the "conscious voice of an oppressed or misunderstood class of Americans".[49]

A note attached to Bruce's poem, "To Whiskey", offers another clue to his choice of pseudonym, citing both the large population of

Ulster-Scots in America and their "attachments" (whether economic or recreational) to Whiskey:

> The Author thought too, as the people, who are distinguished by the name of *Scots-Irish*, were the most numerous in the country, and were remarkable for their attachment to the subject of this Poem, to assume the language and appellation of a Scots-Irishman, would add to his celebrity.[50]

While retaining the comic strains of the preface, the poem itself is also extremely political, and strongly derivative of Burns's language, form and biting satirical power:

> Great Pow'r, that warms the heart and liver,
> And puts the bluid a' in a fever,
> If dull and heartless I am ever,
>   A Blast o' thee
> Maks me as blyth, and brisk and clever
>   As ony bee.   (1–6)

Over eight verses, Bruce's speaker responds to the "Whiskey Rebellion" of 1794, an organised social movement that resisted the Whiskey tax imposed by treasury secretary Alexander Hamilton; a measure the politician imposed to tackle the national debt incurred during the Revolutionary War. Here, Burns's poetic reactions (namely "Scotch Drink" and "The Author's Earnest Cry and Prayer") to the Westminster Wash Act of 1784 more than likely offered Bruce inspiration for his own (strikingly similar) campaign on the opposite side of the Atlantic.[51] Though protestors in Western Pennsylvania—many of Ulster-Scots descent—frequently used violence and intimidation to oppose the tax, Bruce's speaker in fact shows unity with the federal government while maintaining his "everyman" Scots-Irish persona:

> Then foul befa' the ungratefu' deil
> That wou'd begrudge to pay right weel,
> For a' the blessings that ye yiel
>   In sic a Store;
> I'd nae turn round upo' my heel
>   For sixpence more.   (49–54)

This is not the only poem in which Bruce employs Scots to comment on local and national politics, suggesting he deemed the idiom appropriate for both serious and comic purpose in the USA. Unlike the preface to Dinsmoor's volume, which predominantly discussed and dispelled accusations of Burns mimicry, the introduction to Bruce's *Poems* is focused on establishing the poet's political intentions. Citing a comparison to Peter Pindar's poetry that "gibed and ridiculed the sovereign of Britain", the preface, apparently written by Bruce himself, rhetorically states: "and why may not I pass a few jokes on the Sovereign of America for the like *royal* qualities, not to say for worse?"[52] Over twenty of the poems included were written in Scots, including political effusions such as "The Author's Political Opinion" ("Whether Patricians rule the state/ An' mak the laws wi' grave debate") (18–19) and "A Canny Word to the Democrats of the West" ("Is there ony proud Laird/ To mak ye afeard") (13–14). While there is no mention of Burns in the preface, Bruce does include his own "Verses to the memory of Robert Burns the Scottish poet". Written in English, the poem celebrates the "enchanting power" of the "sweet poet of the plain" and is also suggestive of Burns's poetic versatility:

> Whether thy genius chose to paint
>   The grave or comic scene,
> Our ravish'd souls still bless's the Bard,
>   In ev'ry varying strain.[53]   (20–24)

Clearly viewing Scots as far from limiting, both Bruce and Dinsmoor successfully adopt the language, appropriating it to their own, localised ends. This indicates that Scots—as a poetic language—had not only been transported to America through Burns and his predecessors, but that it was continuing to, on some scale, evolve in the USA through Ulster-Scots-American poets.

That said, Dinsmoor and Bruce appear to have had different interpretations of, and uses for, Burns's poetics. Where Dinsmoor's poetic orthodoxy derives directly from the image of a bardic figure concerned with upholding and narrating their immediate locale, Bruce invokes a different aspect of Burns's poetic consciousness through his use of Scots to express widespread political discontent. For Bruce, writing in the Scots vernacular of the "old world" while commenting on contemporary issues was a powerful and satirical poetic tool that simultaneously highlighted and castigated hierarchal class structures. Dinsmoor, channelling the emotive and nostalgic power of Burns, used vernacular language and form to set himself into the mould of a "Rustic Bard" who had organically sprung from the roots of "Western Soil" in New England. Considering this prominent and dualistic influence, it might well be argued that Bruce and Dinsmoor were the first published poets in America to produce entire volumes that owed directly to the Scottish poet.

THE FIRESIDE POETS

As opinions and anxieties over the status of American literature continued to be debated throughout the early decades of the nineteenth century, a coalescence began to emerge around a group of New England-based poets by the 1840s. Known variously as the "Fireside Poets", "Schoolroom Poets" and, less commonly, the "Household Poets", this group consisted of William Cullen Bryant (1794–1878), Ralph Waldo Emerson (1803–1882),[54] Henry Wadsworth Longfellow (1807–1882), John Greenleaf Whittier (1807–1892), Oliver Wendell Holmes Sr. (1809–1894) and James Russell Lowell (1819–1891).[55] Though these individuals knew each other and, in some instances, regularly corresponded, they did not self-identify as a contemporary literary circle.

It was, initially at least, their shared models of poetic value that focused on domestic ("Fireside") and pedagogical ("Schoolroom") spheres that drew them together and conferred a canonical status that was unprecedented in American literature.[56] The call for America to produce its own canon of great poets, so widely argued in the periodical press of the early nineteenth century, had been answered by this group of writers who achieved a level of fame and popularity to rival that of any British or European literary figure.

Few would contest that the half-dozen Fireside Poets were among the first inductees to a national poetic canon in the USA. However, as Josh Timberman Newcomb argues, recent scholarship has demonstrated that "American verse was a much richer and more varied discourse than most histories have admitted" and it has been a disservice to reduce nineteenth-century (American) literary history to "a single canonical narrative focused upon them".[57] While figures like Robert Dinsmoor and David Bruce provide examples of the great tonal, stylistic and ideological variety of American verse in the period, the sheer dominance of the Fireside canon meant that, by the turn of the twentieth century, the New England poets were collectively the best-known literary figures in the nation; with their popularity being supported and maintained by educational institutions across the country. In her book *Schoolroom Poets*, Angela Sorby has mapped out how the poems of Longfellow and Whittier in particular formed "an archive of popular memory" through dissemination and repetition not just in schools, but also "museums, lyceums, theaters, newspapers, and children's magazines, and clubs".[58]

Not only did these poets become beacons of the nation's literary culture, but they also evolved into "icons of middle class taste" with various "Household editions" and textbooks such as the multimillion selling *McGuffrey's Reader* regularly being present in homes across the country.[59] Beyond literature, the Fireside writers were influential in sociopolitical spheres; with many of them leading abolitionist movements and contributing towards the establishment of the highly successful *Atlantic Monthly* magazine in Boston.

The Fireside group's rise to prominence as the first great canonical poets of America holds a certain irony in that, rather than promoting a progressive image or identity, they often espoused nostalgic virtues of childhood, small-town life and pastoral settings. Even their poetic form often adhered to classical convention, predominantly consisting of regular meters, full rhymes and accessible sentiments that, pertaining to a pedagogical function, could easily be remembered and recited. It was these conventions that early twentieth-century modernists would later define themselves against, given the Fireside canon's dominance left them "with virtually no reservoir of imagery, voice, or subject matter"[60] through which they could articulate themselves.

The purpose here is not to further narrate the trajectory of American literary history, but to highlight the sheer presence and pervasive influence that this group of poets had from the 1840s right through to the end of the century. Perhaps unsurprisingly, given the widespread availability of Burns's poetry coupled with his reputation for depicting the "manners of our rustics",[61] it so happened that many of the Fireside writers read and, to some extent, found inspiration in the Scottish poet. In considering whether Burns's "wee-bit ingle, blinkan bonilie" ("The Cotter's Saturday Night", 23)[62] did indeed ignite Fireside imaginations, it is important, first of all, to consider the poetry of an individual who, in his rural self-fashioning and liberal political leanings, would come to be considered by some critics as the "American Burns".[63]

JOHN GREENLEAF WHITTIER & BURNS

Born and raised at a rural homestead in Haverhill, Massachusetts (the same town in which Robert Dinsmoor resided) it is unsurprising that the young John Greenleaf Whittier was to become aware of Scots verse as his poetic sensibilities began to develop and mature in the 1820s. Among the miscellaneous section in Dinsmoor's *Incidental Poems*, a Scots poem titled "To The Rustic Bard" was printed and attributed to "J.G. Whittier". Whittier critics have concurred that this was "the first printing of one of Whittier's poems in book form",[64] significant in that it not only confirms the importance of recovering the volume, but also reveals Whittier's playful adoption of Scots-language poetry in his formative years. In critical editions and biographical accounts, Burns has frequently been cited as being "one of Whittier's important early influences" and it has been suggested that the Scottish poet's "rustic simplicity" and "directness of expression"[65] were inspirational. The conflation of Burns and Whittier partly stems from the American poet's 1840 composition "Burns. On receiving a Sprig of Heather in Blossom", a poem that will be examined in more detail shortly. In Whittier's much earlier "To The Rustic Bard", however, the bard in question is not Burns, but Robert Dinsmoor.

An early catalogue of Whittier's personal library reveals that Whittier, who was twenty-one when *Incidental Poems* first appeared, owned both Dinsmoor's volume and also the 1828 Philadelphia edition of *The Works of Robert Burns* (printed by J. Crissy and J. Grigg). According to a note in the catalogue, the *Works* contained numerous "pencil markings by him" and it was the "first copy of Burns's poems ever owned by Mr Whittier".[66] This might suggest that Whittier was reading the work of both poets (at least in full book form) in the same year. However, biographies of Whittier have claimed that it was his childhood teacher Joshua Coffin who should be first credited with "introducing him to a knowledge of Burns, whose poems he read aloud once as the family sat by the fireside in the evening".[67] Nevertheless, Whittier's early verses to New Hampshire's own "Rustic Bard" remain fascinating for their use and appropriation of Scots as a poetic language.

The Scots verses addressed to Dinsmoor are revealing of both Whittier's early humility and ambitions in regard to becoming a poet. The speaker deems it an "honor to be ca'd/ Yere rhymin' brither" (4–5)[68] while acknowledging that his young muse "Is na possessor" of skill compared with Dinsmoor's ("But yours has been a lang time busy - /An auld transgressor") (10–12). The speaker then turns to dismiss the "heartless sneer" of critics who "urge their wordy weir" (19–20), suggesting that Dinsmoor's self-fashioning as a "rustic" (writing in Scots) had been subject to much "taunt an' jeer" (21). Yet for Whittier's speaker, critical jibes "canna mak the muse less dear" (23) and poets must ignore "What fools may chance to say" in the knowledge that "wise men roose us" (35–39). Whittier implies that to "wear the garb" (34) of a rustic is not a regressive tendency but a pertinent aesthetic device that only "wise men" could understand. The verses that follow convey a typically Burnsian dismissal of the hypocrisy of those in "name, rank, or station":

> But whyles they need a castigation,
> Shall either name, or rank, or station,
> Protect them frae the flagellation,
>   Sae muckle needed?
> Shall vice an' crimes that "taint the nation"
>   Pass on unheeded?
>
> No! let the muse her trumpet take,
> 'Till auld offenders learn to shake,
> An' tremble when they hear her wake
>   Her tones o' thunder;
> 'Till pride, an' bloated ignorance quake,
>   An' gawkies wonder.
>
> (36–47)

The nationalist tone here is significant and, as was the case with Bruce and Dinsmoor, Whittier's use of Scots language while commenting on American affairs effects added satirical bite. It is not entirely clear what specific crimes "taint the nation", but given the literary subject matter it would seem that the speaker is referring to the pomp of critics who, in their "pride an' bloated ignorance", are dismissive of the Scots pastoral effusions of Dinsmoor and like-minded poets. Whittier's speaker concludes with a powerful statement of resistance:

> Farewell! The poet's hopes an' fears
> May vanish frae this vale o' tears;
> An' curtain'd wi forgotten years,
>   His muse may lie;

> But virtue's form, unscaith'd appears –
> It canna die!
>
> (54–59)

The speaker extols the "virtue" in Dinsmoor's poetics, further inflected by Whittier's own adoption of Scots language and the Standard Habbie throughout the poem. Whittier suggests that such criticism is finite; over time it will be "curtain'd wi forgotten years". Though the poem does not directly reference Burns, it is still highly evocative of the poet's acceptance and approval of Scots as a viable language for poetry. In addition to "J.G. Whittier to the Rustic Bard", Whittier also contributed a Scots poem to a local Haverhill newspaper which he signed under the pseudonym "Donald".[69] More significantly, he wrote and signed "The Drunkard to his Bottle" in 1829, a poem which was preceded by a note that referenced Burns:

> I was thinking of the temperance lyrics the great poet of Scotland might have written had he put his name to a pledge of abstinence, a thing unhappily known in his day. The result of my cogitation was this poor imitation of dialect.[70]

The poem is largely comic in tone with a rejuvenated speaker celebrating his "weel-spent day" (35) after refraining from the "witches' broo" (32). Though easily dismissed as a trivial, at best playfully comic, Scots poem, the preceding note reveals the influence of Currie's moralising depiction of Burns having been a victim to the "pollution of inebriation". For Whittier, it was unfortunate that such temperance was "unhappily known" to Burns, foreshadowing later celebrations of the poet that lamented his bacchanalian persuasions.[71] While Whittier's experimentations with Scots account for very little in the grand scheme of his prolific writing career, these poems, at the very least, reveal that Burns was a formative influence.

Unsurprisingly, the one poem critics have commonly referenced when suggesting Burns's influence is "Burns. On a receiving a sprig of heather in blossom", which was written in 1840, almost three decades after Whittier's early Scots poems. Burns critics have predominantly cited the version of the poem found in Donald. A Low's *The Critical Heritage*, which omits several stanzas of the original version. The first stanza of the full-length version is in fact one of the most interesting for its image of Burns's poetry "blooming" in New England soil and beyond:

> No more these simple flowers belong
> > To Scottish maid and lover:
> Sown in the common soil of song,
> > They bloom the wide world over.[72]   (1–4)

As was the case in "The Drunkard to his Bottle", there are echoes of Currie's "prefatory remarks" in Whittier's appreciation for Burns, given the biographer's emphasis on how Burns and his poetry might be influential "beyond the limits" of Scotland, as outlined previously. In the verses that follow, the speaker channels the "old tunes" of Burns in order to appreciate the nature that pervades their own locality:

> I hear the blackbird in the corn,
> > The locust in the haying;
> And like the fabled hunter's horn,
> > Old tunes my heart is playing.
>
> > > (23–26)

Whittier suggests that "Scotland's heathery hills" have been matched by his own "native rills" that echo "wood hymns chanting over" (44–47). In addition to Burns's treatment of nature, the egalitarian language of the poet was also clearly inspirational for Whittier; most evident in his description of "Man Uprising" against "rank and pomp" (49–50) and the sense of virtue to be found "among the lowly":

> With clearer eyes I saw the worth
> > Of life among the lowly;
> The Bible at his Cotter's hearth
> > Had made my own more holy.
>
> > > (49–55)

While Whittier identifies a sense of pious "worth" in Burns's poetry, he also acknowledges the supposed flaws of the man. In a stanza that has previously been neglected by critics (owing to its omission from Donald A. Low's *The Critical Heritage*) the influence of ideological biographical accounts is obvious:

> Lament who will the ribald line
> > Which tells his lapse from duty,

How kissed the maddening lips of wine
Or wanton ones of beauty;

(95–98)

Whittier appears apologetic, suggesting that Burns should, "like Magdalen", be "forgiven" (95–102). Towards the end of the poem, Whittier refers back to the aforementioned trope of setting Burns apart from the European literary establishment:

Not his the song whose thunderous chime
Eternal echoes render;
The mournful Tuscan's haunted rhyme,
And Milton's starry splendor!

(100–105)

Contrasting the "lettered pomp" (115) of "Tuscan's haunted rhyme" (Dante) and "Milton's starry splendour", Whittier conveys an enthusiasm for the successful humility of Burns's pastoral poetry. For Whittier, the "Epic's stately rhyme" (117) cannot rival Burns's poetic appreciation of nature ("But who his human heart has laid/ To Nature's bosom nearer") (105–106).

Frequently in Whittier's poetry, progressive undercurrents and abolitionist sensibilities are intertwined with homely, pastoral themes. By acknowledging this dualistic aspect of Whittier's craft, we might better gauge both the influence of Burns and the parallels between the two poets. Whittier was not a "primitive bard" per se, but, like Burns, frequently alluded to the pastoral realm to reflect on universal themes. In concluding on the importance of Burns's poetry for Whittier, let us turn to 1866; the approximate end date of this study and also the year that the American poet published, arguably, his best-known narrative poem, "Snow-bound".

Set in a rural Haverhill Homestead over three days as a snowstorm rages outside, the poem's chronicling of sublime domesticity is unequivocally resonant of Burns's "The Cotter's Saturday Night". Even the dreary opening scenes of the poems are strikingly similar, with Burns's speaker depicting how "November chill blaws loud wi' angry sugh;/ The short'ning winter-day is near a close" (10–11); and the narrator in "Snowbound" describing how "The sun that brief December day/ Rose cheerless over hills of gray" (1–2).[73] Though both poems begin with simple scenes of pastoral domesticity, the respective verses that follow are densely packed with imagery, metaphor and socio-historical references. Nigel Leask has recently drawn attention to the sociopolitical relevance of Burns's pastoral poem.

Referring to the concluding stanzas, Leask points to how the political language of the poem "breathes radical energy into the quiescent genre of cottage pastoral"[74] through its attack on luxury and aristocratic privilege ("The *Cottage* leaves the *Palace* far behind:/What is a lordling's pomp? a cumbrous load") (168–169). Similarly, Whittier's "Snow-Bound", also previously considered a backward-looking lamentation, has received a revitalised sense of attention in the past few decades, with James E. Rocks asserting the poem's relevance to "the post-Civil War period of anticipated reconciliation and the reuniting of the 'house divided'":

> It is not ours to separate
> The tangled skein of will and fate,
> To show what metes and bounds should
> Stand
> Upon the soul's debatable land,
>
> (579–582)

Rocks goes further to suggest that "the poem's rhetoric of reconciliation and consolation" points towards "a future in which all wrongs will be righted and freedom will replace slavery".[75] This reading differs widely from earlier responses that reductively labelled the poem as a representation of the simplicity of "New England Country life".[76]

The dualistic evolution of criticism towards both poems is, perhaps inadvertently, revealing of a uniting parallel that adds much to our understanding of the interrelationship between Burns and Whittier. In their fusion of the domestic, pastoral sphere with the political sublime, both poets unite the various discourses of their ages to present deceivingly complex compositions. This observation, in addition to his much earlier experiments with language, form and the vernacular, might give further credence to the idea that John Greenleaf Whittier was, more so than any other poet at least, closest to being the "American Burns" of the nineteenth century.

JAMES RUSSELL LOWELL AND AMERICAN VERNACULAR VERSE

One of James Russell Lowell's earliest poems was his 1837 composition, "Imitation of Burns" which was first published in the Harvard "college periodical" *Harvardiana*,[77] though it did not make the cut for his first collected edition.[78] Like Whittier, it seems that Lowell's poetic apprenticeship included a playful engagement with (and imitation of) Burns's Scots-language poetry. While Whittier's foray into the vernacular was brief, Lowell remained a proponent of vernacular poetry and a scholar of linguistics throughout his life, eventually co-founding the American Dialect Society in 1898, just two years prior to his death.[79] Arguing that formal poetic language (or "standard English") was insufficient for depicting "American customs", Lowell's early engagement with Burns must surely have shaped his views on dialect poetry.[80] Without exaggerating their transatlantic interconnectedness, it is worth remembering that Lowell's vernacular effusions appeared shortly after he (and Whittier) had experimented with Scots-language poetry.

In the 1840s, Lowell, also an ardent abolitionist, was increasingly involved in reformist politics and anti-slavery movements, rising to become chief editorial writer of *The Pennsylvania Freeman* and *The National Anti-Slavery Standard* between 1846 and 1848. It was during this period—and in these newspapers—that the poet first began to publish his American vernacular verses under the pseudonym "Hosea Biglow".[81] By the end of 1848, the first series of *The Biglow Papers* were published in book form and edited by Lowell under the persona of "Rev. Mr Homer Wilbur". Largely abolitionist and anti-war (the poet opposed the Mexican-American War of the same decade) in thematic content, *The Biglow Papers* are a formal and linguistic medley of prose, satirical verse, "Yankee" dialect, English and Latin. Annotated with an array of bemusing referential notes and self-reflexive intrusions, the book almost reads like an experiment in proto-postmodernism.

Reviewing one of the last scholarly editions of *The Biglow Papers* in 1978, John W. Crowley highlighted the immediate and widespread success of it upon publication in 1848, stating that the vernacular verses "were copied everywhere" and that their popularity extended to Britain. Yet Crowley further notes that Lowell's "literary reputation has plummeted in the twentieth century",[82] and it seems this trend has continued with little commentary on (or revised editions of) *The Biglow Papers* to date.[83]

The Biglow Papers begin with a series of hyperbolic mock-reviews that convey the divisive nature of Lowell's use of vernacular language. Evoking Burnsian "rustic garb" that impacts "on the heart", a quote from the grandiosely named "Universal Literary Universe" suggests that the following poems point towards an "indigenous" American literature:

> We hail the appearance of this work as a long stride toward the forma-
> tion of a purely aboriginal, indigenous, native, and American literature.
> We rejoice to meet with an author national enough to break away from
> the slavish deference, too common among us, to English grammar and
> orthography.[84]

In contrast, a subsequent extract from the "Saltriver Pilot and Flag of Freedom" suggests that the writer has "raked all the gutters of our language"; with another review stating that "the general style of diction was susceptible of a higher polish".[85] In what appears to be an irreverent elevation of the work into the realms of high literary appraisal, what follows is a series of Latin reviews. Here, Lowell simultaneously derides criticisms aimed at the poetic vernacular, yet refrains from rendering it a serious literary device through his use of comic hyperbole. On the title page that follows, a bold epigraph once again evokes and lavishes praise on "rustic" simplicity:

> The Ploughman's whistle, or the trivial flute,
> Finds more respect than great Apollo's lute
> *Quarles's Emblems*, B. ii. E. 8.[86]

The image of a poetic "ploughman's whistle" smacks of a "rustic" literary figure in the vein of Burns or Whittier. Even in this brief but powerful epigraph, there remains a suggestion that vernacular language contains an egalitarian sense of virtue in its rejection of hierarchal form (symbolised by "Apollo's lute") and promotion of rural literacy. What follows is a description of "Yankee" dialect by "Homer Wilbur" that fluctuates between the comic and sincere. In the more eloquent and serious passages, "Wilbur" defends the use of American vernacular ("Undoubtedly we have a right to make new words, as they are needed by the fresh aspects under which life presents itself here in the New World"), suggesting that "wherever a language is alive it grows".[87] For all the comic inflections of the introductory notices and preface, the

dialect poems that follow are altogether more serious. In "A Letter from
Mr. Ezekiel Biglow", for example, the speaker attacks proponents of slavery in both the North and South:

> They may talk o' Freedom's airy
>> Tell they're pupple in the face, -
> It's a grand gret cemetary
>> Fer the barthrights of our race;
> They jest want this Californy
>> So's to lug new slave-states in
> To abuse ye, an' to scorn ye,
>> An' to plunder ye like sin.
>
> Aint it cute to see a Yankee
>> Take such everlastin' pains,
> All to git the Devil's thankee,
>> Helpin' on em weld their chains?
> Wy, it's jest ez clear ez figgers,
>> Clear ez one an' one make two,
> Chaps thet make black slaves o' niggers
>> Want to make wite slaves o' you.
>
>   (64–79)

The phonetic spelling here is, to some extent, employed to imitate the
speech of a Northern farmer. However, following Nadia Nurhussein's
theory of dialect poetry as a "paradoxical genre", it is important to note
the variable processes by which poets "evoke so-called nonstandard
speech in written English and not speech itself".[88] Lowell, in his *literary*
evocation of a Northern farmer, strategically harnesses linguistic fluidity
to launch a scathing attack on those complicit in a slave-based agricultural system.

The frequent intrusions of "Homer Wilbur" also seek to legitimise
"Yankee" as a purposeful literary language, which might well be compared to Francis Jeffrey's defence of Scots as a "highly poetical" language
in 1809.[89] The case of an emerging "American" literary dialect was, of
course, more complex in that several variants of English developed from
divergent regional strains including "the Negro [dialect], the Southern,
the Western, the Hoosier, in addition to the Yankee".[90] Attempting to
determine the political agency, and indeed linguistic salience, of a unified
nineteenth-century "American English" or literary language remains,

then, a far more complex and multi-factorial undertaking.[91] As David E. E. Sloane observes, traditions of "dialect" or "vernacular" verse in America were born in various regions of "American life, both agrarian and urban, using language and images that were simple, earthy, local and comic".[92] A common factor among the most interesting verse, Sloane suggests, was the use of language to "deflate the pretensions of those who failed to value the egalitarian nature of democratic life".[93] Indeed, Lowell was not the only writer to use "Yankee" dialect for political purpose.[94]

Another example, also revealing a possible Burnsian influence, is Joel Barlow's "The Hasty-Pudding" (1793). Like Burns in "To a Haggis" ("Auld Scotland wants nae skinking ware/That jaups in luggies")[95] (45–46) Barlow draws on the most of egalitarian of local foods—"The Hasty-Pudding" being a cornmeal mush popular in New England—to suggest democratic virtue and reject monarchical rule:

> London is lost in smoke and steep'd in tea;
> No Yankee there can lisp the name of thee;
> The uncouth word, a libel on the town,
> Would call a proclamation from the crown.[96]

Written in three cantos, the mock-heroic poem satirises the lofty manners of eighteenth-century British literature and calls for a more democratic form of poetry; reflected through the sustained metaphor of an earthly culinary dish available to all. With specific regard to language, Barlow is unapologetic in his use and promotion of a burgeoning new American lexicon: "Squaw"; "mush"; "succotash"; "maize"; "raccoon"; "skunk"; and of course "Hasty Pudding" to name but a few examples.[97]

Homer Wilbur's intrusions in the *Biglow Papers* go even further to assert the literary worth—not just inclusive democratic virtue—of "Yankee" poetry. At one point Wilbur even goes as far to fully translate Shakespeare's opening soliloquy from *Richard III* into "Yankee". The effect is at once humorous and intriguing. Undercutting the obvious comic intent of translating Shakespeare into a dialect of "the country bumpkin of New England",[98] there is a more serious statement; Lowell hints that American vernacular might flourish as a literary language. In hindsight, Lowell was right given his linguistic experimentations later inspired writers such as Walt Whitman (1819–1892), Mark Twain (1835–1910) and William Dean Howells (1837–1920).

However, as I have argued in a recent essay on Walt Whitman, literary critics and the wider reading public, ever eager to find connections, are often quick to pick up on complimentary links between Burns and American poets, without providing a fully balanced literary and historical context.[99] Though Lowell's vernacular verse might be traced to his engagement with Scots, the American vernacular tradition, as noted, had multiple roots that stemmed back well beyond the widespread circulation of Burns's poetry. Nonetheless, Wilbur's annotations highlight that "Yankee", at least as a literary language, had evolved from variants of English and its related dialects, of which Scots might be included. The same might be said for some of the other widely recognised dialects in nineteenth-century America.

Even the early use of "Negro Dialect" caused William Dean Howells to remark that the language was "of like impulse and inspiration with the work of Burns when he was most Burns, when he was most Scotch, when he was most peasant".[100] Here, there is a potentially reductive conflation between Burns's Scots verse and a form of "peasant" or "labouring class" poetry ("most Scotch'/'most peasant"). In an illuminating essay, Nigel Leask has explored "the complex interrelationship" between language, class, region and nationality that underpinned Burns's links with "labouring-class" poets such as Stephen Duck (c. 1705–1756), John Clare (1772–1802) and Robert Bloomfield (1776–1823).[101] Currently, an online database of "British and Irish labouring-class poets who wrote between 1700-1900" is being compiled under the general editorship of John Goodridge at Nottingham Trent University.[102]

While the reach of these poets in America was (in comparison with Burns) limited, editions of their work were still available; with Bloomfield's *The Farmer's Boy* being reprinted in New York, Philadelphia and Baltimore several times in the first decade of the nineteenth century.[103] Moreover, around fifty of the "labouring-class" poets listed in the database are noted to have spent time or emigrated to America, with the vast majority of them being from Scotland.[104] Notably, Paisley poet Alexander Wilson (discussed previously in Chapter 2) is included among this group of poets.

In writing about the inception of American literary dialects, David Simpson states that Burns and John Clare were the "prototypes of which American writers must have been conscious as they mediated the question of dialect".[105] Simpson's speculative suggestion conflates Burns with a renowned "labouring-class poet" in Clare. Regardless of Burns's considered, aesthetic choice of linguistic register(s) and personal opinions on class identity, the fact remains that many American readers would have viewed him as a "ploughman" who, as a consequence of his "rank" and vocation, wrote poetry in Scots. For the likes of William Dean Howells, it was clear Burns wrote poetry using the language of "peasants".[106]

While potential "labouring class" (or whichever contemporary cognate might be deemed appropriate) poets in nineteenth-century America deserve much further attention, it is also important to note that Lowell, despite his use of the vernacular, was certainly not among them. Lowell belonged to the elite caste of "Boston Brahmins" in New England, graduating from Harvard college in 1838 and later obtaining a law degree from Harvard Law School. Thus, if he owed any debt to Burns for his experimentation with dialects, then it was a purely aesthetic one. The earlier appropriation of Scots by the likes of David Bruce and Robert Dinsmoor, on the other hand, might well have owed more to a "labouring-class" tradition or "experience" that gave poetic voice to actualised regional subjects and experience.

It is also crucial to note that Lowell (and some of the other Fireside poets) simultaneously drew on lofty European poetic trends. Towards the end of the nineteenth century, Lowell published a collection of "Literary Essays and Addresses", one of which reads like a sweeping appraisal of the previous century's best European poets. It is worth quoting a substantial passage in order to fully grasp the sheer variety of Lowell's critical summary:

> Whatever the eighteenth century was, there was a great deal of stout fighting and work done in it, both physical and intellectual, and we owe it a great debt [...] In what is called the elegant literature of our own tongue (to speak only of the most eminent), it gave us Addison and Steele, who together made a man of genius; Pope, whose vivid genius almost persuaded wit to renounce its proper nature and become poetry; Thomson, who sought inspiration in nature, though in her least imaginative side; Fielding, still in some respects our greatest novelist; Richardson, the only author who ever made long-windedness seem a benefaction; Sterne, the most subtle humorist since Shakespeare; Goldsmith, in whom the sweet humanity of Chaucer finds its nearest parallel; Cowper, the poet of Nature in her more domestic and familiar moods; Johnson, whose brawny rectitude of mind more than atones for coarseness of fibre.[107]

Surprisingly, there is no mention of Burns throughout the entirety of a substantial overview of the "elegant literature of our own tongue". Cowper is deemed the poet of "Nature in her more domestic and familiar moods"; Pope as a "vivid genius"; while Goldsmith is credited for his "sweet humanity". Yet Burns, who might have easily vied for similar distinctions, remains notably excluded from the eighteenth-century British canon. This omission might indeed hint at the idea that Burns was considered within a coarser "labouring-class" tradition. At the very least it highlights the Scottish poet's disassociation from the esteemed, "elegant literature" of the previous century. While Burns's Scots verse, egalitarian ethos and intriguing biographical narrative (in its variously published fragmentary forms) were certainly of interest and occasional inspiration to the Fireside group; the extent of his poetic influence needs to be contextualised appropriately.

Though Lowell wrote a poem on Burns, for example, he also wrote extensively about Keats[108]; and Longfellow arguably owed more to Tennyson than Burns, as one Edgar Allan Poe (1809–1849) was quick to point out during the "Poe-Longfellow War" of the 1840s.[109] Carol McGuirk has made a parallel between the "morbidity and mortality" of Burns's "Highland Mary" songs—widely reprinted in the United States—and William Cullen Bryant's precocious 1811 meditation on death, "Thanatopsis".[110] Though there are certainly echoes of Burns's lamentation of a loved one "moldering now in silent dust" ("Highland Mary", 29),[111] Bryant's poem, in tone, imagery and form, owes equally as much if not more to Henry Kirk White (1785–1806) and Burns's Scottish predecessor Robert Blair (1699–1746) in his poem "The Grave".[112]

Yet crucially, in 1859, the majority of these renowned and revered American poets (the first American national canon) came together one evening, fresh compositions in hand, not to celebrate the life of Keats, Tennyson or any American poet, but Robert Burns. The wider cultural significance and processes behind the 1859 Burns centenary in America will be discussed in the following chapters. However, in order to edge towards a conclusion regarding the significance of Burns for major mid-nineteenth-century American poets, it is vital to reconsider the poetic works composed for The Parker House Hotel Centenary Dinner on 25 January 1859.

THE PARKER HOUSE HOTEL CENTENARY DINNER

In his contemporary recording of "a spectacle unprecedented in the history of the world",[113] James Ballantine's *Chronicle of the Hundredth Birthday of Robert Burns*, published in May 1859, notes that 61 celebratory events took place across the USA to commemorate the birth of Robert Burns. In Chapter 7, I will consider, through comparison, how these events were notably diverse in their scale, location and appropriations of the poet. However, for the purpose of the present focus on Burns and nineteenth-century poets, The Parker House Hotel Centenary Dinner, organised by the Boston Burns Club, emerges as the most significant single event in regard to poet's association with the renowned American literati of the period. Having established the widespread national recognition, reach and literary fame of the Fireside poets— "among the chief cultural powers of our nineteenth century"[114]—the spectacle of these individuals gathering together in a Boston hotel function room one evening, for the purpose of paying homage to an eighteenth-century Scottish poet, becomes all the more striking.

The transcript of the evening's speeches and recitations, first published in Boston by H. W. Dutton and Son in 1859, is prefaced by a description of the "Origin Of The Club". Having grown to foster a "reputation far beyond what its originators had ever contemplated", the club's success is attributed to a "unique feature of our Republicanism" that promotes encouragement in "men whose approbation is a safe endorsement of true value". Here, we can begin to see a distinct association between the club's constitution and the recently formed Republican party of the 1850s. Founded in 1854 by Northern abolitionists, the main catalyst in the party's formation was its opposition to the Kansas-Nebraska Act that repealed the Missouri Compromise by which slavery was restricted in Western territories. Viewing the Act as an expansionist move by slave-owning states, the Republican party (like its predecessor the Free Soil party) "condemned slavery as an evil, attempted to restrict its expansion, and sought to eventually abolish it according to some long and imprecise time frame".[115]

Notably, several members and attendees at the Parker House Hotel were also active Republicans and abolitionists. Edward Everett (1794–1865), for example, was partly responsible for the nomination of Abraham Lincoln at the 1860 Republican Party Convention[116]; while during the centenary celebrations he celebrated the "truer

Republicanism" of Burns's "A man's a man for a' That".[117] Similarly, Holmes, Bryant and Emerson all supported the Republican stance on abolition although, as James H. Read astutely notes, Emerson later "drifted away from the Republican insistence on the constitutional right and moral duty of Congress" through his attachment to "the philosophy of self-reliance".[118]

Appropriating Burns into this Republican context, the Boston Burns Club preface further notes how Burns might act as a democratic conductor between men from "learned professions" and "humbler walks of life". The preface subsequently alludes to "the little Fireside association" that has "sprung into enviable repute"; further noting the Club's association with "some of the greatest minds which adorn the literature of the day". Rather than being strictly symbolic of Scotland, then, Burns is adopted as a democratic conductor between "nearly two hundred and fifty men"[119] in Boston. This idea is made explicit in the club's constitution:

> We admire the honest independence of BURNS. Liberty—American liberty! —fought side by side with his sentiments of freedom and manly self-respect, and found in them a powerful ally.[120]

The poet's own engagement with America, outlined in Chapter 2 of this book, is further used as justification for the club's heralding of the poet, with one club member celebrating his "glowing language" that extolled the "virtues of the American Congress" and "the glorious results of the Revolution".[121] Absent from earlier American critical responses to the poet, it seems the comprehensive list of biographical epithets, poems and editions (in particular William Pearson's 1832 collected edition and the appearance of Cunningham's "Life" two years later in 1834) available by 1859 provided much fodder for those seeking to appropriate Burns as kin to an ideological, American political ideals.

The extent to which Burns is adopted by the Boston Burns Club as a decidedly masculine figure of political dignity is also notable. The repetition of "men" beats throughout the all-male club's constitution, and the poet's own political leanings are described as stemming from a sense of "manly self-respect". A list of the names, nationality and birthplace of 177 club members follows, providing contrary evidence to the idea that Burns Clubs in the USA were solely formed and populated by first generation Scottish émigrés in order to keep their

"Scottish connections alive".[122] Of the 177 members, 123 were born in America, 28 from Scotland and the remainder comprised of a mixed minority from England, Ireland, Canada and Spain. Though a portion of the 123 Americans might have descended from Scottish heritage (surnames included McGregor, Mitchell and Brown), this was not exclusively a club for expats keen to connect back to their ancestral homeland, though it would appear that women were indeed the victims of exclusivity.

POETIC COMMEMORATION: OLIVER WENDELL HOLMES SR. & JAMES RUSSELL LOWELL

Returning to Burns in specific relation to the Fireside poets, then, it is worth considering how Emerson, Lowell, Holmes and Whittier (the latter *in absentia*) paid tribute to the poet at the 1859 Centenary Dinner. The appearance of Oliver Wendell Holmes Sr. at The Parker House Hotel was just one of many instances of him offering up "occasional" verse to commemorate or celebrate a given cause. Particularly between 1836 and 1857, when Holmes was more (professionally) focused on medical endeavours, the majority of his poems were written for public events and observances. It was, in fact, through his commemorative and "occasional" verse that Lowell built his reputation as a wordsmith; fast becoming the "unofficial laureate" to select fraternities and clubs such as the "Harvard Class of 1829, the Saturday Club, or the Boston Medical Society".[123] As Holmes himself acknowledged at Whittier's seventieth birthday celebration: "I'm a florist in verse, and what *would* people say / If I came to a banquet without my bouquet?"[124]

Taking his poetic reputation into account, then, there was obviously an expectation of Holmes to bring a fitting "bouquet" to the Boston Burns Club on 25 January 1859. In his 2002 book *Democratic Voices and Vistas*, Darrell Abel notes that "occasional" verse rarely offers a "confessional revelation" of the poet's "private and natural self" but rather presents a "social display" for "an audience of persons who hear rather than read his poetry".[125] It is worth considering this before pitching Holmes's 1859 commemorative poem as evidence for his unabashed personal admiration for Burns. Undoubtedly dictated by audience, occasion and following the tropes of *vers de société*, his poem is strewn with laudatory allusions inviting stock responses from his intended audience, in this case the Boston Burns Club. However, to render Holmes as being limited to prescribed "occasional" verse would, by 1859 at least, also be a great disservice.

In the year preceding the Burns centenary, Holmes had published *The Autocrat of the Breakfast-Table*, which had catapulted his literary reputation to new heights. Originally published serially in *The Atlantic Monthly*, Holmes's philosophical essays and poems showcased his flair for thought-provoking poetic and prosaic compositions. After the success of *The Autocrat*, Holmes's poetry "took a somewhat higher and wider flight" and he finally began to "consider himself a professional author".[126] Regardless of whether his sentiments were designed specifically for the occasion or not, then, Holmes's praise for Burns would have undoubtedly been impactful on wider public perception and opinion.

Holmes's poem opens with grand, sweeping imagery to describe how the "tumultuous tide" of Burns's "wild emotion" has been swept across the Atlantic through "Rolls in the western Ocean" (4–8).[127] Echoing Burns's hailing of "The Royalty of Man" in "Ode For General Washington's Birthday", the speaker encourages all to "greet the monarch-peasant" as "The Past becomes present". Once again, it seems, Burns is used to bolster a form of democratic Republicanism. The image of Burns the debauchee also features heavily in the remainder of the verses; perhaps both a reflection and reaction against the more conservative biographical narratives that highlighted the poet's supposed penchant for "drunkness—in the tavern—and in the brothel".[128] Holmes appears to go on the defensive while somewhat begrudgingly acknowledging Burns's vices. For Holmes, no amount of "faults" can tarnish nature's "bonniest bair". Urging the audience to join in adoration with the repetition of "we love", the speaker states:

> We love him, not for sweetest song,
> Though never tone so tender;
> We love him, even in his wrong –
> His wasteful self-surrender.
>
> (39–32)

It is notable that Burns's poetic abilities are downplayed here. He is not loved for the "sweetest song" or "tone so tender", but rather for his sheer humanity. Holmes is almost apologetic in his suggestion that "even in his wrong", Burns must be "loved" and understood for his humanity rather than condemned ("His manhood breathes in every line, — / was ever heart more human?") (33–36). Throughout the poem, it is Burns "the man" who is praised and defended rather than his poetry; not only reflecting the considerable influence of biographical narratives but also rendering the idea of a stylistic or "poetic" influence on Holmes rather obsolete. As stated in the final lines, it is the biographical "minstrel's story" that will live on through "The mountain-mist of glory!" (49–56), manifested by the very fact that Holmes commemorates the "virtues" and "frailties" of Burns's supposed character rather than reflecting on his verse, form or possible linguistic influence.

Offering by far the most imaginative tribute to Burns at the Boston centenary dinner, James Russell Lowell arrived at the Parker House Hotel "double-barreled, with a piece about seven minutes long and one about two minutes and a half long".[129] Critics have missed the literary nuances of Lowell's longer poem, which appears to be an adaptation of the medieval French *fabliau* "Le villain qui Conquest Paradis par Plait" or "The Peasant who Plead his Way into Heaven"; a tale that recounts the trials of a peasant who avoids ejectment from Heaven through his superior wit, culminating in God conceding his rightful place in paradise.[130]

Lowell's poem, over the course of eighteen verses, depicts Burns appearing at the gates of Heaven only to find that "Holy Willie" has taken guard and relieved the apostles of their duties for the day. It is unsurprising that Lowell might have drawn on medieval French *fabliaux* given, in the years preceding the Centenary, he was awarded the title of Smith Professor of French & Spanish at Harvard, where he helped to "introduce a course in medieval French literature".[131] Moreover there is evidence to suggest that Lowell's literary allusion was indicative of the wider perception of Burns as a "peasant" who rose above his class; thus fitting with the above suggestion of Burns as a "labouring-class" or "peasant" poet. Sarah Gordon's study of the medieval French genre points towards the "interaction between rural and urban at the center of the fabliaux"; with "farmers", "clergy", "merchants" and "rural poor" often containing strong "aspirations of social mobility".[132] Lowell's adaptation was most likely conceived with a similar sense of the poet having successfully risen from a "claybuilt hovel" in the "humblest society".[133]

Adopting the role of *jongleur*, Lowell introduced his poem with a witty religious quip that simultaneously paid homage to his Scottish heritage ("I am a son of a clergyman who was educated in Edinburgh, and from whose principles I hope I have not departed")[134] before reflecting on how "Burns's memory" had become common topos among America's most renowned poets:

> A theme like this would Bryant choose,
> Longfellow, Holmes or Whittier;
> If my poor muse can't fill their shoes,
> Pray pardon her and pity her.[135]   (20–24)

Lowell's speaker, while "musing on what to say" then experiences a "vision" of "Burns's soul/at the wicket-hole/where sits the good St. Peter" (27–32), but crucially, "The Saint, methought, had left his post/ That day to Holy Willie" (33–34). What follows is a verse-by-verse account and rebuttal of the various sinful accusations levelled against Burns, beginning with his irresponsible fondness for "the water o' life" (82). After demanding Burns should "Go rouse the other house" (52):

> Old Willie's tone grew sharp's a knife;
> "*Imprimis,* I indict ye
> For makin' strife wi' the water o' life
> And preferrin' *aqua vitae.*'
> Then roared a voice with lusty din,
> Like a skipper's when tis' blowy,
> "If *that's* a sin, *I'd* ne'er ha' got in,
> As sure's as my name is Noah!"
>   (80–87)

Alluding to the biblical passage (Genesis 9:21) in which Noah "lay in a drunken stupor",[136] the hypocrisy of those fiercely critical and unforgiving of Burns's supposed drunken pursuits is exposed. Maintaining its theological undertones, the poem then turns to address the idea of Burns as an irreligious blasphemer, with Holy Willie this time refusing Burns entry to heaven on account of him saying "hard things o' the clergy":

> Sly Willie turned another leaf, -
> "There's many here ha'e heard ye,

> To the pain and grief o' true belief,
>   Say hard things o' the clergy!"
> Then rang a clear tone over all, -
>   "One plea for him allow me,
> I once heard call from o'er me, 'Saul,
>   Why persecutes thou me?"

(90–95)

The reference to Saul the blasphemer of Christ and persecutor of Saints, who, despite his sin, found a place in Heaven, once again provides a rebuttal to the charges levelled at Burns by Holy Willie. In a final attempt to condemn the poet, Holy Willie turns to accusations of philandering and adultery:

> To the next charge vexed Willie turned
>   And, sighing, wiped his glasses, -
> "I'm much concerned to find ye yearned
>   O'er warmly tow'rd the lasses!"
> But David cried, "Your ledger shut,
>   E'en Adam fell by woman,
> And hearts close shut with if and but,
>   If safe, are not so human!"

(96–103)

Similar to the pervading theme in Oliver Wendell Holmes's commemorative poem, it is Burns's tender humanity that we are urged to acknowledge, despite any supposed sinful tendencies. Significantly, despite its frequent biblical allusions to reformed sinners, Lowell's poem does not plead forgiveness for Burns on the grounds of religious absolution. Rather, his treatment of the poet's flaws aligns with Thomas Carlyle's concept of the heroic struggle "all great men" face through their "wild, wrestling naked with the truth of things".[137]

Furthermore, both Holmes and Lowell's emphasis on the sincere humanity of Burns resonates with Carlyle's idea that "the chief quality of Burns is the *sincerity* of him" even if he was flawed through such "great tragic sincerity".[138] By 1859, of course, Carlyle's influential collection of essays *On Heroes, Hero-Worship, and The Heroic in History* was widely available in the USA, in addition to the 1829 appraisal outlined in the previous chapter. Echoes of Carlyle can once again be heard in the conclusion to Lowell's adapted *fabliau*:

> The earth must richer sap secrete
> (In time, could ye but know it!)
> Must juice concrete with fiercer heat
> Ere she can make her poet;
> These larger hearts must feel the rolls,
> Of stormier-waved temptation,
> These star-wide souls between their poles
> Bear zones of tropic passion.
>
> (136–143)

Here, it is the "richer sap" and "fiercer heat" of Burns that results in his "stormier-waved temptations". The "star-wide souls" and "tropic passion" that Lowell refers to is reminiscent of Carlyle's idea that "great men" are swept up in "a whirl of distracted atoms",[139] that sometimes results in flawed, detrimental attributes. While Emerson's acquaintance with Carlyle has been widely documented, Lowell too was "an avid reader of Carlyle" and, according to Sharon Gravett, was "especially attracted to his essay on Robert Burns".[140] In a final defence and rebuttal of Burns's flaws, Lowell's speaker, adhering to the idea Burns as a "genius" (thus natively flawed) poet, triumphantly praises "nature strong" and dismisses all who "Against thy faults be railing!" (144–151).

One the most striking elements of both Lowell and Holmes's poems is the apparent need to defend Burns, suggesting that negative portrayals of the poet, variously transmitted by fragmentary biographical accounts, remained influential in the period leading up to the 1859 Centenary Dinner. John Greenleaf Whittier's centenary poem (sent by letter and read aloud by Emerson directly after Lowell's poem) also took on a defensive, partly apologetic stance. The Haverhill poet pleaded "To-day be every fault forgiven/Of him in whom we joy"; (25–26).

Whittier's full poem, perhaps the most arbitrary tribute of the evening, offers little more to his earlier compositions about Burns, unsurprisingly focusing on his admiration for the Scottish poet's treatment of nature. The "pastoral pipe of Burns" is praised for singing the "love of man" while Whittier's prefatory letter declared Burns "the sweetest of all who have ever sung of home, and love, and humanity".[141] Rather than Whittier's epistolary tribute, however, it was to be the orator of the poem, Ralph Waldo Emerson, that would make the biggest impression on the audience at The Parker House Hotel.

POETIC COMMEMORATION: RALPH WALDO EMERSON

Billed as the keynote speaker of the evening, Ralph Waldo Emerson conceded to being "the worst Scotsman of all" before going on to identify Burns as a transnational beacon for social mobility. For Emerson, Burns represented that "great uprising of the middle class against the armed and privileged minorities" that "worked politically in the American and French Revolutions".[142] In a recent study, Linda Young has suggested the rise of a nineteenth-century Anglophone "middle class" (in Britain, the USA and Australia); attributing the transnational development to the "culture of gentility".[143]

Emerson's description of revolutionary, "middle-class" rebellions against the "privileged", however, negates any sense of polished refinement. Cindy S. Aron notes that the term "middle-class" did not appear in American dictionaries up until 1889, thus Emerson's use of the term might loosely have referred to a "middling sort" of men characterised by ambition and social mobility rather than a definitive and well-defined sociocultural status.[144] Emerson's subsequent description of Burns's rise from humble ploughman to political agitator further supports this reading:

> The "Confession of Augsburg." the "Declaration of Independence," the French "Rights of Man," and the "Marseillaise," are not more weighty documents in the history of freedom than the songs of Burns [...] He is so substantially a reformer, that I find his grand plain sense in close chain with the greatest masters—Rabelais, Shakespeare in comedy, Cervantes, Butler, and Burns. [145]

Here, Emerson's rhetorical flamboyance must (like Holmes above) be considered within the parameters of contemporary American oratory trends that often veered towards the "bombastic".[146] It should also not go unnoticed that Emerson was being paid considerable amounts of money for his increasingly renowned oratory appearances, and would have wanted to avoid disappointing a room full of Burns enthusiasts.

In the months preceding the centenary dinner, for example, "Emerson the lecturer had success after success" following his 1858 December tour of New York, Philadelphia, Hamilton and Toronto. His impressive delivery at the Burns centenary itself, praised by Lowell, Holmes and widely reprinted in the European press, reportedly earned him another course of Boston-based "lectures which brought him nearly $700 above expenses".[147] That Emerson might have been showcasing his oratory charisma in a bid to increase his reputation surely had some influence on his grandiose opening sentiments.

Less speculatively, Emerson's personal journals suggest that he was not quite as enamoured by Burns's poetry as the Boston centenary transcription would have us believe. While Emerson's public appraisal of Burns ranks the poet alongside "the greatest masters" ("Rabelais, Shakespeare [...] Cervantes, Butler"), his private correspondence reveals a less enthusiastic critical approach. Musing on famous literary figures, Emerson noted in a private journal that some men "do not in the record of the facts equal their own fame". Sir Philip Sidney is described as having "accomplished very little to have made so profound an impression in Europe"; The Earl of Essex and Sir Walter Raleigh are "men of great figure, but of few deeds"; while "the fame of Burns also is too great for the facts". Emerson goes on to suggest that while these men certainly had the "power to impress" through strength of "*character*", their talents can no longer be discerned through "visible or analysable" methods.[148] On the basis of this journal entry, it seems that Emerson believed Burns's widespread fame to be disproportionate to the quality of his poetic output; a sentiment that opposes his later conflation of Burns's songs with the "Declaration of Independence" and the "Confession of Augsburg".

The idea that Emerson was not particularly enthused by Burns (prior to the centenary) is backed up by an anecdote in Franklin B. Sanborn's 1971 book *The Personality of Emerson*. Prior to the centenary, Emerson allegedly stated he did not have "a very good opinion of the Scottish songster" and thus he had to renew his "acquaintance with him by a fresh reading"[149] in preparation for his speech. It must be noted, however, that the source of this anecdote is not referenced and does not appear to be included in any other editions of Emerson's collected correspondence. Regardless of its validity, an awareness of the oratory expectations placed on Emerson, coupled with the heightened sense of occasion helps to better contextualise—perhaps curtail—any grand assumptions one might have regarding the American writer's debt to Burns.

Another aspect of Emerson's speech that appears to have gone unnoticed is its adherence to Thomas Carlyle's visionary account of Burns. Just as Carlyle's 1828 essay depicted Burns as "a seer" who was born with a "gift of vision",[150] Emerson too draws on Burns's "secret of genius"; lavishing praise on his ability to "draw from the bottom of society the strength of its speech" through a transcending "beauty" that was "better than art".[151] Carlyle, of course, was a hugely important figure for Emerson, the two having struck up "a lifelong friendship" after the American writer's 1833 trip to Carlyle's residence in Scotland; a visit that occurred exactly a day after Emerson had visited "Burns's tomb".[152] Though Emerson's visit to Dumfries, where he allegedly saw a "son of Robert Burns standing on the doorstep" of the King's Arms, made for a footnote in most accounts of his European travels, his meeting and subsequent correspondence with Carlyle garnered much contemporary interest.[153]

As early as 1848, James Russell Lowell parodied their epistolary exchanges in his book length poem *A Fable for Critics* ("If C.'s an original, E'.s more peculiar";).[154] Even in his centenary tribute, Emerson subtly made reference to Carlyle by suggesting that if another name should be added to his list of the "greatest masters" then it would be "in a living countryman" of Burns who is "an exceptional genius".[155] Though Emerson situates Burns as being on an even intellectual plain with Carlyle, there is little doubt, when considering all evidence, which one of the two Scots was more influential on him. Thus, Carlyle's influence is inherently woven into Emerson's appreciation for Burns in his 1859 speech. His statements on how Burns's "genius" had the ability to depict "the homely landscape which the poor see around them"[156] adheres to his broader philosophical belief that the "elevation of soul" could determine "power over language".[157] It was this belief that saw him similarly praise the likes of innovative French essayist Michel de Montaigne for his natural "robustness of sentiments" over what one might derive from "an evening lecture or a young men's debate".[158] For Emerson, both Burns and Montaigne's "genius" was as "native and intuitive" as, in typically transcendentalist terms, the "orbit of stars", "the growth of grass" and "the angles of crystals".[159]

Concluding with a prophetic statement on how the "memory of Burns" was no longer learned "from a book" but passed on "from mouth to mouth",[160] Emerson's speech was to (somewhat ironically) become a major factor in the way Burns has been remembered, appropriated and considered as being an important figure for nineteenth-century

American poets and writers. The enduring significance of the speech seemingly did not escape his contemporaries. US Attorney journal E. R. Hoar (1816–1895) later recalled that he had "never witnessed such an effect of speech upon men"[161]; James Russell Lowell reminisced that his (Emerson's) words seemed to have "dropped down to him from the clouds"[162]; while Emerson's friend and epistolary muse Thomas Carlyle clipped a transcription "from his journals" having been completely "charmed by it".[163] Moreover, modern scholarly references to the speech continue to pollinate discussions about the connections between Burns and American poets. Carol McGuirk, for example, has called the speech "the warmest and most perspicuous of nineteenth century American appreciations"[164] while Robert Crawford has noted the significance of Emerson's speech in rendering the image of Burns as "rebelliously political" in North America.[165]

Crucially, however, it must not go unnoticed that Emerson's engagement with Burns prior to the centenary speech was minimal in comparison with his reading of other European writers and philosophers; which might also be said for Lowell, Holmes, Bryant and to a lesser extent, Whittier. In regard to Emerson specifically, Susan Manning has argued that a certain "Burnsian Romanticism" can be identified in the American's "poetic" and "philosophic" self-presentation and received character as "Transcendentalism personified". In challenging the parameters of literary "influence", Manning's study of the relationship between "poetic character", biography and performance is illuminating.[166] Indeed, the "character" of Emerson might well have owed more to Burns than an analysis of his writings can suggest. This idea is bolstered when reconsidering Emerson's appreciation (in his personal journal) of Burns's strength of "character"—but not his "talents".[167] On the basis of the above discussion, then, it could even be argued that Burns's literary output was less of an obvious "influence" than his perceived "poetic character" and biography.

When held as evidence for Burns's strong impact and influence on the Fireside group, the Boston Centenary Dinner has, to some extent, served to exaggerate his strictly poetic or literary influence. It was in fact the performed "memory of Burns" that would be the stronger factor in establishing a lasting connection between the poet and the first canonical poets of America.

NOTES

1. James Russell Lowell, *The Biglow Papers*, ed. Ernest Rhys (London: The Walter Scott Publishing Company, 1892), 5.
2. *The American Review of History and Politics, and General Repository of State Papers* 1 (1811): 166–167.
3. Joseph Rezek, *London and the Making of Provincial Literature: Aesthetics and the Transatlantic Book Trade, 1800–1850* (Philadelphia: University of Pennsylvania Press, 2015), 6.
4. Ibid., 22.
5. Philip Freneau, "Literary Importation" quoted from Sarah M. Corse, *Nationalism and Literature: The Politics of Culture in Canada and the United States* (Cambridge: Cambridge University Press, 1997), 18.
6. Sydney Smith, "Review of Statistical Annals of the United States, by Adam Seybert", *The Edinburgh Review* 33 (1820): 69–80.
7. See also *The British Critic* 10 (1818): 497: "The Americans have No National Literature, and No Learned Men" and *The Athenaeum* 173 (1831): 115: "This Want of Originality in American Literature Is, We Think, Likely Long to Continue…".
8. Alan. K. Snyder, *Defining Noah Webster: A Spiritual Biography* (Fairfax: Allegiance Press, 2002), 49.
9. *The North American Review and Miscellaneous Journal* 7 (1818): 206.
10. William Cullen Bryant, *A History of the Celebration of Robert Burns's 110th Natal Day, at the Metropolitan Hotel, New York* (Jersey City: John H. Lyon, 1869), 31.
11. Gilbert H. Muller, *William Cullen Bryant: Author of America* (Albany: State University of New York Press, 2010), 185–186.
12. Chris Bryers, "Augustan American Verse", in *The Oxford Handbook of Early American Literature*, ed. Kevin J. Hayes (New York: Oxford University Press Inc., 2008), 189–215.
13. *The North American Review and Miscellaneous Journal* 34 (1832): 75.
14. Crawford, "America's Bard", 104–105.
15. *The Biglow Papers*, 5.
16. For a discussion of the debate between "primordial" and "constructivist" approaches to nineteenth century American "national identity", see Anatol Lieven, *America Right or Wrong: An Anatomy of American Nationalism* (London: Harper Perennial, 2005), 108.
17. Boggs, "Transatlantic Romanticisms", 226.
18. *The New York Magazine: Or, Literary Repository* 1 (1790): 668.
19. *Scotland and America*, 128. See also Rhona Brown, "Allan Ramsay, Robert Fergusson and Robert Burns", in *Burns and Other Poets*, ed. Fiona Stafford and David Sergeant (Edinburgh: Edinburgh University

Press, 2012), 23–38; and Rhona Brown, "Robert Burns and Robert Fergusson", in *The Edinburgh Companion to Robert Burns*, ed. Carruthers, 86–97.

20. For discussion of Burns's poetic relationship to his Scots predecessors see Kenneth Simpson, "Poetic Genre and National Identity: Ramsay, Fergusson, and Burns", *Studies in Scottish Literature* 30 (1998): 31–42; and Douglas Dunn, "'A Very Scottish Kind of Dash': Burns's Native Metric", in *Robert Burns and Cultural Authority*, ed. Crawford, 58–85.

21. *Port Folio* 1 (1806): 196.

22. Michael Montgomery, "The Rediscovery of the Ulster Scots Language", in *Englishes Around the World: General Studies, British Isles, North America*, ed. Edgar Werner Schneider (Amsterdam: John Benjamins Press, 1997), 215.

23. See Robert Dinsmoor, *Robert Dinsmoor's Scotch-Irish Poems*, ed. Frank Ferguson and Alister McReynolds (Belfast: Ulster Historical Foundation, 2012), Introduction.

24. See, for example, T. W. Moody, "The Ulster Scots in Colonial and Revolutionary America: Part II", *Studies: An Irish Quarterly Review* 34, no. 134 (1945): 85–94.

25. Robert Dinsmoor, *Incidental Poems: Accompanied with Letters…Together with a Preface, and Sketch of the Author's Life (Written by Himself)* (Haverhill: A. W. Thayer, 1828), Preface.

26. Ibid.

27. Ibid.

28. Ibid.

29. Ibid.

30. Another poem titled "The Bobolink" by Thomas Hill appeared in a bird-themed American poetry collection: Dana Estes, ed., *Among the Birds: Selections from the Standard Poets* (Boston: Dana Estes, 2009), 33. Bryant's "Robert of Lincoln" appears on 40.

31. Ibid.

32. *Scotland and America*, 127–129.

33. See Jennifer Orr, "Constructing the Ulster Labouring-Class Poet: The Case of Samuel Thomson", in *Class and the Canon: Constructing Labouring-Class Poetry and Poetics, 1780–1900*, ed. Kirsty Blair and Mina Gorji (London: Palgrave Macmillan, 2012), 37; Carol Baranuik, *James Orr: Poet and Irish Radical* (London: Routledge, 2014); and Valentina Bold, "Janet Little 'the Scotch Milkmaid' and 'Peasant Poetry'", *Scottish Literary Journal* 20, no. 2 (1993): 21–30.

34. Andrews, "'Far-fam'd RAB'", 41–67.

35. Ibid., 42.

36. *Incidental Poems*, "Preface".

37. Ibid., 13.
38. *The Poems and Songs*, 1:49.
39. *Incidental Poems*, 102.
40. David Hill Radcliffe, "Imitation, Popular Literacy, and 'The Cottar's Saturday Night'", in *Critical Essays on Robert Burns*, ed. Carol McGuirk (New York: G.K. Hall & Co., 1998), 274.
41. Susan Manning, "Burns and God", in *Robert Burns and Cultural Authority*, ed. Crawford, 129.
42. *Incidental Poems*, 110.
43. Ibid., 49.
44. Ibid.
45. Ibid., 123.
46. *The Poems and Songs*, 1:104.
47. See "David Bruce". Accessed 29 December 2015. http://www.ulsterscotslanguage.com/en/texts/biography/david-bruce-ulster-scot-american-poet/.
48. *America Right or Wrong*, 96.
49. David Simpson, *The Politics of American English, 1776–1850* (Oxford: Oxford University Press, 1986), 109.
50. Ibid.
51. The Wash Act of 1784 "cracked down on illegal Scottish distilleries and taxed the legal ones more heavily than before". See Marilyn Butler, "Burns and Politics", in *Robert Burns and Cultural Authority*, ed. Crawford, 93.
52. David Bruce, *Poems Chiefly in the Scottish Dialect, Originally Written Under the Signature of the Scots-Irishman, by a Native of Scotland. With Notes and Illustrations* (Washington: John Colerick, 1801), 6.
53. Bruce, *Poems*, 28.
54. Having pioneered the later Transcendentalist movement of the mid-nineteenth century, it is uncommon for Emerson to be referred to as a Fireside writer. However, for the purpose of this chapter, which focuses on the collective significance of Burns to these six writers, I have adhered to John Timberman Newcomb's situating of Emerson within the "Fireside canon".
55. John Timberman Newcomb, *Would Poetry Disappear?: American Verse and the Crisis of Modernity* (Columbus: Ohio State University Press, 2004), 4.
56. Stephen Cushman, Clare Cavanagh, Jahan Ramazani, and Paul Rouzer, eds., *The Princeton Encyclopedia of Poetry and Poetics*, 4th edn (Princeton: Princeton University Press, 2012), 491.
57. *Would Poetry Disappear?*, 4.
58. Angela Sorby, *Schoolroom Poets: Childhood, Performance and the Place of American Poetry, 1865–1917* (Durham: University of New Hampshire Press, 2005), Introduction.

59. *The Princeton Encyclopedia*, 491.
60. *Would Poetry Disappear*, 4.
61. *The Critical Heritage*, 97.
62. *The Poems and Songs*, 1:146.
63. *The Critical Heritage*, 432.
64. John Greenleaf Whittier, *The Letters of John Greenleaf Whittier: 1828–1845*, ed. John B. Pickard, 3 Vols (Cambridge, MA: Belknap Press of Harvard University Press, 1975), 1:8.
65. Eric L. Haralson, ed., *Encyclopedia of American Poetry: The Nineteenth Century* (London: Routledge, 2014), 479.
66. *Catalogue of Manuscripts, Books and Autographs from the Library of the Late John Greenleaf Whittier, Comprising Original Manuscripts... Autograph Letters of the Highest Literary Interest; Works Hitherto Undescribed. Mr. Whittier's Own Copies; Author's Presentation Copies*, etc., etc., *To Be Sold at Auction ... February 6th, 1903 ... John Anderson, jr. Auctioneer* (New York: Taylor, 1903), 4.
67. John Greenleaf Whittier, *The Complete Poetical Works of John Greenleaf Whittier*, ed. H. E Scudder (Boston: Houghton Mifflin, 1894), 12.
68. "J.G. Whittier to the 'Rustic Bard'", in *Incidental Poems*, 243 (4–5).
69. *Catalogue of Manuscripts, Books and Autographs*, 8.
70. *The Complete Poetical Works of John Greenleaf Whittier*, 490.
71. Whittier was not alone in his sober lamentation. In 1859, Edinburgh's Total Abstinence Society attracted over 2500 guests to its Burns centenary celebration. See Murray Pittock and Christopher A. Whatley, "Poems and Festivals, Art and Artefact", *The Scottish Historical Review* 93, no. 236 (2014): 72.
72. *The Complete Poetical Works of John Greenleaf Whittier*, 196.
73. John Greenleaf Whittier, *The Poetical Works of John Greenleaf Whittier* (London: Macmillan and Co., 1874), 351.
74. *Robert Burns and Pastoral*, 231.
75. James E. Rocks, "Whittier's 'Snow-Bound': 'The Circle of Our Hearth' and the Discourse on Domesticity'", *Studies in the American Renaissance* (1993): 343.
76. *The Complete Poetical Works of John Greenleaf Whittier*, 17.
77. *Harvardinia* 4 (Cambridge: John Owen, 1838), 31.
78. For a full list of early Lowell poems published in *Harvardinia*, see Luther Samuel Livingston and Jacob Chester Chamberlain, eds., *A Bibliography of the First Editions in Book form of the Writings of James Russell Lowell, Compiled Largely from the Collection Formed by the Late Jacob Chester Chamberlain, with Assistance from His Notes and Memoranda* (New York: The De Vinne Press, 1914), 3.
79. See Jayne Crane Harder, "James Russell Lowell: Linguistic Patriot", *American Speech* 29, no. 3 (1954): 181–186.

80. Ibid., 181.
81. See Todd N. Thompson, "From Brahmin to Biglow (and Back Again): James Russell Lowell as Temporary Satirist", *A Journal of the American Renaissance* 58, no. 2 (2012): 154–184.
82. John W. Crowley, "James Russell Lowell's The Biglow Papers [First Series]: A Critical Edition (Review)", *The New England Quarterly* 51, no. 2 (1978): 279–281.
83. See also Nils Erik Enkvist, "The Biglow Papers in Nineteenth-Century England", *The New England Quarterly* 26, no. 2 (1953): 219–236.
84. *The Biglow Papers*, 5.
85. Ibid., 5–7.
86. Ibid., Title Page.
87. Ibid., 36.
88. Nadia Nurhussein, *Rhetorics of Literacy: The Cultivation of American Dialect* (Columbus: The Ohio State University Press, 2013), 6.
89. *Select Reviews, and Spirit of the Foreign Magazines* 2 (1809): 17.
90. Killheffer, "A Comparison of the Dialect of 'The Biglow Papers'", 225.
91. See Nurhussein, *Rhetorics of Literacy*.
92. David E. E. Sloane, "Dialect, Doggerel, and Local Colour: Comic Traditions and the Rise of Realism in Popular Poetry", in *The Cambridge History of American Poetry*, ed. Alfred Bendixen and Stephen Burt (New York: Cambridge University Press, 2015), 445.
93. Ibid.
94. See, for example, John Adams' 1763 "Humphrey Ploughjogger Letters" and Royall Tyler's 1787 play *The Contrast*; both of which occasionally use "Yankee" as a voice of political and moral reason.
95. *The Poems and Songs*, 1:312 (45–6).
96. Joel Barlow, Esq., *The Hasty-Pudding, a Poem, in Three Cantos* (New Haven: William Storer, 1838), 2.
97. Sloane, "Dialect, Doggerel, and Local Colour", 447.
98. Marie Killheffer, "A Comparison of the Dialect of 'The Biglow Papers' with the Dialect of Four Yankee Plays", *American Speech* 3, no. 3 (Duke University Press, 1928): 222.
99. Sood, "A Modern Poet on the Scotch Bard", 230–236.
100. William Dean Howells quoted from Paul Laurence Dunbar, *The Complete Stories of Paul Laurence Dunbar*, ed. Gene Andrew Jarrett and Thomas Lewis Morgan (Athens, OH: Ohio University Press, 2005), 15.
101. Leask, "Was Burns a Labouring-Class Poet?", in *Class and the Canon*, ed. Blair and Gorji, 17.
102. "Laboring Class Poets Online". Accessed 15 December 2015. https://laboringclasspoetsonline.omeka.net/.

103. See, for example, *The Farmer's Boy, A Rural Poem by Robert Bloomfield, Fourth American Edition* (Baltimore: Thomas, Andrews & Butler, 1803).
104. See "Laboring Class Poets Blog". Accessed 15 December 2015. https://lcpoets.wordpress.com/.
105. *The Politics of American English*, 109.
106. *The Complete Stories of Paul Laurence Dunbar*, 15.
107. James Russell Lowell, *Latest Literary Essays and Addresses* (London: Macmillan & Co., 1891), 12.
108. See "To the Spirit of Keats", in James Russell Lowell, *Poems* (London: C. E. Mudie, 1844), 245; and *The Poetical Works of John Keats with a Memoir by James Russell Lowell*, ed. James Russell Lowell (New York: J. Miller, 1873).
109. See Kent Ljungquist and Buford Jones, "The Identity of 'Outis': A Further Chapter in the Poe-Longfellow War", *American Literature* 60, no. 3 (1988): 404–415.
110. McGuirk, "Haunted By Authority", 146.
111. *The Poems and Songs*, 2:660.
112. See William Cullen Bryant II, "The Genesis of 'Thanatopsis'", *The New England Quarterly* 21, no. 2 (1948): 163–184.
113. *Chronicle of the Hundredth Birthday of Robert Burns*, Introduction.
114. Frank Lentricchia, *Modernist Quartet* (Cambridge: Cambridge University Press, 1994), 2.
115. James H. Read, "The Limits of Self Reliance: Emerson, Slavery and Abolition", in *A Political Companion to Ralph Waldo Emerson*, ed. Alan Levine (Lexington: University Press of Kentucky, 2011), 163.
116. Richard A. Katula, *The Eloquence of Edward Everett: America's Greatest Orator* (New York: Peter Lang Publishing Inc., 2010), 110.
117. *Celebration of the Hundredth Anniversary of the Birth of Robert Burns, by the Boston Burns Club. January 25th, 1859* (Boston: H. W. Dutton and son, 1859), 3.
118. Read, "The Limits of Self Reliance", 165.
119. *Celebration of the Hundredth Anniversary of the Birth of Robert Burns, by the Boston Burns Club*, 3.
120. Ibid., 6.
121. Ibid., 40.
122. Jenni Calder, *Scots in the USA* (Edinburgh: Luath Press Ltd., 2014), 193–194.
123. Darrel Abel, *Democratic Voices and Vistas: American Literature from Emerson to Lanier* (Lincoln: iUniverse, 2002), 283.
124. Oliver Wendell Holmes Sr. quoted from Susan Goodman, *Republic of Words: The Atlantic Monthly and Its Writers, 1857–1925* (Hanover and London: University Press of New England, 2011), 102.

125. *Democratic Voices and Vistas*, 284.
126. Ibid., 283.
127. *Celebration of the Hundredth Anniversary of the Birth of Robert Burns, by the Boston Burns club*, 44.
128. *The Works of Robert Burns, Containing His Life by John Lockhart Esq* (Hartford: Judd, Loomis & Co.), 144.
129. *Celebration of the Hundredth Anniversary of the Birth of Robert Burns, by the Boston Burns Club*, 44.
130. Scott L. Taylor, "*Judicium Dei, vulgaris popularisque sensus*: Survival of Customary Justice and Resistance to its Displacement by the "New" *Ordines iudiciorum* as Evidenced by Francophonic Literature of the High Middle Ages", in Albrecht Classen and Connie Scarborough, eds., *Crime and Punishment in the Middle Ages and Early Modern Age: Mental-Historical Investigations of Basic Human Problems and Social Responses* (Berlin and Boston: De Gruyter, 2012), 109–130.
131. Kim Ileen Moreland, *The Medievalist Impulse in American Literature: Twain, Adams, Fitzgerald, and Hemingway* (Charlottesville: University of Virginia Press, 1996), 99.
132. Sarah Gordon, "Rural and Agricultural Space in the Old French *Fabliaux* and the *Roman de Renart*", in *Rural Space in the Middle Ages and Early Modern Age: The Spatial Turn in Premodern Studies*, ed. Albert Classen (Berlin and Boston: De Gruyter, 2012), 290.
133. "Parallel Between Cowper and Burns", *The Monthly Anthology and Boston Review* 3 (1806): 68.
134. *Celebration of the Hundredth Anniversary of the Birth of Robert Burns, by the Boston Burns Club*, 55.
135. Ibid.
136. Paul Haupt, "Alcohol in the Bible", *Journal of Biblical Literature* 36, nos. 1 and 2 (1917): 75.
137. Thomas Carlyle, *On Heroes, Hero-Worship and the Heroic in History* (London: Chapman and Hall, 1840), 226.
138. Ibid.
139. Ibid., 198.
140. Mark Cumming, ed., *The Carlyle Encyclopedia* (Madison: Farleigh Dickinson University Press, 2004), 297.
141. *Celebration of the Hundredth Anniversary of the Birth of Robert Burns, by the Boston Burns Club*, 61–62.
142. Ibid., 35–37.
143. Linda Young, *Middle-Class Culture in the Nineteenth Century: America, Australia* (New York: Palgrave Macmillan, 2002), 33.

144. Cindy S. Aron, "The Evolution of the Middle Class", in *A Companion to 19th—Century America*, ed. William Barney (Malden and Oxford: Blackwell, 2008), 179.
145. *Celebration of the Hundredth Anniversary of the Birth of Robert Burns, by the Boston Burns Club*, 36.
146. See Zoltan Kovecses, *American English: An Introduction* (Peterborough: Broadview Press, 2000), 261; and James Darsey, *Prophetic Tradition and Radical Rhetoric in America* (New York: New York University Press, 1999), 160.
147. Ralph L. Rusk, *The Life of Ralph Waldo Emerson* (New York: Columbia University Press, 1957), 440.
148. Ralph Waldo Emerson, *The Journals and Miscellaneous Notebooks of Ralph Waldo Emerson*, ed. William H. Gilman and J. E. Parsons, 16 Vols (Cambridge, MA: Harvard University Press, 1970) 8:46.
149. Franklin B. Sanborn, *The Personality of Emerson* (New York: Hasker House Publishers, 1971), 121.
150. *The Edinburgh Review* 96 (1828): 278.
151. *Celebration of the Hundredth Anniversary of the Birth of Robert Burns, by the Boston Burns Club*, 37.
152. *The Life of Ralph Waldo Emerson*, 194.
153. Ibid.
154. James Russell Lowell, "A Fable for Critics" quoted from Alexander Ireland, *Ralph Waldo Emerson: His Life, Genius, And Writings to Which Are Added Personal Recollections of His Visits to England, Extracts from Unpublished Letters and Miscellaneous Characteristic Records* (London: Simpkin, Marshall, & Co., 1882), 333.
155. *Celebration of the Hundredth Anniversary of the Birth of Robert Burns, by the Boston Burns Club*, 36.
156. Ibid.
157. *The Life of Ralph Waldo Emerson*, 156–157.
158. Ibid.
159. *The Journals and Miscellaneous Notebooks of Ralph Waldo Emerson*, 14:180.
160. *Celebration of the Hundredth Anniversary of the Birth of Robert Burns, by the Boston Burns Club*, 37.
161. E. R. Hoar quoted from *Estimating Emerson: An Anthology of Criticism from Carlyle to Cavell*, ed. David LaRocca (New York and London: Bloomsbury, 2013), 191.
162. Ibid.
163. John McAleer, *Ralph Waldo Emerson: Days of Encounter* (Boston: Little, Brown and Company, 1984), 564.

164. McGuirk, "Haunted By Authority", 150.
165. Crawford, "America's Bard", 111.
166. *Poetics of Character*, 244–267.
167. *The Journals and Miscellaneous Notebooks of Ralph Waldo Emerson*, 8:46.

PART III

Memory and Nation

CHAPTER 6

"The West Winds": Burns and American Cultural Memory, c.1800–1866

> The memory of Burns ... The west winds are murmuring it ....[1]
> —Ralph Waldo Emerson (1859)

Arguably more so than any other eighteenth-century literary figure, the popular legacy of Robert Burns has continually straddled the blurry boundaries between myth, "memory"[2] and history. As recently as the 2015 UK General Election, the Scottish branch of the right-wing populist United Kingdom Independence Party (UKIP) attempted to win the hearts (if not the minds) of Scottish voters by producing posters emblazoned with lines from Burns's "The Dumfries Volunteers",[3] while, previously, the opposing Scottish Nationalist Party had launched an electoral campaign on 25 January, with former leader Alex Salmond claiming there was "no better day" to do so "than on the birthday of Robert Burns".[4] Contests were also waged over the poet's presumed political leanings during the 2014 Scottish Referendum as he was variably cast as a Unionist or Nationalist across media outlets,[5] causing Gerard Carruthers to astutely note the irony of appropriating an individual who "never actually had any kind of political vote in life".[6]

In the nineteenth century, divergent memories and appropriations of the poet similarly co-existed and conflicted with one another. Christopher A. Whatley has discussed, for example, how Burns was claimed by both Radicals and Scottish conservatives between 1796 and 1859; citing the Ayr Festival of 1844 and the 1859 Centenary as instances of where Burns was simultaneously appropriated by Scotland's

© The Author(s) 2018
A. Sood, *Robert Burns and the United States of America*,
https://doi.org/10.1007/978-3-319-94445-6_6

Whigs and Tories among other groups.[7] The "memory of Burns" in the nineteenth-century USA was equally multiflorous and complex. The idea that Burns was "a friend to liberty in the United States"[8] has been both popular and enduring, partly due to the frequency with which he has been yoked with ideological praise from influential nineteenth-century Americans such as Whitman, Emerson and Abraham Lincoln. However, as the previous chapter discussed, Emerson's praise for Burns was more occasional than innate while Whitman was by no means wholly enamoured as I have argued elsewhere.[9]

There is, of course, no doubting the significance of these figures having read and, to some extent, praised Burns. Yet the conflation of these—albeit important—individual "memories" should not be mistaken for proof that Burns was cohesively and unanimously remembered as a beacon of democracy and egalitarianism in the early USA, however appealing the notion may be. Such a sweeping assertion belies the complexity of the multiple, at times competing, layers of memory that diversely preserved and promoted the poet and his works between 1800 and 1866.

As we shall see, groups and individuals divergent as Frederick Douglass (1818–1895), the Freemasons and the Ku Klux Klan also held their own, often idiosyncratic, "memories" of Burns that were variously articulated through speeches, essays, dinners and other forms of objectified culture. Regularly implicit in these articulations of remembrance, however, was the subjective promotion of group and individual values. Where Frederick Douglass remembered Burns as being kin to an African American slave who had "broke loose from the moorings which society had thrown around him",[10] the first Ku Klux Klan used "To a Louse" as a rite of initiation; seemingly drawing on the fact that all six founding members were of white Scottish descent and thus should have knowledge of the poem.[11] The examples here are, admittedly, purposefully polarising and require much further analysis. Nonetheless, pointing out such deviations in appropriation and memory (Who else might connect UKIP, SNP, Frederick Douglass and the KKK?) unquestionably renders Burns a worthy subject when discussing the complex interrelationships between memory, history and identity.

It is unsurprising, then, that Burns has attracted the attention of leading twenty-first-century cultural theorists and proponents of memory studies. Scholars such as Ann Rigney, Leith Davis, Murray Pittock and Susan Manning have applied and advanced the foundational work of Maurice Halbwachs and Pierre Nora, providing new frameworks with which to comprehend both the legacy and reception of Burns and his works. Having traced the initial appearances, widespread reprinting and consequential literary influence of Burns's poetry, it seems an apt moment to turn to the slightly more conceptual issue of how Burns was "remembered" in the USA and, in doing so, highlight the significance of various nineteenth-century modes of remembrance and commemoration.

Cultural Memory Theory and Burns

Employed and appropriated across disciplines as diverse as literature, neuroscience and philosophy, the term "cultural memory" has become academically convoluted over the past few decades. In literary studies, it broadly refers to how "memory" or knowledge about past events, people or things, is preserved through "cultural" means in any given space or place. In referring to the cultural memory of Burns in the USA, then, one might think of the term as an umbrella for considering the ways in which American society—through festivals, songs, rituals, text, rites, objects or otherwise—"remembered" the poet and his works.

The idea of there being a complex interrelationship between memory and history, or rather, that there is a connection "between the act of memorisation and the writing of history"[12] is not a new one and can be traced through several works from Classical Greece to Renaissance Europe.[13] Our current understanding and use of the term "cultural memory", however, broadly derive from a reinvigorated interest in, and response to, Maurice Halbwachs's twentieth-century concept of "collective memory" (*mémoire collective*); a phrase first coined in his 1925 book *Les cadres sociaux de la mémoire* and later advanced in the posthumously published *La mémoire collective* (1950).

Formulated in the same period that Sigmund Freud (1856–1939) famously began to introduce memory theory through his development of metapsychology, it is only in recent decades that Halbwachs has received a rejuvenated sense of attention as contemporary historians continue to grapple with "the politics of memory in the waning or abandoned traditions of the modern age".[14] Halbwachs challenged Freud's view of memory being a resource of the individual psyche, arguing that it operates according to a social rather than a psychological dynamic. Where Freud believed that memory was something inherent in the individual, hidden but always recoverable, Halbwachs proposed that recollected memories are constructed "within social contexts". That is, he believed that memories could "become whole only when they are located within the social framework of our present lives".[15]

Building on this principle, Halbwachs suggested that perceptions of the past are continually revised by "social forces" that act upon us and moderate our present conceptions. It is these "social forces", Halbwachs argued, that bind and form the "collective memory" of both groups and individuals in any given context. The dynamics of social structures—families, demographics, social classes and religious sects, for example—determine the ways in which we "remember" the past, creating a shared memory and identity that might differ from the "collective memory" of other groups. For Halbwachs, our conception of the past is not fixed, hidden and in need of "recovery" (as Freud suggested), but malleable to the point where the original memory source might be reconstituted. It is this idea that led Halbwachs to distinguish between "memory" and "history". Where history, or historical knowledge about the past, is a set of generalised facts that follows some form of fixed standardisation (such as the remembering and recitation of a specific set of dates), "collective memory" contains a "subjective dimension" and promotes a sense of identity which is "intimately tied to a particular group" and its values.[16]

Returning to Emerson's 1859 speech and reconsidering it within the parameters of Halbwachs' theory of *mémoire collective*, then, we might consider the American writer's "memory of Burns" with renewed interest. The previous chapter outlined how Emerson and his fellow speakers at the Parker House Hotel described Burns as being kin to the "armed and privileged minorities" who "worked politically"[17] in the American Revolution. Here, Emerson's individual "memory" clearly reflects the influence of wider social structures, namely the Boston Burns Club which, as discussed, prided itself on the newly formed Republican party's political idealism. Though Burns made subtle, favourable references towards the outcome of the American Revolution, the manner in which he is fervently remembered and likened to American Revolutionaries at The Parker House Hotel clearly smacks—in line with Halbwachs' theory—of a memory source being re-modified into an "idealized image, or imago".[18]

Thus, even a brief *précis* of Halbwachs' idea of "collective memory" offers up several intriguing points of consideration when discussing the ways in which Burns was remembered in the nineteenth-century USA. However, questions remain over the types of commemorative practices that led to the reconstitution of these memories. We might consider, for example, the differing yet interrelated effects of print media (James Currie's *The Works*), memorial architecture (the erection of statues) and festivals (Burns Suppers and the 1859 Centenary itself) on preserving and influencing the memory of the poet. Moreover, the vital question of whether such diverse methods of remembrance (and divergent appropriations) can be legitimately grouped together and considered as forms of national collective remembrance, unique to the USA, is also open to debate. To use the "nation" in such a way, as a binding parameter, would require much further discussion about the evolution of American nationalism in the nineteenth century, and how it might have affected Burns commemorations. It is these overriding questions that render the issue of Burns and cultural memory in the nineteenth-century USA both complex and problematic. In order to approach this topic with greater clarity, then, it is worth considering the more recent advancements on Halbwachs' theory and corresponding scholarly articulations on Burns and cultural memory.

Expanding on Maurice Halbwachs' model, Jan Assmann and John Czaplinka put forth the idea that collective memory might be split into two further, interrelated categories: "Communicative memory" ("based on everyday oral communications") and "Cultural memory" (formed when "living communication crystalliz[es] in the forms of objectivized culture – whether in texts, images, rites, buildings, monuments, cities or even landscapes").[19] In other words, where "communicative memory" is oral and comprised of multiple narratives articulated by active participants,[20] "cultural memory" relies on symbolisation and requires "institutions of preservation"[21] (relics, books and other modes of objectification) in order for past experience to be conveyed or reconfigured. Admittedly, the incisive categorical tagging here of "communicative memory" being primarily transmitted through oral means and "cultural memory" as stemming from "objectified" culture can be misleading, due to the fact "cultural memory" is often preserved or inscribed orally.

Returning, once again, to Emerson and his (orally transmitted) 1859 speech, for example, his "memory of Burns" was not—as would be the case for a "communicative memory"—a living, autobiographical "embodied memory", but in fact both a response to and result of extant objectified commemorative forces (such as the centenary itself, the Boston Burns Club or biographical texts on Burns). Moreover, through his "ceremonial communication"[22] at The Parker House Hotel, Emerson was functioning as, what Assmann calls, an "institution of preservation", not only in the form of his ceremonial delivery but also by the fact his speech was later transcribed and disseminated widely. Thus, the processes by which Emerson's 1859 speech (and its subsequent circulation in print form) "re-embodied" the memory of Burns are clear.

There were, of course, several other "institutions of preservation" that functioned to "re-embody" the memory of the poet in the nineteenth century. Chapter 4 of this book demonstrated the extent to which Currie's edition and several other biographical accounts were reprinted in the USA between 1801 and 1866. Having documented the empirical methods by which the poetry of Burns was reprinted and distributed, we might now turn to think more critically about the repercussions of such a vast dissemination in the light of the theoretical discussion above. The widely available American editions of Burns's poetry might easily be considered as what Assmann calls "institutions of preservation",[23] each one an "objectified memory" serving to reconstitute remembrance in the absence of any communicative memory and further complicated by a multiplicity print-forms that circulated information about the poet (anthologies, newspapers and periodicals). That the biographies contained vast ideological differences is also demonstrative of Assmann's assertion that cultural memory undergoes repeated, subjective "revisions" that often reflect back on those doing the "remembering".

A microcosmic example, when specifically considering the American editions as "institutions of preservation", is the contrasting differences between James Currie's Enlightenment-inspired "remembering" of Burns as a product of civic educational structures and Thomas Carlyle's Romantic revision of the poet's legacy. Here, in terms of the way Burns is "remembered", "the distinction between myth and history vanishes"[24] as objectified memories (in this case in the form of biographical text) are reconstructed to reflect a changing present (the obvious variation here is from an Enlightenment-era reading of Burns to an overtly Romantic one).

The abundance of American biographical editions, each transmitting their own ideological "memory" of the poet, was certainly one method by which Burns was continually and variously remembered. However, having devoted Part II of this book to print culture, it is more useful here to discuss other modes of commemoration or "institutions of preservation" within these specific geo-cultural and chronological parameters. Books, postcards, ceramic ware, snuff boxes and statues might be the most tangible examples of how material "objects" can preserve the cultural memory of significant events, experiences and literary or historical figures. Equally, but perhaps less obviously in relation to the noun "object", associational clubs, fraternities, rites, landscapes and sites of tourism must also be counted among mediated forms of memory preservation. Spanning over a wide expanse of material and memorial culture, the following discussion will address several of the above, ranging from the establishment of the first "Burns Clubs" (in the early nineteenth century) to the beginnings of the transatlantic vogue for erecting statues in the poet's honour (the mid to latter half of the century).

SUPPERS AND FRATERNAL SOCIETIES

The coming together of migrants with the same ethnic background is a widely documented and common sociological occurrence, and thus it comes as no surprise that several Scottish clubs, associations and kinship networks had formed by the time that Burns's poetry first arrived in North America at the end of the eighteenth century. As early as 1657, when the Scots Charitable Society of Boston was established, Scots emigrants came together to promote fraternal bonds and offer charitable aid to one another.[25] Similar clubs continued to be formed in the following century, predominantly adopting the name of Scotland's patron saint to unify emigrants seeking fraternal kinship. In the years preceding the arrival of Burns's poetry in the USA, St. Andrew's Societies had been established in New York (1756), Philadelphia (1749), Baltimore (1750) and South Carolina (1729).[26] Naturally, as the reputation of Burns increased through the periodical press and American reprints, these Scoto-centric groups were swift to recognise, celebrate and subsequently memorialise a poet they could claim as their own.

It is stated in the *The History of Saint Andrew's Society of The State of New York*, compiled and edited by Harlan Douglas Whatley in 2008, that the one annual occasion that "was never allowed to pass without due celebration"[27] by the organisation and its sister societies was a grand feast in honour of the patron saint's birthday (30 November) each year. Used to promote "conviviality and friendship", celebrations included, among festive eating and drinking, the performance and recitation of Scottish poetry and song. Clark McGinn has recorded how Burns's poems were recited at these North American events as early as 1790 (at the St. Andrew's Night Dinner in Pittsburgh).[28]

The incorporation of Scottish songs also draws attention to the performative elements of memory transfer in relation to Burns. The formal "suppers" provided a wider platform for the performance of his songs outside of the domestic sphere, allowing for a performative form of communication and preservation.[29] From the initial inclusion of selected poems and songs at annual feasts, toasting the poet swiftly became a customary gesture after his death in 1796. Several transcripts of separate St. Andrews Society proceedings in different states reveal similar tributes and toasts to "The Memory of Robert Burns, The Ayrshire Poet".[30] Rather than just the recitation of his poetry and songs, then, the very act of commemorating Burns became a way of asserting and maintaining Scottish cultural value in the far-removed context of the USA.

Though these early festive toasts were woven into extant celebrations of St. Andrew's birth, it was not long before autonomous "Burns Suppers"—solely concerned with commemorating the life and works of the poet—were established. The phenomenon of the "Burns Supper", of course, was not exclusive to the USA and was catalysed by the widely publicised inception of organised feasts in Ayrshire, first arranged by Reverend Hamilton Paul in 1801. McGinn notes that, as early as 1803, articles documenting these events were printed in newspapers across several American States, consequently "opening the concept of dining in memory of Burns around his birthday to the American market".[31] That the nature of these "Suppers" was based "on Masonic Lines",[32] resembling lodge ceremonials, meant that Freemasons were active in organising annual Suppers in honour of the poet. Yet the Freemasons were not the only associational society involved in organising such events and, as we shall see, by the 1859 centenary, there were multiples of Burns Suppers organised by different clubs and social groups; all of which functioned as separate "institutions of preservation" that promoted a memory of the poet that was infused with a slightly altered "subjective dimension".[33]

That "social forces",[34] and in particular geopolitical circumstances, dictated the (sometimes contrasting) ways in which Burns was "remembered" at contemporary Burns Suppers has previously been discussed by Murray Pittock, Leith Davis and Nigel Leask. With imperial synchronicity, by the mid-nineteenth-century events celebrating the birth of Burns had been marked on social calendars across locations as diverse as India, Jamaica and Australia. In noting the subjective nature of these occasions, Leask notes how the 1812 Calcutta Burns Supper "buttressed Scottish identity in the British Empire",[35] a purpose quite different to some of the American commemorations that featured songs dedicated to those who "fought and bled" against the British in the Revolutionary War. Yet even within the national context of the USA, the memory of the poet being toasted was far from uniform and variously shaped by differing "social forces" (variable by associational groups, regional interests or otherwise).

An interesting convergence of Scottish and American patriotism, for example, can be found at the first American (free-standing) "Burns Supper" held by the Philadelphia Burns Club in 1817. Beginning with tributes and toasts to (in addition to Burns) "Scotland's Daughters!", "The memory of Buchanan, Lindsay, Ramsay and Ferguson" and "The immortal memory of Bruce and Wallace"; the format initially appears similar to the Scoto-centric agenda of the earlier St. Andrews Society events. A notable addition to the proceedings, however, was a tribute to "the immortal memory of General Washington" followed by the performance of "Hail Columbia".[36] Used as the de facto national anthem of the USA up to the turn of the twentieth century, the song, composed by Philip Phile (1734–1793) with lyrics added by Joseph Hopkinson (1770–1842), extols those "who fought and bled in Freedom's cause" and celebrates "Rallying round our Liberty".[37] Hopkinson, who became a member of the House of Representatives in 1816, wrote his lyrics and sent them to George Washington just four years after Burns had penned his own "Ode" to the first president, further revealing the symbolic and inspirational power of Washington in the "revolutionary" 1790s, as discussed in Chapter 2. "Hail Columbia" was to be a regular feature at Burns Suppers and an introduction to the song can be found in a transcript of the 1822 celebration held at Harmony Hall, New York.

Commenting on Burns's love for his "native country, his patriotism and independence of spirit", the speaker, Mr William Orr, observed how "love of country is a passion pretty generally diffused among mankind". Expanding further, Orr explained that while Americans should "indulge our own patriotism", they might also admire those "who cherish the same principle with regard to their countries, even although these countries be at war with our own".[38] Here, rather than Burns being directly praised for his supposed political kinship with American ideals (as he was at the 1859 Boston Centenary), Orr channels his "memory" of the poet's relationship to Scotland to promote his *own* values. In recognising the subjective, at times ideological, nature of these commemorative occasions, then, we might once again consider Jan Assmann's assertion that "cultural memory reaches back into the past only so far as the past can be reclaimed as 'ours'".[39]

STATUES AND MEMORIALS

While Burns Clubs and Suppers were established in America in the early decades of the nineteenth century, it was not until later that statues and memorials of the poet appeared. This can be attributed to a much wider (late nineteenth century) vogue for erecting public memorials of literary figures in America; evidenced by the statues of Burns, Dante, Goethe and Shakespeare that were commissioned within years of each other across several states from 1860 onwards.[40] Though the present discussion is concerned with Burns and cultural memory in the USA up to 1866, it remains useful to briefly touch upon the circumstances from which some of the later monuments to the Scottish poet arose, particularly having acknowledged the interrelationship(s) between different forms of objectified culture in the context of cultural memory. As Jan Assmann notes, "transitions and transformations account for the dynamics of cultural memory"[41]; a process marked here by the intersecting re-mediations of the memory of Burns (from texts and suppers to statues and other forms of objectified culture).

The first detailed study of worldwide Burns statues, titled *The World's Memorials of Robert Burns,* was, incidentally, published in the USA (Detroit) by Edward Goodwillie in 1911. James Mackay also devoted a significant chapter of his book *Burnsiana* (1986) to the subject and, as previously noted, the twenty-first century has seen the comprehensive listing and digitisation of Burns monuments, memorials and memorabilia as a result of the "Robert Burns: Inventing Tradition and Securing Memory, 1796-1909" project conducted by the Universities of Glasgow and Dundee. In specific relation to North America, Thomas Keith has provided an informative survey of monuments in a paper first given as part of the pre-conference symposium and exhibit, "Robert Burns and America" organised for the Robert Burns World Federation Limited meeting in Atlanta, Georgia 20 July 2001. Elucidating the number of statues in North America, Keith notes that there are now a total of fourteen in the USA and eight in Canada, pointing to the fact that there are more statues of Burns in North America (22) than that are in Scotland (15).[42]

Perhaps the most pertinent aspect of Keith's survey (and the digital database) to the present discussion, however, is the extent to which Burns Clubs and Caledonian/St. Andrews Societies were involved in raising capital for the erection of statues. The link here is revealing of the "transitions and transformations" that allowed for the cultural memory of the poet to be continually reconfigured and preserved, a point worth emphasising given that most discussions of cultural memory tend to focus on "isolated acts of remembrance rather than on the processes by which one type of remembrance feeds into another".[43]

The first statue of Burns in the USA was unveiled in New York's Central Park in 1880 and was predominantly sponsored by members of the New York Caledonian Club and St. Andrews Society. Revered Scottish sculptor Sir John Steele (1804–1891) was commissioned for the job and depicted Burns on the stump of an elm tree (which Sir Walter Scott linked with the harp of Caledonia in the opening lines of his poem "The Lady of the Lake").[44] The unveiling of the New York statue, featuring "speeches, poems, songs and bagpipes",[45] was not dissimilar to previous convivial St. Andrews Day celebrations in its heralding of perceived "Scottishness" or Scottish heritage. McGinn and Pittock have both touched on how American Scottish Societies were influential on the increasing "tartan-isation" of the Burns Supper as the poet became, arguably to a greater degree in the far-removed context of the USA, a symbolic and unifying figure for Scottish culture in representing both Highland and Lowland identities. The ceremonial unveiling of the early Burns statues in the USA reveals similar associational appropriations, with the 1888 event in Albany "organised to coincide with the annual gathering of the North American Caledonian Association". This meant that Caledonian Societies, St. Andrew Societies and other Scots charitable societies gathered together from cities such as "Boston, Milwaukee, New York, Buffalo and from as far as Montreal and Toronto".[46]

On this evidence, the "memory" of Burns, as it was initially objectified into statuary medium in the USA, was seemingly a way of maintaining a sense of Scottish identity or heritage, bringing to mind Assmann's idea of "remembering" being "a realization of belonging, even a social obligation".[47] Yet, as was the case with Suppers, even the static medium of statues would, at times, take on subjective inflections. The Scotocentric elements of the earliest statues discussed above, for example, might be considered apart from some of the later tributes, such as John Horrigan's twentieth-century statue in Massachusetts which is inscribed with a long excerpt from "Ode for General Washington's Birthday" or the 1928 monument erected by the St. Louis Burns Club that depicts Burns with a sheaf of wheat and a scythe, closely resembling a "minuteman from the American Revolution".[48] Both the Massachusetts and St. Louis statues clearly promote a localised sense of identity transposed through a form of objectified culture.

Though the transatlantic vogue for Burns statues began after the 1859 centenary (and thus beyond the current study's parameters), it is hoped that this brief outline of its inception provides a clear example of how cultural memory undergoes frequent processes of remediation while retaining traces of the source memory (Burns). Ann Rigney has pioneered this media-based approach towards considering cultural memory by emphasising how investigations into "the way memories are communicated, circulated and exchanged" allow us to see the way collective identities are "redefined through memorial practices, and not merely reflected in them".[49] In considering this idea further, it is useful to turn to another process of mediation that rose to particular prominence in the nineteenth century and, as we shall see, played a significant role in preserving the cultural memory of the poet, the practice of literary tourism and its associated material culture.

LITERARY TOURISM AND MATERIAL CULTURE

In her comprehensive study of American tourists in nineteenth-century Britain, Allison Lockwood notes that the birthplace of Burns became "all but an obligatory stop for the American tourist", citing a visit by Andrew Bigelow in 1817 as an early example.[50] Several written accounts of these visits were reproduced across the Atlantic, further contributing to the cultural preservation of the poet in American print culture. In 1829, New York publishers G. & C. & H. Carvill published Nathaniel Carter's tour journal, which contained a detailed account of his visit to the cottage, in full book form.[51]

Perhaps the most famous American visitor in the period was prominent African American abolitionist Frederick Douglass whose written account, titled "A Fugitive Slave Visiting the Birth-Place of Robert Burns", was repeatedly reprinted in the USA: first in *The New York Tribune* of 9 July 1846 and subsequently in other (predominantly abolitionist) newspapers, such as the *Albany Evening Journal* and the Ohio-based *Anti-Slavery Bugle*, which was widely distributed across Iowa,

Illinois, Wisconsin and Indiana.[52] As Thomas Keith has noted, the original recipient of Douglass's epistolary account was Abigail Mott (1775–1846), who wrote and published Biographical *Sketches and Interesting Anecdotes of Persons of Colour* in 1826. It is likely that Mott was responsible for sending it to abolitionist newspapers given its strong anti-slavery message and her active participation in the abolitionist cause.[53]

The fuller significance of Douglass's memory of Burns in relation to US abolitionism will be discussed later in this chapter. However, when considering literary tourism, it is more useful to first touch upon an anecdote from his written account. In describing meeting Mrs. Begg (the poet's sister) and two nieces of Burns, Douglass noted how one of the latter individuals remarked that her "uncle was more highly esteemed in America than in Scotland".[54] This curious remark was likely a reaction to the frequency with which enthusiastic American tourists had visited the Burns Cottage, given it was promoted as a site of tourism as early as 1801.[55]

Some decades later, an article specifically about Mrs. Begg and the cottage appeared in the Virginia-based *Daily Dispatch* stating, in line with this idea, how she had received more visitors from "the States than any other part of the world".[56] Later in the nineteenth century, as literary tourism continued to boom, American traveller Leonard A. Morrison noted in his published memoir how Miss. Begg (by then Burns's only remaining niece) once again spoke highly of the large amounts of American visitors she had received.[57] In another telling anecdote, nineteenth-century American traveller Loretta J. Post commented that "hawkers quite disturb the poetic spell"[58] of the cottage, suggesting that the capitalistic rise of material culture was, to some extent, interwoven into the practice of literary tourism.

Pittock and Mackay have touched upon this connection in describing how nineteenth-century tourists sought to reify memories through "a wealth of objects" that were "claimed to be relics [...] of particular locations associated with Burns's poetry and life".[59] Objects and tourist merchandise such as jewellery and snuff boxes were adorned with multiple Burns-related locations (e.g. Alloway Kirk and The Braes of Ballochmyle) while some objects were allegedly made from wood extracted from the rafters of Alloway Kirk or the cottage floorboards, thus allowing literary pilgrims to maximise their memorial experience and proximity to the poet. Though the mass production of Mauchline ware did not occur until the later decades of the nineteenth century (partly in response to the growing literary tourist market), evidence of a desire to participate in this objective form of commemoration can be found in these early accounts.

In 1827, Nathaniel Carter observed how parts of the grave of Burns's father had "been broken off for relics" by "the curiosity of strangers who, in some instances have carried fragments of it to the banks of the Ganges, or to the shores of Ontario and Huron". Displeased at the mutilation of the grave, Carter obtained his own "highly prized" relic in the form of a walking stick "cut from the site of the monument" before filling a "cup from the cottage" and drinking to "the memory of Robert Burns".[60] Douglass also made reference to material culture on his visit, admiring a "finely executed marble bust of Burns" and "two statues carved out of free stone" of Souter Johnny and Tam o' Shanter, which can still be seen in the Alloway Monument today. He further described a bible "given by Burns to his sweet Highland Mary", which was displayed in a glass case along with "a lock of her hair neatly fastened to a cord". Constructing a melancholic memory from these objects, Douglass remarked:

> As I gazed on the hair of her he so dearly loved, and who by death was snatched from his bosom, and up to his bust glowing with expression, I received a vivid impression'.[61]

In a fascinating transatlantic exchange, the bible (and accompanying "lock of hair") that Douglass responded to had initially been transported to Canada by William Anderson in 1832, before being purchased for 100 dollars by "seventy Scotsmen living in Canada" who then forwarded it to the Provost of Ayr to be displayed to reflect "great credit and honour on those seventy exiled Scots".[62] Much of the Burns-related merchandise circulating in the USA was a result of the frequency with which American travellers returned home from Scotland with "relics".[63] This process is evidenced by Nathaniel Carter and later on (and to a far greater degree) by William R. Smith who, while visiting Scotland, went to the effort of obtaining everything from manuscripts, stamps, pins and postcards to a fragment of curtain thought to belong to Jean Armour. In one of his "scrapbooks", Smith also claimed that a square of the same curtain was made into a sofa-cushion for one John Greenleaf Whittier.[64]

Burns-related relics were also on display at multiple nineteenth-century Burns Suppers, usually having been shipped from Scotland specifically for the event. Memorabilia and objects associated with Highland Mary proved particularly popular including items as tenuous as "wild flowers from the banks of the Fayle, the scene of the parting of Burns and Highland Mary" and a "branch of Highland Mary's Thorn".[65] Pittock and Mackay have convincingly demonstrated how the popularity of "Highland Mary" was "due not so much to the archival record" but rather to "the images, objects and memorialisation through which her relationship with the poet was constructed as an act of public memory in the nineteenth century".[66]

There is, however, also evidence to suggest that the popularity of the "Highland Mary" songs in the USA preceded the full blooming of postcards, statues, plaques and other objects that would cement her iconic reputation as Burns's tragically lost muse. As touched upon in Chapter 4, several newspapers specifically alluded to the "Highland Mary" songs as the poet's most "moving" and "tender"[67] works, particularly after the reprinting of Cromek's *Reliques* which boasted the editor's "discovery" of Mary Campbell. Commenting on the US "enshrinement" of Burns's "sentimental songs to Highland Mary as his finest works", Carol McGuirk has suggested that the "urgent addresses to a dead girl" achieved the "focus on morbidity and mortality that nineteenth-century Americans found so perversely attractive". McGuirk's suggestion is fascinating in that it weaves "the cult" of Highland Mary into the thematic oeuvre of American Gothic or "Dark Romanticism", a movement that found expression in a literary sense through Poe, Hawthorne and Melville, but extended to broader manners of taste such as the rise in popularity of pre-interment photographs of dead children.[68]

Fascinating though the suggestion may be, considering the poems as gothic "addresses to a dead girl" is a slightly obscure reading given it was never really a live theme in Burns's poems. Thus, the idea is best read in conjunction with Pittock's explanation that the popularity of "Highland Mary" in the USA might also be linked with her image as a potential emigrant to the New World who died before she could take the opportunity to leave with her beloved.[69] Regardless, the case of "Highland Mary" serves as a useful microcosmic example of the processes by which modes of cultural remembrance can feed into one another and preserve reconstituted memories. That is, memories of "Highland Mary", pertaining to Rigney's "media-based approach", were continually (re)communicated through songs, relics, statues, landscapes and even dances (the "Highland Mary" Mine and Lakes in Colorado and the "Highland

Mary" Morris Dance.).[70] When outlining these multiple forms of memorial practice, it is crucial to note that, while remaining connected by the source, they all preserved slightly altered "memories".

The singular question of how Burns was remembered in the USA thus demands a pluralistic answer in that we must consider not only several forms of mediation, but also the wide array of separate communities, individuals and groups that variously reconstituted the memory of the poet. In line with Halbwachs' foundational idea that "every group has its own collective memory and that collective memory differs from the collective memory of other groups",[71] we might then begin to address how diversely the cultural memory of Burns was appropriated in the period to articulate and promote, often conflicting, group and individual identities.

CIVIL DIVISIONS OF MEMORY: FREDERICK DOUGLASS AND US ABOLITIONISM

In his exploration of how Burns was remembered and appropriated in Scotland between 1796 and 1859, Christopher Whatley has highlighted how both Chartists (along with their successors the Radical Liberals) and the Scottish Tories drew on selective interpretations of Burns's life to bolster divergent political values and principles. Implicit in Whatley's discussion, then, is how tensions in the sociopolitical climate of early to mid-nineteenth-century Scotland shaped the disputed legacy or "memory" of Burns. While Scottish conservatives aimed to counter social unrest caused by the linked processes of rampant industrialisation and rapid urbanisation, liberals argued for justice and reform, with both groups commandeering and shaping in their own interests the memory of Burns.[72]

Unsurprisingly, in the light of Assmann's articulations on the dynamics of cultural memory, similar patterns of social and political appropriation emerged in the USA. In unpacking (divergent) group and individual memories of Burns, it is possible to see how the foremost sociopolitical issues of the period were interwoven into articulations of remembrance, particularly in the decades that straddled the 1859 Centenary and American Civil War. It would be grandiose to suggest that the poetry (or indeed legacy) of Burns was highly influential on shaping political opinion given the multitude of sociopolitical factors that contributed towards rising tensions, territorial divisions and unrest. However, in highlighting how commemorations of the poet variously served to bolster extant identities, beliefs and values, we might further demonstrate how cultural memory is frequently an expression of "one's own diachronic identity",[73] thus underpinning the important point that there was never a cohesive, singular "cultural memory" of the poet or his works in the USA due to a constant flux of subjective dimensions and circumstances.

Perhaps the most striking posthumous competition over the memory of Burns was between African American abolitionist Frederick Douglass and opposing groups and individuals from the slave-holding states of the American South. There has been a recent surge of interest in the speeches that Douglass delivered in Scotland during his anti-slavery tour of Britain and Ireland, primarily due to the continuing scholarly attempts to "recover" the memory of Scottish connections with slavery and the black Atlantic.[74] It was during this tour that Douglass visited the birth-place of Burns in 1846, as touched upon above. A fuller examination of Douglass's account reveals the extent to which his individual "memory" was shaped by sociopolitical tensions and, in particular, abolitionist discourses.

It would be a stretch, even an injustice, to suggest that Douglass systematically constructed his written "memory" of Burns to bolster white Scottish support for the movement. Douglass was long acquainted with Burns's poetry, having purchased the 1833 Philadelphia edition, printed by J. Crissy, as his "first book" after his "escape from slavery", and later gifting it to his son as a "keepsake" over three decades later in 1867.[75] Yet, the rhetorical and thematic parallels between "A Fugitive Slave Visiting the Birth-Place of Robert Burns" and his contemporary oratory proclamations in 1846 still serve to highlight a distinct correlation between Douglass's individual memory and the sociopolitical discourses that surrounded him.

A brief consideration of Douglass's 1846 speech in Paisley, delivered just weeks before his visit to Ayr, alongside his letter about Burns drives home the point. Where Burns had been trapped "in the moorings which society had thrown around him",[76] African Americans were described (in Paisley) as "clanking their chains, and calling upon Britons to aid them".[77] Where "Burns lived in the midst of a bigoted and besotted clergy",[78] the Paisley speech condemned the bigotry of a church (the Free Church of Scotland) that "comes forward and holds up the slave-holder as being Christian".[79] Douglass's description of how Burns battled a "corrupt generation" plagued by "a shallow brained aristocracy"[80] also resonates with his protests in Paisley against "the man whose pockets are lined with the gold with which I ought to have been educated".[81]

The theme of pious hypocrisy is also implicit throughout. Acknowledging the poet's alleged misgivings, Douglass maintained that Burns was "yet more faultless than many who have come down to us in the pages of history as saints".[82] In a similar condemnation in Paisley, he remarked: "The Free Church is doing more for infidelity and atheism than all the infidels in Scotland combined".[83] Douglass's targeted attack on the Free Church of Scotland, founded in 1843 after the Great Disruption, was the result of Free Church missionaries accepting monetary donations from American slaveholders, thus partly inspiring Douglass's "Send Back the Money!" campaign and tour in Scotland. In order to acquire the fullest understanding of the social discourses that shaped Douglass's memory of Burns, then, it is crucial to acknowledge that "A Fugitive Slave Visiting the Birth-Place of Robert Burns" was written at the height of his mission to exert pressure on the USA by increasing international sympathy and support for abolition. In his own emphatic words, he was intent on uniting the people of "Scotland, England, Ireland, Canada, Mexico, and even the red Indians [to join] with us and against slavery".[84] This ardent concern and sociopolitical factor lingers throughout his memory of Burns, as the poet is symbolically enlisted into Douglass's discourse on slavery and abolition.

That the reprinting of Douglass's letter functioned, and continues to function, as an "institution of preservation" is clear in that it has influenced several transatlantic constructions of the poet, specifically among African Americans who came to regard Burns as a voice of liberty, equality and brotherhood. As Alan Rice astutely points out, Douglass ignited a "strategic Celto-philia"[85] for African American writers, perhaps most famously iterated in recent years by the late Maya Angelou who, like Douglass before her, made "a pilgrimage to "Burns Country"" and identified the poet as the "first white man" who understood that "a human being was a human being and we are more alike than unalike".[86]

Specifically in regard to nineteenth-century abolitionism in the USA, Thomas Keith has traced instances of where "Man was made to mourn" and "Is there for honest poverty" were used to rouse public support[87]; with the former song being simultaneously claimed as a "Masonic Anthem" on both sides of the Atlantic. Similarly, Clark McGinn has provided an informative list of quotes in which Burns was invoked by prominent black and white nineteenth-century abolitionists, including Samuel

Ringgold Ward (1817–1866); Gerrit Smith (1797–1874); Henry Ward Beecher (1813–1887); and William Lloyd Garrison (1805–1879), with the former even writing an anti-slavery anthem set to the tune of "Auld Lang Syne".[88] In the build-up to—and during—the American Civil War, pro-Union writers and orators regularly drew on the memory of Burns and specifically the phrase "a man's a man for a that" to win support for the abolitionist cause and promote messages of equality and brotherhood beyond the boundaries of racial confines.

Also referencing "Scots Wha Hae", William Lloyd Garrison rhetorically questioned "Who would be a traitor knave? Who so base as be a slave?" before declaring that "a man's a man for a that".[89] An article in the *National anti-slavery Standard* urged Americans to recognise that regardless of "complexion [sic] a man's a man for a that" while Frederick Douglass, in encouraging "colored" men to enlist in the Union Army, powerfully suggested that the "self-evident truths" contained in the Declaration of Independence ought to be reduced to practice, and that, whatever may be the colour of his skin, "a man's a man for a' that".[90]

Though these examples are centred on the aphorismic adoption and appropriation of one specific line ("a man's a man's for a that'"), the cultural preservation of Burns (or rather a line of his poetry in this case) through public speeches and text remained clearly linked to contemporary sociopolitical discourses or values. This is most explicit in William Wells Brown's 1848 adaption of Burns's egalitarian anthem. Where Burns derides the "coward-slave" who bows to hierarchal authority, Brown—echoing Wedgewood's emblematic sentiment—disrupts any distinction between man and dark-skinned slave:

> Though stripped of all the dearest rights
> > Which nature claims and a' that,
> There's that which in the slave unites
> > To make the man for a' that.
> For a' that and a' that,
> > Though dark his skin, and a' that,
> We cannot rob him of his kind,
> > The slave's a man, for a' that.[91]

Quite remarkably, Brown's collection, which predominantly adapted Scottish and Irish melodies, also contained anti-slavery lyrics set to Burns's "Auld Lang Syne" ("I Am An Abolitionist"; "Scots Wha Hae"

("On To Victory") and "Sweet Afton" (I'll Be Free! I'll Be Free!). Of course, the posthumous use of Burns by abolitionists remains an uncomfortable topic given the poet's increasingly debated and somewhat ambiguous attitudes towards slavery and abolition. With specific regards to Burns's poetic use of "coward slave", Nigel Leask notes the "transferential" use of "slave" (i.e. not literally denoting African chattel slavery) in eighteenth-century political discourse to describe negative relationships of feudal dependence.[92] Yet, if Burns's poetics might be explained, his plans to travel, prior to the success of the "Kilmarnock edition", to Jamaica in 1786 to work on a plantation remain more problematic.[93]

Yet the wider discussion of Burns and slavery itself reveals much about the selective dynamics of cultural memory and collective remembrance, as Michael Morris has outlined in a chapter of his recent study *Scotland and the Caribbean, c.1740–1833: Atlantic Archipelagos*. Where Morris, responding to Pierre Nora's concept of *Les Lieux de mémoire*, unpacks the memory of Burns in its relation to Scottish national remembrance and identity ("the failure to recognise the wider significance of Burns' planned emigration to Jamaica" mirrors "the marginalisation of the Caribbean plantations in Scottish national historiography"),[94] we might here note the vicarious nature of cultural memory on an individual level through Douglass's memorialisation of Burns as an enslaved underdog who broke through his "moorings".

Reflecting on the circulation of memories in mediated form (whereby text, objects, public speeches or other media are the "carriers"[95] of the memory) Rigney further notes that individuals and groups who have "no actual connection in any biological sense with the events in question" may "learn to identify with certain vicarious recollections".[96] Regardless of the uneasy ambiguity that continues to pervade the issue of Burns in relation to slavery and abolition, the (mediated) memorialisation of the poet by Douglass and other prominent abolitionists in the nineteenth-century USA unquestionably generated a "working memory"[97] that could be (re)constructed and (re)constituted through future acts of public commemoration and remembrance.

Even in the twenty-first century, we might then view, for example, Kofi Annan's (then secretary general of the United Nations) enlistment of Burns into a global canon of humanitarianism with renewed interest. Speaking in 2004 at the United Nations Headquarters in New York, Annan, without acknowledging but clearly drawing on Douglass's commemoration of Burns, described the poet as "an opponent of slavery, pomposity and greed".[98] Rather than doggedly attempt to defend, condemn or verify such a statement, it might serve us well, in terms of historical understanding, to consider more fully the cultural mechanisms at work behind the construction of such a "memory".

In concluding on Burns in relation to nineteenth-century American abolitionism and the North, it is worth reflecting on the popularly known association between Burns and the 16th president of the USA, one Abraham Lincoln. What is perhaps most thought-provoking is the extent to which "artistic mediators"—editors, biographers and cultural critics—have influenced the conflation of the two figures on the grounds of democracy and egalitarianism. While Lincoln quoted Burns only once, in a rather inconsequential 1837 letter[99] to James Adams, there is, admittedly, evidence to suggest that he owned, read and occasionally recited Burns's work (among other "large swaths" of poetry that he shared with friends).[100] However, it has been biographers and critics that have emphasised, arguably created, the poet's profound "influence" on Lincoln.

In 1928, for example, Lincoln biographer Albert J. Beveridge described how the writings of Burns had shaped the president's views on "religious conceit" and political hypocrisy[101]; while just over a century later, Fred Kaplan, in his 2008 *Lincoln: The Biography of a Writer*, argued that Burns's egalitarian themes had strongly inspired Lincoln's own political and moral vision.[102] Adopting a more scaled approach, Ferenc Morton Szasz has recently highlighted some of the "overstatements" regarding the influence that Burns's poetry had on Lincoln, while maintaining that his verses did help to "*reinforce* many of the ideas that Lincoln absorbed growing up".[103] Szasz subsequently touches on the comparable malleability of posthumous constructions of Burns and Lincoln, drawing attention to how the "memory" of both men (individually or conflated) has been used to bolster various political causes; is often contested; argued over; and is frequently (re)mediated through biography, statuary culture and other modes of objectified commemoration.[104]

Rather than Lincoln's actual reading and absorption of Burns's poetry, then, it is the very processes (and consequences of) cultural memory that continue to bind the two individuals together; with their posthumous reputations intertwined in that most influential of spaces—the space "between memory and history".[105]

CIVIL DIVISIONS OF MEMORY: BURNS THE "SOUTHERN MAN"

The appropriation of Burns by Frederick Douglass and other prominent abolitionists has been established, yet equally important, if somewhat less palatable, is to recognise that the poet was also adopted by opposing groups and individuals in the Southern slave-holding states. In addressing how one source of remembrance can become invested with multiple, at times conflicting historical "memories", Rigney, following Michel Foucault's dictum of *loi de rareté*, has outlined how the "principle of scarcity" affects memory through processes of "selectivity, convergence, recycling and transference".[106]

In juxtaposing two broadly opposing "memories" of Burns formed within the same geo-cultural and (and chronological) parameters, Rigney's "principle of scarcity" might be demonstrated to some effect in that the poet's persona and works were selectively recycled to articulate and inform conflicting identities, values and experiences. Partly due to long and continuing associations between Burns and humanitarianism, the appropriation of the poet by prominent US abolitionists in the Civil War-era comes as relatively unsurprising. Conservative constructions of Burns, on the other hand, tend to brush against the grain of the more popular perception of Burns as a beacon of liberal egalitarianism (thus making his attitudes to slavery and abolitionism a particularly thorny issue). However, as was the case in the Northern States, "memories" of Burns in the South correlated directly with localised values.

That the Southern, agrarian male planter class prided themselves on ideals of honour, loyalty and integrity is a popular notion verging on stereotype that, arguably, remains powerful today judging by the Republican Party's (GOP) emphasis on restoring "honour" and "integrity" to "a federal system of government"[107] in the lead up to the Southern Republican Leadership Conference, held at Oklahoma City in 2015.[108] More detailed studies have, of course, challenged this monolithic view of Southern masculinity, highlighting the complexity and variety of male experience in the nineteenth-century American South. In an excellent 2004 volume titled *Southern Manhood: Perspectives on Masculinity in the Old South*, editors Craig Thompson Friend and Lorri Glover compiled a provocative collection of essays that map some of the intricate and shifting frameworks—variable by class, religion, race and era—that shaped male identities before, during and after the American Civil War. The opening essay by Harry S. Laver documents how eighteenth-century masculine ideals of civic virtue (whereby Southern manhood was identified with being "head of household" and placing the good of the community and nation "above individual desires") were swept aside in the early nineteenth century by a renewed sense of individualism (spurred on by a growing market economy) that promoted the unapologetic pursuit of "wealth, power and self-advancement".[109] Laver argues that the American Civil War provided a new opportunity for men to demonstrate their manhood. Enlisting could, Laver suggests, "authenticate the civic virtue of those who embraced the competition and selfishness of the market economy".[110]

Here, the complex interrelationships between agriculture, commerce and conceptions of "virtue" in post-revolutionary America, as outlined by J. G. A. Pocock in his seminal *The Machiavellian Moment*, are implicit.[111] More pertinently for this study, if Southern strains of traditional civic virtue comprised of "manly" pride; fierce patriotism; expressions of military competence; independence; a humble agrarian "work ethic" and success in the domestic sphere, then the poetry and persona of Burns were ripe for appropriation on various levels.

Evidence of the memory of Burns functioning to articulate Southern ideals of masculinity can be found in a recent biography of Confederate colonel William Calvin Oates (1835–1910), largely remembered as the officer defeated at Little Round Top during the Battle of Gettysburg. The biography, written by Glenn W. LaFantasie and published by Oxford University Press in 2006, was based on the "exclusive access of family papers" and "archives" and thus delved into the previously unexplored personal life of the confederate soldier. LaFantasie notes how Oates regularly "called to mind some lines written by his favourite poet, Robert Burns" whenever "the romance of war flooded his emotions",[112] thus demonstrating the memory of Burns being tied to a heavily romanticised "masculine" military experience. LaFantasie also suggests that Oates "manufactured and crafted" his identity in later life in accordance with "Southern manly ideals" which explained his frequent "waxing romantic by quoting Burns" whenever he was "inspired by the Shenandoah women".[113]

An 1852 article in the Virginia-based *Daily Dispatch* similarly described Burns as "extremely gallant, always in love, and a great favourite with the ladies" while acknowledging—notably without any trace of moral judgement—how "the susceptible heart of the poet was bandied from one to the other".[114] Joseph Du Rant has recently undertaken a useful comparative study of the way Burns was portrayed in Northern and Southern Antebellum newspapers. Most powerfully, Du Rant notes that articles on Burns regularly appear within pages—at times on the same page—as advertisements selling "Negroes" and notices of "captured" slaves. Du Rant makes the overall point that Burns as a symbol of universal equality—so widely remembered by Douglass and the Northern abolitionists—does not seem to have any presence in the Southern newspapers.[115] Rather, Burns is portrayed akin to a charismatic Southern white male complete with all the admirable trappings of idealised masculinity. In a slightly absurd parable in the pro-slavery *Daily Dispatch*, this selective Southern commemoration of Burns appears explicit:

> Robert Burns, on his way to Leith one morning met a country farmer: he shook him earnestly by the hand and stopped to converse a while. A young Edinburgh blood took the poet to task for this defect of taste. "Why, you fantastic," said Burns, "it was not the great coat, the scone bonnet, and the saundaer boot hose, I spoke to, but the man that was in them; and the man, sir, for worth would weigh down you and me, and ten more any such day".[116]

Though Burns's egalitarian virtues are hinted at here, the parable also smacks of traditional Southern discourses of masculinity. It is not the city-dwelling "blood", tainted by individualism, materialism and a market economy that reigns supreme, but rather the honourable agrarian concerned with community and honour. The fact of him being a "country farmer" is also notable. Farming, in particular manual labour, was predominantly undertaken by slaves in the period, and they were rarely referred to as "farmers". Thus, the "country farmer" that the imagined Burns speaks highly of seems to resemble a Southern white plantation overseer, a darkly ironic posthumous cultural appropriation given the poet's early intentions to emigrate to Jamaica.

By far the least palatable form of Southern Burns commemoration, however, came in Pulaski, Tennessee after the defeat of the confederacy in 1865. In his empirical outlining of how cultural memories are articulated, Jan Assmann cites "rites" and "rituals" as being a primary method of preservation.[117] In a ceremonial induction lacking in any true sense of "honour" or "integrity", Burns's "To a Louse" was incorporated into being a rite of initiation for potential new members of the freshly formed white supremacist fraternity, the Ku Klux Klan:

> A skullcap with donkey's ears sewn on it was placed on the head of a candidate, who was then escorted to a large dressing mirror the Klan dubbed as "the royal altar" and ordered to recite a poem written by Scotsman Robert Burns. The blindfold was then removed to reveal to the candidate that he'd literally been dressed up as an ass, much to the amusement of the Klansmen. The embarrassed man could then accept or deny membership. Most agreed to join with those in the financially depressed rural areas showing a particular interest.[118]

Furthermore, the original "Prescript of the **" (the first constitutional document of the Ku Klux Klan) also reveals a Burnsian influence. Printed secretly in the office of the *Pulaski Citizen* in 1867, the prescript begins with two unattributed literary quotes; Shakespeare's Hamlet ("What may this mean,/That thou, dead corse ...") and an altered stanza from Burns's "Address to the Deil':

> An' now auld Cloots, I ken ye're thinkin',
> A certain *Ghoul* is rantin', drinkin',
> Some luckless night will send him linkin,'
>   To your black pit;
> But, faith! he'll turn a corner jinkin',
>   An' cheat you yet.[119]

Here, Burns's original use of "*Bardie's* rantin, drinkin" is replaced with "*Ghoul*" to denote the white-cloaked members of the organisation who, as outlined in the document, were to meet in "Dens" under the command of the "Grand Wizard of the Empire". The mock-imperial language of the constitution also provides a clue to the choice of "Address to the Deil". Originally appearing in the "Kilmarnock edition" of 1786, the Burns's poem is more burlesque than God-fearing through its proverbial register, Scots idiom and comic derision of the Devil as "Auld Hornie, Satan, Nick, or Clootie".[120] While the Devil is, of course, a time-honoured habitué of Scottish writing from William Dunbar's "Dance of the Sevin Deidly Sins" through James Hogg's *Confessions of a Justified Sinner*, Burns's "Deil"—in this poem at least—is cast as comical folk-trickster than malevolent or evil genius.[121] Yet transposed to the context of a white secessionist fraternity, darker undertones might also emerge. Where Burns's "bardie" comically expressed hope for salvation from the Devil's "black pit", the juxtaposition of the white "Ghoul" in the constitutional adaption evokes racial undertones. That is, the Devil's "black pit", in the transatlantic context of this document, is linked to a degenerative black experience that the "Ghoul" must "cheat".

Speculative as the reading may be, the question of why Burns's poetry was adopted by vengeful Confederate veterans, intent on venting their frustrations on African Americans, merits further discussion. On the one hand, the first Ku Klux Klan initiation ceremony might be viewed as mere comical farce in its primary purpose of entertaining existing members of the organisation. In this view, Burns (and his poem) may not have been considered as holding any major thematic or political significance in relation to white supremacist ideals. The recitation of the lines ("O wad some Power the giftie gie us/To see oursels as ithers see us!") complied perfectly with the "light-hearted" prank which culminated in the potential new member finally seeing himself (humiliated) in a large dressing mirror "as ithers" did: literally dressed up as an ass.

This base appropriation is highly ironic given Burns was partly glossing Adam Smith's *Theory of Moral Sentiments* in verse form.[122] Furthermore, the founding members did not necessarily need to have a great deal of familiarity with Burns's wider oeuvre and poetic sensibilities to include the poem while devising their "comical" initiation rite. The two lines, taken from the final stanza of the poem, had by this period long evolved into a popular proverb with evidence of it being used in other humorous contexts in the American South. An 1859 advertisement in the *Daily Dispatch*, for example, quoted the lines before promoting "photographs", "pearl ambrotypes" and "patent leather pictures" by an artist who "paints the face to-day',[123] with the comical emphasis being on how technological advances in photography (the daguerreotype) meant that individuals might now see themselves as "ithers" did ("The gift is made that Burns was wont to find").[124]

Yet wholly reducing the Ku Klux Klan "rite" to mere farce would be ignorant of both the constitutional use of "Address to the Deil" and more broadly the extent to which Scottish writers, images and icons played an important part in shaping the identity of Southern extremists. As Clarence Ghodes remarked in 1953, the "Pulaski Den did well to make use of Bobby Burns, for many of them were of Scotch Presbyterian background".[125] A more recent 2005 essay by Andrew Hook discusses how ex-confederate soldiers often drew on parallels between the loss of "Highland" culture in eighteenth-century Scotland and the loss of Southern independence after the Civil War.[126] This formed a mould for the foundational identity of various Southern far-right groups such as the League of the South, the John Birch Society and the anti-semitic Christian Identity; all of whom drew on selective interpretations of Scottish history to justify their defence of what they see as their threatened white Anglo-Celtic culture. Hook has elsewhere summarised that there is "general agreement" that the final version of the flag "was meant to be seen as incorporating the blue St Andrews cross of the Scottish Saltire".[127]

This is particularly resonant in the light of the recent debates over the origins and continued use of the Confederate Flag ignited by the racially motivated 2015 shooting at the Emanuel African Methodist Episcopal Church in Charleston, South Carolina. Another fact relating to Burns and Southern white extremism is that the first president of the Burns Club of Atlanta (Hamilton Douglas) was "a staunch advocate of both white supremacy and the Democratic Party's white primary".[128] While the club's only qualification for membership upon its inception was "good citizenship" and "admiration and love for the great poet",[129] it is highly doubtful that such citizenship extended to the African Americans that Douglas was actively attempting to disenfranchise.

Returning to the first incarnation of the Ku Klux Klan (1865–1874), the very employment of the word "clan" with its dualistic connotations of both a sense of "lost" (Highland and Southern) society is also notable and might easily be linked to the Scots ancestry of members. As Michael Morris notes, the "second" Klan (1915–1944) "adopted its gruesome icon of the burning cross from the third canto of Walter Scott's *The Lady of the Lake* [...] in which Highland clans are summoned by a Fiery Cross".[130] This brings to mind Mark Twain's famous remark that Scott was "in great measure responsible" for the Civil War. For Twain, Scott's depiction of "honourable" (but threatened) Highland culture created "rank and caste down there"[131] in the US South, where feudalism could only be maintained by slavery. Joseph Rezek's recent work on how nineteenth-century American readers refashioned Scott's "romantic Scottish nationalism"[132] provides further evidence of how a Southern spirit of defiance was, in part, shaped by the romantic precedent of Highland resistance. It should come as little surprise that Burns too was enlisted for the cause.

In her insightful articulations on "the principle of scarcity" and cultural memory, Ann Rigney states that one of the ways "emergent groups" confirms their identity "*as* group is by celebrating and reinforcing their sense of a common past". Rigney goes further to suggest that "the sense of sharing memories, of having a past in common, is arguably a precondition for the emergence of such groups in the first place".[133] Taken as an "emergent group" formed from the ashes of the Civil War, then, we might see why the six founding members of the Ku Klux Klan would draw upon their perceived sense of shared heritage. Here, we might also note the deeper significance of the Ku Klux Klan's burlesque initiation ceremony. That ritual is linked to emergent collective identity formation has been well established, with Jan Koster noting that "speaking in choruses", "common dress" and a general "collectivizing of physical appearance" are key elements to the symbolic unification of emergent groups.[134] In the case of the Ku Klux Klan, it seems the shared humiliation of comical dress (itself a uniting experience) and incorporation of Scottish poetry (familiar to all) shored up a sense of genealogical unity.

Southern historian Grady McWhiney has previously gone so far as to (perhaps questionably) suggest that the cultural difference between the South and the rest of the USA is predominantly due to the South's Celtic cultural heritage.[135] Even if McWhiney's argument is only partially true, the Klan's appropriation of Burns was clearly embedded within a much wider, Southern tradition, fully developing after the Civil War, of drawing on Scottish and culture to articulate and maintain a distinctly white, often supremacist, identity.

NOTES

1. *Celebration of the hundredth anniversary of the birth of Robert Burns by the Boston Burns club*, 37.
2. A fuller theoretical contextualization of what is meant here by "memory" and "cultural memory" will be put forth later in the chapter.
3. For an informed discussion of the contested "Unionist" sympathies of "The Dumfries Volunteers" see *Burns the Radical*, 238–240.
4. "SNP Campaign Launch". Accessed 31 December 2015. http://www.snp.org/media-centre/news/2005/jan/salmond-launches-snp-general-election-campaign.
5. "Was Robert Burns a Nat or Unionist". Accessed 31 December 2015. http://www.scotsman.com/news/politics/top-stories/scottish-

independence-mps-gripped-by-the-question-was-rabbie-burns-a-nat-or-a-unionist-1-2077809; and "How Would Robert Burns Vote in the Scottish Referendum?". Accessed 31 December 2015. http://www.theguardian.com/commentisfree/2014/jul/23/robert-burns-vote-scottish-referendum-identity.

6. Gerard Carruthers, "The Myth-Eaten Corpse of Robert Burns". Accessed 31 December 2015. http://blog.oup.com/2015/01/robert-burns-appropriation/.

7. Christopher A. Whatley, "'It Is Said That Burns Was a Radical" Contest, Concession, and the Political Legacy of Robert Burns, ca. 1796–1859,' *The Journal of British Studies* 50, no. 3 (2011): 639–666. For more on this see also Whatley's more recent and expanded study *Immortal Memory: Burns and the Scottish People* (Edinburgh: Birlinn Ltd., 2016).

8. Pittock, "Introduction, Global Burns", 19.

9. Sood, "A Modern Poet on The Scotch Bard", 230–236.

10. Frederick Douglass, "A Fugitive Slave Visiting the Birth-Place of Robert Burns", *New York Weekly Tribune* 5, no. 45 (1846). Accessed 30 December 2015. http://library.sc.edu/spcoll/douglass/fugitive.pdf.

11. Wyn Craig Wade, *The Fiery Cross: The Ku Klux Klan in America* (Oxford: Oxford University Press, 1998), 34–35.

12. Matthew Kempshall, *Rhetoric and the Writing of History* (Manchester: Manchester University Press, 2011), 456.

13. As Kempshall outlines in *Rhetoric and the Writing of History*, the availability of Aristotle's work in the twelfth and thirteen centuries had a dramatic impact on the conception of memory and influenced historiography up to the fifteenth century. See also Mary Carruthers, *The Book of Memory: A Study of Memory in Medieval Culture* (Cambridge: Cambridge University Press, 2008) and Francis Yates, *The Art of Memory* (London: The Bodley Head, 2014).

14. Patrick H. Hutton, "Sigmund Freud and Maurice Halbwachs: The Problem of Memory in Historical Psychology", *The History Teacher* 27, no. 2 (1994): 148–149.

15. Ibid., 149.

16. Nicolas Russell, "Collective Memory Before and After Halbwachs", *The French Review* 79, no. 4 (2006): 797.

17. *Celebration of the Hundredth Anniversary of the Birth of Robert Burns, by the Boston Burns Club*, 35–37.

18. Patrick Hutton, *History as An Art of Memory* (Hanover and London: University Press of New England, 1993), 7.

19. Jan Assmann and John Czaplicka, "Collective Memory and Cultural Identity", *New German Critique* 65 (1995): 126.

20. See also Ann Rigney, "Plenitude, Scarcity and the Circulation of Cultural Memory", *Journal of European Studies* 35, no. 1 (2005): 14.
21. Assmann, "Communicative and Cultural Memory", 111.
22. Ibid., 117.
23. Ibid., 111.
24. Ibid., 113.
25. Carol Thomson Gallagher, *The Scots Who Built New York* (New York: St. Andrew's Society of the State of New York, 2006), 19.
26. Ibid. See also Tanja Bueltmann, *Clubbing Together: Ethnicity, Civility and Formal Sociability in the Scottish Diaspora to 1930* (Liverpool: Liverpool University Press, 2014).
27. Harlan Douglas Whatley, Duncan A. Bruce and Randall Lenox Taylor, eds., *Two Hundred Fifty Years 1756–2006: The History of Saint Andrew's Society of The State of New York* (New York: Saint Andrew's Society of The State of New York, 2008), 21.
28. Clark McGinn, "Early American Burns Celebrations", *The Burns Chronicle* (2015), 48.
29. There is evidence that Burns's songs were played as entertainment at these social gatherings. See, for example, John Melish *Travels in the United States of America* (Philadelphia: Thomas & George Palmer, 1812), 284–285.
30. See, for example, *The Pennsylvania Packet*, 25 December (1790); *Albany Spectator*, 12 December (1804); *Commercial Advertiser*, 8 December (1804).
31. McGinn, "Early American Burns Celebrations", 50.
32. Pittock and Whatley, "Poems and Festivals, Art and Artefact", 60–61.
33. Russell, "Collective Memory Before and After Halbwachs", 799.
34. Hutton, "Sigmund Freud and Maurice Halbwachs", 149.
35. Nigel Leask '"Their Grove o' Sweet Myrtles": Robert Burns and the Scottish Colonial Experience', in *Robert Burns in Global Culture*, ed. Pittock, 181.
36. *New-York Daily Advertiser*, 3 February (1818).
37. "Three Centuries of Broadsides and Other Printed Ephemera". Accessed 21 January 2015. http://memory.loc.gov/cgi-bin/ampage?collId=rbpe&fileName=rbpe07/rbpe077/07701000/rbpe07701000.db&recNum=1&itemLink=r?ammem/rbpebib:@field(NUMBER+@band(rbpe+07701000))&linkText=0.
38. *The New-York American*, 2, no. 588 (1822), 3.
39. Assmann, "Communicative and Cultural Memory", 111.
40. See "Smithsonian Institution, Inventory of American Art". Accessed 31 January 2015. www.AmericanArt.si.edu.
41. Assmann, "Communicative and Cultural Memory", 117.

42. Thomas Keith, "Burns Statues—North America", *The Burns Chronicle* (2001), 71.
43. Rigney, "Plentitude, Scarcity and the Circulation of Cultural Memory", 20.
44. "Robert Burns Memorials". Accessed 30 December 2015. http://www.robertburnsmemorials.arts.gla.ac.uk/details.php?ID=8.
45. Keith, "Burns Statues—North America", 74.
46. "Robert Burns Memorials". Accessed 30 December 2015. http://www.robertburnsmemorials.arts.gla.ac.uk/details.php?ID=8.
47. Assmann, "Communicative and Cultural Memory", 114.
48. Keith, "Burns Statues—North America", 81.
49. Rigney, "Plentitude, Scarcity and the Circulation of Cultural Memory", 11.
50. Allison Lockwood, *Passionate Pilgrims: The American Traveler in Great Britain, 1800–1914* (New York: Cornwall Books, 1981), 78.
51. Nathaniel Hazeltine Carter, *Letters from Europe, Comprising the Journal of a Tour Through Ireland, England, Scotland, France, Italy, and Switzerland in the years 1825, '26, and '27* (New York: G. & C. & H. Carvill, 1829).
52. "Chronicling America". Accessed 31 December 2015. http://chroniclingamerica.loc.gov/lccn/sn83035487/.
53. Thomas Keith, "Burns in the Abolitionist's Arsenal", Robert Burns Conference Paper, University of Glasgow (2009).
54. Douglass, "A Fugitive Slave Visiting the Birth-Place of Robert Burns". Accessed 31 December 2015. http://library.sc.edu/spcoll/douglass/fugitive.pdf.
55. Pittock and Whatley, "Poems and Festivals, Art and Artefact", 60.
56. *The Daily Dispatch*, 15 October (1856).
57. Leonard A. Morrison, *Rambles in Europe: In Ireland, Scotland, England, Belgium, Germany, Switzerland, and France* (Boston: Cupples, Upham & Co., 1887), 104.
58. Loretta J. Post, *Scenes in Europe; or, Observations by an Amateur Artist* (Cincinnati, OH: Hitchcock & Walden, 1874), 111.
59. Mackay and Pittock, "Beyond Text: Burns, Byron and Their Material Culture Afterlife", 150–151.
60. *Letters from Europe,* 312.
61. Douglass, "A Fugitive Slave Visiting the Birth-Place of Robert Burns". Accessed 31 December 2015. http://library.sc.edu/spcoll/douglass/fugitive.pdf.
62. Pittock and Mackay, "Highland Mary: Objects and Memories", *Romanticism* 18, no. 2 (2012): 194.
63. "Robert Burns Beyond Text". Accessed 31 December 2015. www.gla.ac.uk/robertburnsbeyondtext.

64. Sood, "An American Trove of Burnsiana", 44.
65. *Celebration of the Hundredth Anniversary of the Birth of Robert Burns*, 27.
66. Pittock and Mackay, "Highland Mary: Objects and Memories", 194.
67. *Salem Gazette* 1 (1823)
68. McGuirk, "Haunted by Authority", 146.
69. Pittock and Whatley, "Poems and Festivals, Art and Artefact", 65–67.
70. Pittock and Mackay, "Highland Mary: Objects and Memories", 194.
71. Russell, "Collective Memory Before and After Halbwachs", 796.
72. Whatley, "'It Is Said That Burns Was a Radical'", 640–641.
73. Assmann, "Communicative and Cultural Memory", 113–114.
74. See Morris, *Scotland and the Caribbean*, 128–177. In 2015 The University of Glasgow's History Department launched "Runaway Slaves in Britain: Bondage, Freedom and Race in the Eighteenth Century". The project aims to provide a database of information related to the enslaved in eighteenth century Britain. See also Nikki Brown, "'Send Back the Money!" Frederick Douglass's Anti-Slavery Speeches in Scotland and the Emergence of African American Internationalism'. Accessed 2 January 2016. http://www.iash.ed.ac.uk/star/archive/Papers/Brown_Douglass.in.Scotland.pdf.
75. "Collection Highlight: Robert Burns and Frederick Douglass" quoted from University of Rochester Rare Books, Online Special Collections. Accessed 2 January 2016. https://www.lib.rochester.edu/index.cfm?PAGE=4646.
76. Douglass, "A Fugitive Slave Visiting the Birth-Place of Robert Burns". Accessed 31 December 2015. http://library.sc.edu/spcoll/douglass/fugitive.pdf.
77. Frederick Douglass, *The Frederick Douglass Papers*, ed. John Blassingame, 5 Vols (New Haven: Yale University Press, 1979), 1: 240.
78. Douglass, "A Fugitive Slave Visiting the Birth-Place of Robert Burns". Accessed 31 December 2015. http://library.sc.edu/spcoll/douglass/fugitive.pdf.
79. *The Frederick Douglass Papers*, 1: 240.
80. Douglass, "A Fugitive Slave Visiting the Birth-Place of Robert Burns". Accessed 31 December 2015. http://library.sc.edu/spcoll/douglass/fugitive.pdf.
81. *The Frederick Douglass Papers*, 240.
82. Douglass, "A Fugitive Slave Visiting the Birth-Place of Robert Burns". Accessed 31 December 2015. http://library.sc.edu/spcoll/douglass/fugitive.pdf.
83. *The Frederick Douglass Papers*, 240.
84. Ibid.

85. Alan Rice, *Radical Narratives of the Black Atlantic* (London: Continuum, 2003), 213.
86. "Angelou on Burns". Accessed 2 January, 2016. http://ssa.nls.uk/film/7076.
87. Thomas Keith, "Burns in the Abolitionist's Arsenal", Robert Burns Conference Paper, University of Glasgow (2009).
88. Clark McGinn, "Burns and Slavery". Accessed 2 January 2015. http://www.electricscotland.com/familytree/frank/burns_lives92.htm#sdendnote43anc.
89. *The New York Times*, 15 February (1854).
90. Frederick Douglass, "Why Should a Colored Man Enlist?". Accessed 2 January 2016. http://rbscp.lib.rochester.edu/4396.
91. William Wells Brown, *The Anti-Slavery Harp: A Collection of Songs for Anti-Slavery Meetings* (Boston: Bela Marsh, 1849), 44.
92. Nigel Leask, "Burns and the Poetics of Abolition", in *The Edinburgh Companion to Robert Burns*, ed. Gerard Carruthers (Edinburgh: Edinburgh University Press, 2009), 47–61.
93. As discussed in the introduction of this book, Prior to the success of the 1786 "Kilmarnock Edition", Burns intended to sail for Jamaica to take up a position as a plantation "bookkeeper". For more on this contentious issue, see Gerard Carruthers, "Robert Burns and Slavery", in *Fickle Man: Robert Burns in the 21st Century*, ed. Johnny Rodger and Gerard Carruthers (Dingwall: Sandstone Press, 2009), 163–176; Murray Pittock, "Slavery as Political Metaphor in Scotland and Ireland in the age of Burns", in *Robert Burns and Transatlantic Culture*, ed. Alker, Davis, and Nelson (Farnham, Burlington: Ashgate, 2012) 201; and Clark McGinn, "The Scotch Bard and 'The Planting Line': New Documents on Burns and Jamaica", *Studies in Scottish Literature* 43, No. 2 (2017): 255–266.
94. *Scotland and the Caribbean*, 128–176.
95. Assmann, "Communicative and Cultural Memory", 118.
96. Rigney, "Plentitude, Scarcity and the Circulation of Cultural Memory", 16.
97. Assmann, "Communicative and Cultural Memory", 118.
98. "United Nations Robert Burns Memorial Lecture". Accessed 2 January 2016. http://www.un.org/press/en/2004/sgsm9112.doc.htm. Accessed 2 January 2016.
99. Ferenc Morton Szasz, *Abraham Lincoln and Robert Burns: Connected Lives and Legends* (Carbondale: Southern Illinois University Press, 2008), 76–77.
100. "Abraham Lincoln and Poetry". Accessed 24 January 2016. http://www.loc.gov/rr/program/bib/lincolnpoetry/.

101. Albert J. Beveridge, *Abraham Lincoln*, 2 Vols (Boston: Houghton Mifflin, 1928) 1: 300.
102. Fred, Kaplan, *Lincoln: The Biography of a Writer* (New York: Harper Collins, 2008), 49–86.
103. *Abraham Lincoln and Robert Burns*, 77.
104. Ibid., 7–122.
105. See Pierre Nora, "Between Memory and History: Les Lieux de Mémoire", *Representations* 26 (California: University of California Press, 1989), 7–24.
106. Rigney, "Plentitude, Scarcity and the Circulation of Cultural Memory", 11.
107. See "Federalism and The Tenth Amendment". Accessed 2 January 2016. https://www.gop.com/platform/we-the-people/.
108. "Republican Leadership Conference". Accessed 2 January 2016. http://www.srlc.gop/events/southern-republican-leadership-conference/event-summary-c98988953d0f406c8aedc02da46c0a7e.aspx.
109. Harry S. Laver, "Refuge of Manhood: Masculinity and the Militia Experience", in *Southern Manhood: Perspectives on Masculinity in the Old South*, ed. Craig Thompson Friend and Lorri Glover (Athens: University of Georgia Press, 2004), 1.
110. Ibid., 15.
111. J. G. A. Pocock, *The Machiavellian Moment: Florentine Political Thought and the Atlantic Republican Tradition* (Princeton: Princeton University Press, 1975), 506–553.
112. Glenn W. LaFantasie, *Gettysburg Requiem: The Life and Lost causes of Confederate Colonel William C. Oates* (Oxford: Oxford University Press, 2006), 75.
113. Ibid., 40.
114. *The Daily Dispatch*, 4th November (1852).
115. Joseph Du Rant, "Burns North and South, in Mid 19th C American Newspapers", *The Burns Chronicle* (2016), 26–33. Thank you to Joseph for providing me with an early version of this article prior to its publication.
116. *The Daily Dispatch*, 4th February (1853).
117. Assmann, "Communicative and Cultural Memory", 118.
118. Martin Gitlin, *The Ku Klux Klan: A Guide to an American Sub-culture* (California: ABC-CLIO, 2009), 52.
119. *Prescript of the* ** (Pulaslki, 1867). Accessed 4 February 2016. https://archive.org/details/prescriptoforder00kukl.
120. Robert Burns, "Address to the Deil", in *The Poems and Songs of Robert Burns*, vol. 1, ed. James Kinsley (Oxford: Oxford University Press, 1968), 168.

121. For more on this see Nigel Leask, *Robert Burns and Pastoral: Poetry and Improvement in Late Eighteenth-Century Scotland* (Oxford: Oxford University Press), 190–194.
122. *The Poetics of Character*, 251.
123. *The Daily Dispatch*, 24th December (1859).
124. *The Daily Dispatch*, 24th December (1859).
125. Clarence Gohdes, "The Ku Klux Klan and the Classics", in *The Georgia Review* 7, no. 1 (1953), 23.
126. Andrew Hook, "Troubling Times in the Scottish-American Relationship", in *Transatlantic Scots*, ed. Celeste Ray (Tuscaloosa: University of Alabama Press, 2005), 217.
127. Andrew Hook, "Down With That Flag". Accessed 2 January 2016. http://www.scottishreview.net/AHook148.html.
128. Lorraine Nelson Spritzer, *The Belle of Ashby Street: Helen Douglas Mankin and Georgia Politics* (Athens: University of Georgia Press, 2008), 5.
129. Franklin M. Garrett, *Atlanta and Environs: A Chronicle of Its People and Events, 1880s–1930s* (Athens: University of Georgia Press, 2010), 340–341.
130. *Scotland and the Caribbean,* 172. Morris further highlights that, rather ironically, Frederick Douglass (born into slavery as Frederick Bailey) had also adapted his name from the hero of *The Lady of the Lake* (the leader of 'Clan Douglas') on the advice of his friend Nathan Johnson who was reading Scott at the time. Similar to the multifarious nature of remembrance surrounding Burns, the memory of Scott—and his hugely popular narrative poem—was also evidently subject to various modes of selective remembrance.
131. Mark Twain, *Life on the Mississippi* [1883] (Oxford: Oxford University Press, 1996), 390.
132. *London and the Making of Provincial Literature*, 174.
133. Rigney, "Plentitude, Scarcity and the Circulation of Cultural Memory", 23.
134. Jan Koster, "Ritual Performance and the Politics of Identity: On the Functions an Uses of Ritual", *Journal of Historical Pragmatics* 4, no. 2 (2003), 218–248.
135. See Grady McWhiney, *Cracker Culture: Celtic Ways in the Old South* (Tuscaloosa: University of Alabama Press, 1988).

CHAPTER 7

The Burnsian Palimpsest and 1859
Centenary Celebrations

I will close by repeating the sentiment I started with, "The Memory of Burns".[1]

—Ralph Waldo Emerson (1859)

On the 25 January, 1859, toasts to "The Memory of Robert Burns" were heard at over 60 separate locations spread across different regions of the USA. Yet even within the "national" parameters of the supposedly "united" States, the (re)constitution of these memories and the ways in which they were communicated differed greatly. Drawing on Benedict Anderson's now famous concept of "imagined communities",[2] Ann Rigney has suggested that the 1859 Burns Centenary provided "a way of briefly turning imagined communities (usually seen as the key to modern identities) into actual embodied communities, and vice versa".[3] Broadly considering "imagined communities" as differing from actualised ones in existing through processes of imaginative cohesion rather than physical interaction, we might further consider Rigney's idea in the specific context of the USA.

That the 1859 centenary united prominent but (geographically) far-removed US abolitionists across several states, for example, might be considered as an "imagined community" becoming "embodied", while the previous chapter has already discussed how the Boston Burns Club's—taking it as an actualised "community"—celebrations bolstered group identity and cohesion. In cultivating the public memory of Burns then, different "communities", both real and "imagined"

© The Author(s) 2018   195
A. Sood, *Robert Burns and the United States of America*,
https://doi.org/10.1007/978-3-319-94445-6_7

(from abolitionists to Freemasons to Southern planters among others), used the centenary celebrations to articulate a sense of identity and thus became "embodied" through the process of commemoration.

Following Rigney's study, Leith Davis has explored the centenary in relation to the "connections and disjunctions involved in the transatlantic circulation of the poet's memory". Davis not only maps how Burns was remembered differently "depending on which side of the Atlantic he was being toasted" but also explores some of the more nuanced differences between North American celebrations, noting, for example, how commemorations in the "British provinces in North America" frequently acknowledged connections to the "Mother Nation", while the US celebrations predominantly staked out "their singular position in relation to their British predecessors".[4]

However, it is equally important to avoid the binary idea that Canadian, or British North American, celebrations heralded a poet who represented the wider imperium while the USA reformulated him to embody Republican ideals. This would miss the deeply layered complexity of the memory of Burns in America. As we shall see, a closer inspection of selected events provides a useful overarching and summarising perspective on how, by the latter half of the nineteenth century, the memory of Burns was not only upheld by multiple "memory communities" in the USA, but also communicated through a wide range of media.

Indeed, the question of whether such conflicting memories and appropriations can even be considered instances of "national" cultural remembrance must also be addressed. Correspondingly, this chapter, in continuing to engage with recent scholarship on national memory, proposes that the cultural memory of Burns in nineteenth-century America might best be conceived as a transnational site of memory, or what Jay Winter describes as a "palimpsest".[5] I propose that Winter's metaphorical concept—a transnational advancement on Pierre Nora's principle of national *lieux de mémoire*—is beneficial to understanding the plurality of Burns commemorations in nineteenth-century America in that they are comprised of an overlay of memories that transmit variable messages, but are bound together by a common source. This commemorative variability was demonstrated in the previous chapter through detailed case studies of Frederick Douglass and the Ku Klux Klan.

Analysing the different geographical sites and modes of remembrance during the 1859 Centenary provides further evidence of the "palimpsestuous" nature of Burns commemoration in nineteenth-century America.

Before doing so, and in order to gain a fuller understanding of the centenary celebrations, it is worth further expanding on Winter's theory of transnational sites of memory and its applicability to Burns.

THE BURNSIAN PALIMPSEST

Studies on cultures of national remembrance have continued to boom in recent decades, partly catalysed by a rejuvenated sense of engagement with Pierre Nora's monumental seven-work volume, *Les lieux de mémoire*. Nora pointed to how, as a by-product of modernisation, national feeling is actively cultivated and maintained through forms of objectified culture. For Nora, "national memories" of the past could no longer be communicated through spontaneous, or "lived", experience. Consequently, Nora argued, national communities had to construct and draw upon forms of objectified culture, or rather, *lieux de mémoire* (which translates as "sites" or "realms" of memory) in order to establish and maintain meaningful relationships with the past (and thus harmonise feeling).

These *lieux*, or "sites", might range from ceremonies, statues, museums, anniversaries, flags, buildings to outstanding individuals and myths, with the binding principle that they, whether physically or spiritually, uphold shared memories of the past that are consecrated as the quintessence of the nation.[6] Nora based his project on French national identity, pointing to "sites" of memory such as the Court of Versailles, the Eiffel Tower and Joan of Arc and articulating their interdependent relationship(s) with French nationhood. However, Nora also suggested that his project might easily be used to establish the "typical style of relating to the past in each country", which consequently led to similar undertakings in the Netherlands, Germany, Russia, Italy and elsewhere.[7]

Alex Tyrell has suggested that in nineteenth-century Scotland "Burns had become what Pierre Nora has called a 'lieu de mémoire'" in that the public celebration and commemoration of the poet "helped to give Scots a notion of the past" and shaped "forms of Scottish national identity." Tyrell observes, however, the ideological elements implicit in the construction of national memory sites, pointing to how the Robert Burns Festival at Ayr in 1844 interlocked with other events (such as Queen Victoria's first visit to Scotland) to promote an ideological identity that asserted "aristocratic paternalism in Scotland".[8] Leith Davis has also commented on Burns as a nineteenth-century *lieu de mémoire*, further outlining the multifaceted processes by which this was achieved.

Davis points to the evolution of Burns Clubs from local gatherings to "international sites where ex-patriot Scots joined together" and the effects of "international print networks" that, through the circulation of biographies, "helped make Burns and Scotland synonymous".[9] In accordance with this, Murray Pittock and Christopher A. Whatley, with a particular emphasis on "space, gesture, image and object", have described the nineteenth-century "Burns phenomenon" as being a "complex and multi-dimensional" *lieu de mémoire* in that a "complex realm of memorialisation"—celebratory events, images, objects, texts among others—combined to reinforce certain "dimensions of Scottish national memory."[10] However, the issue of Burns functioning as a *lieu de mémoire* for Scotland in the USA is more complex and problematic.

On the one hand, we must acknowledge how Burns and his works helped to cement and articulate the identity of expatriate Scots in America (or their descendants). From the early 1800s onwards, expatriate Scots attended St. Andrew's Society dinners to toast the poet and their country; local poets preserved and adapted Scots language verse and songs inspired by Burns; tartan and other Scottish imagery often adorned commemorative events; and biographical texts provided (and thus preserved) detailed, if subjective, accounts of the "Scotch character" of Burns (namely James Currie's *The Works*).

To another extreme, the prevalence of American flags at the centenary outlined later in this chapter toasts to the President and assertions that Burns "fought side by side" with the "sentiments of freedom" and "Liberty—American Liberty!"[11] might even suggest a (rather fragile) case for him representing a *lieu de mémoire* for nineteenth-century American national identity. However, as the previous chapter demonstrated to an extreme, nineteenth-century American "national identity" was barely uniform and comprised of a plurality of forms.[12] Indeed, the widely differing sectional appropriations of Burns (simultaneously a symbolic figure for the Northern abolitionist and the Southern planter, for example) within the USA make it problematic to consider the poet as a signifier of a unifying "national" narrative, whether Scottish *or* American. It is thus the very ambivalence of a singular "collective" or "national" identity (in the context of Burns commemoration) that makes considering Burns as a *lieu de mémoire* in the USA so complex.

One of the major discrepancies that twenty-first century scholars have raised with Nora's concept is its limiting and restrictive emphasis on "national" frameworks.[13] In a 2009 collection titled *Memory, History, and Colonialism: Engaging with Pierre Nora in Colonial and Postcolonial Contexts* (edited by Indra Sengupta and Hagen Schulze), an interlinking series of essays argued for the extended and adapted use of Nora's *lieux de mémoire* through a theoretical revision that "could fit the contours of colonial and postcolonial societies, which were and remain transnational in character".[14]

Focused on imperial history, the collection widens the concept to better address the "conflicting nature of collective memory" that is characteristic of colonial and postcolonial contexts.[15] Several examples of *lieux de mémoire* are given that, rather than maintaining a cohesive feeling of national continuity, capture the pluralistic and subjective nature of remembrance and identity. One case study, for example, is focused on war memorials to Indian troops (both on the Western front and in India) that emanate inherent ambiguities. Questions over "Why did the men buried there die? Did they help liberate India or renew its oppression?" riddle the same memory site as multiple conflicting, yet inseparable, narratives are embedded within.[16] Sir Edwin Lutyens' India Gate or All India War Memorial in New Delhi, for example, does not stabilise national identity but instead reflects plural identities, contradictory histories and contested "national" narratives.

To return, then, to the similarly complex idea of Burns as a figurative *lieu de mémoire* in the nineteenth-century USA, we might also identify, within one "nation", multiple and at times competing layers of memory. The (re)constitutions of Burns as a "site of memory" were not assigned with fixed meanings and symbols pertaining to a national population. Rather, "the memory of Burns" was fluid, repeatedly reshaped, and reflective of multiple identities. In developing a "wider vocabulary" for a "transnational" age and advancing the foundational principles of Nora's *Les Lieux de mémoire*, Winter has introduced the conceptual term "palimpsest", connoting a repeated overlay of memories that transmit variable messages but are bound together by an original source. Due to the hybrid, conflicting nature of cultural memory in transnational contexts, Winter suggests that colonial and postcolonial sites of memory, or *lieux de mémoire*, might each be considered as a "palimpsest, an overwritten text [...] something that is reused or altered but still bears visible traces of its earlier form". For Winter, "memories are overwritten time and again" and even when "considering the same event or object, each memory is unique".[17] Thus, conceiving of memory sites as "palimpsests" is more appropriately fluid than retorting to more rigid, inflexible terms or metaphors that fail to reflect on the layered, multidimensional nature of cultural memory.[18]

Winter's proposed transnational evolution of *lieux de mémoire* is, of course, formulated around the more rigidly defined postcolonial nations, and therefore America's "troubled postcoloniality" must not go unnoticed here.[19] Scholars have rightly warned against constructing false, transhistorical comparisons between nineteenth-century America's struggle for cultural independence and postcolonial Africa or India. Eric Cheyfitz, for example, reminds us that indigenising early European immigrants and settlers "denies the previous and ongoing existence of indigenous cultures in America",[20] while Peter Hulme argues that post-revolutionary America—through its heightened effort to continue the European project of imperial expansion—was "postcolonial and colonizing at the same time".[21]

In adopting Winter's postcolonial metaphor, I wish to follow Gesa Mackenthaum distinction of "taking a postcolonial *perspective* on nineteenth-century America"[22] rather than claiming it a postcolonial country. Mackenthaum notes the importance of postulating "a fundamental difference between the bilateral colonial, and later postcolonial, relationship between the English mother country and its American colonists" and the "multilateral or transnational colonial relationship between the Anglo-Saxon colonists (later American nationalists) and African and American indigenous groups"[23] that were subjected to violent dispossession and slavery.

Indeed, acknowledging the double-stranded postcoloniality of nineteenth-century America (simultaneously liberated but also colonising) allows us to better examine the complexity of contemporary race relations and the country's continuing involvement in the slave-based Atlantic colonial system up to the Civil War. Particularly when discussing appropriations of Burns by Frederick Douglass and the Ku Klux Klan—each with contrasting visions of a national future—Winter's perspective of postcolonial memory sites as "palimpsests" is particularly effective. That is, it is near impossible to find one "shared" or national story when unpacking the poet as a multidimensional *lieu de mémoire* or "site of memory" in the USA.

Yet equally, these multidimensional "memories" and remediations should not be considered as entirely separate or isolated acts, given they stem from the same source, espouse various conceptions of the American "nation", and are bound together by specific geo-chronological parameters. This dichotomy is evidenced explicitly through analysis of the centenary celebrations, where Burns was remediated in multiple and often divergent ways across the USA on the very same day: 25 January 1859.

The Burnsian Palimpsest: The 1859 Centenary Celebrations

In Adrian, Michigan, the Burns centenary celebrations were firmly focused on preserving a sense of Scottish identity akin to the early St. Andrews Society dinners discussed above. The event was attended exclusively by "Scotchmen" who spent the evening "recurring to the days of "Auld Lang syne"" and who, by the end of the evening, had formed a committee "for the purpose of organizing a St. Andrew's Society for this county",[24] providing another example of how one mode of remembrance (the centenary), or "institution of preservation", can feed into another (the establishment of a new St. Andrew's Club). Just as earlier "Suppers" had provided a platform for the performance of Burns's songs, as opposed to just their recitation, several of the centenary events also featured "songs, instrumental music, and social chat" between speeches. Rather unsurprisingly, "Auld lang syne" was one of the most common inclusions.[25]

In Detroit, Michigan, preserving a version of Scottish identity was also at the forefront of the evening, with the orator claiming that "the oblation at the shrine of genius" will "do more to arouse and preserve the nationality of Scotland than a thousand monuments to Wallace or Bruce". Celebrations in Cleveland, Ohio, were similarly Scoto-centric with an added touch of locality evidenced by both "Scotch and American flags". Special mention was also given to—as one of the few exceptions amidst a majority of homosocial events—the presence of Scottish women, albeit in slightly subjective terms: "The Scots lads and lasses gathered in great numbers […] The bonnie lasses with their soncey faces, were crowded thick through the hall, while 'every lassie had her laddie', and good 'braw lads they were too'".[26]

Of course, the memory of Burns was not solely used to bolster a specifically "Scottish" sense of identity at centenary events.

In some instances, the commemorations were used to symbolically maintain diplomatic relations between the USA and Great Britain. In Cincinnati, "the American and British colours were tastefully displayed forming an arch above the presiding host".[27] In Jersey, "The Queen of England" was toasted to "enthusiastic cheers", while in in Brooklyn "the stars and stripes and the union jack" were "blended in harmonious union around a life size bust of Burns".[28] These events bring to mind Robert Crawford's acute observations about the bicultural appeal of Burns as both a Scottish and British poet; only here a further transnational complication arises through the presence of Saltires, Union Jacks and Stars and Stripes (at different venues) over the course of one evening.[29]

The "life size bust" in Brooklyn also serves as a reminder of the role of material culture at the centenary. In Boston, "a mass of Burns related relics" had been "shipped from Scotland" for the event[30] while in Albany, New York, the "chief feature of the evening was the exhibition of the autograph copy of 'Auld Langsyne'", which had been bought for the occasion by club member J. V. L. Pruyn. Even the smaller-scale celebrations contained forms of material culture such as locally drawn "illustrations" of "Highland Mary".[31] In Mobile, Alabama, a Rev. H. N. Pierce presented a "graphic sketch" of "the road which Tam o' Shanter travelled" that was composed "from personal recollection",[32] further evidencing the influence of literary tourism and, in particular, the Burns Cottage as a point of pilgrimage for American tourists.

Chapter 5 highlighted the significance of three of America's most prominent (Fireside) poets—Holmes, Lowell and Whittier—composing new poems especially for the 1859 centenary at The Parker House Hotel in Boston. Yet the promotion of American Literature at the centenary was not unique to Boston. Other renowned writers, namely Washington Irving (1783–1859) and Henry Wadsworth Longfellow (1807–1882), sent messages to be read out at selected events[33] while William Cullen Bryant celebrated "The Poets and Poetry of America" ("loved at home, revered abroad")[34] in his toast at Astor House, New York. In Baltimore, Irving was celebrated as "the Patriarch of American Literature" while in Newhaven, Connecticut, a toast to "The Literature of America" was met with "admiration" and applause from the crowd.[35]

That the centenary inspired a sense of unity among American writers might be seen, to follow Rigney's line of theory, as the "embodiment" of an "imagined community" through the physical process of commemoration. The promotion of an American literary "canon" was, of course, one of many instances of group or "community" values being articulated. In Chicago, the centenary was marked by a procession which saw several of these "memory communities" come together. Marching alongside each other were the "Chicago Dragoons", "Highland Guard", "Knights Templars", "Masonic Lodges", "Odd Fellows", "St Andrew's Society" and "The Citizen's Fire Brigade".[36] Not only did the celebrations serve to "embody" and articulate the respective identities of these groups but—in paying tribute to the memory of the Scottish poet—they were also, albeit briefly, united in one procession.

One of the most telling comparative observations can be found in noting the broad differences between some of the Northern celebrations (often focused on tying the memory of the poet to abolitionism) and Southern events (which usually commemorated a "rural" and masculinised Burns). At Rockford, Illinois, a city known for its abolitionist leanings and support of the Free Soil Party, orator Anson S. Miller described Burns as "prophetically sounding the key-note of the popular sentiments of our country and our age" through "his uniform affection for man, irrespective of external conditions" and his "hatred of oppression in every form".[37] His references to "external conditions" and "popular sentiments" clearly allude to the contemporary battle for racial equality and abolition. Even more explicitly, a speaker in Boston profoundly claimed that Burns was not the type of man to "laud a declaration of independence, without applying its ground truths to all—irrespective of their condition, their colour, or their clime".[38] At the New York Cooper Institute, a remarkable 3000 people were in attendance to hear prominent abolitionist Henry Ward Beecher (1813–1887) delivering a keynote speech. In what reads like a condensed, narrative biography of the poet, Beecher unsurprisingly emphasised the "universal sympathy" of Burns and his "love for man in all his moods".[39]

In one of the most pertinent remarks of all the centenary speeches, particularly in the light of recent studies on Burns and slavery (noted in the introduction to this book), Beecher refuted the idea that Burns came close to being an "overseer of a plantation" in stating "I think I see Robert Burns following a gang of slaves, and chanting "A man's a man for a' that"".[40] Here, Beecher, daring to answer the question that still plagues twenty-first century critics, speculates that if Burns had sailed for Jamaica and personally encountered slavery then he would have "chanted" for their liberation. That Beecher commented on the issue also hints that there was a wider contemporary awareness of the fuller implications of Burns's tentative emigration plans. Regardless, the possibilities of what the poet "might have been" (i.e. complicit in the transatlantic slave trade) were clearly not an issue for the abolitionists who chose to commemorate him, bringing to mind Rigney's "scarcity principle" whereby cultural memory is subjectively recycled through "selectivity", "convergence" and "transference".[41]

In a concluding flurry of metaphorical hyperbole, Beecher, renowned for his charismatic prowess, suggested that if every living memory of Burns within these twenty-four hours "could each be changed into a flower" then "a mountain would arise, and he would sit upon a rose blossoms now at length without a thorn".[42] To playfully extend Beecher's curious metaphor, each memory, or rather flower, would also have to be a different hue given the divergent, at times conflicting, nature of memories evident at the US centenary celebrations.

In St. Louis, Missouri, Burns was not so much remembered as a "universal" upholder of rights but commemorated more, pertaining to the traditional discourses of Southern masculinity discussed above, as a hard-working "Poet Ploughman" concerned with providing for his family. The orator described how "that family of Burns" was "all hard workers", even converting the equivalent of what Burns earned for his "labours" into dollars ("thirty-five dollars for one year's labour of the poet Burns"). In the orator's words, "Not only were they celebrating the memory of the hale fellow, but of manhood in its most glorious personification"; a striking irony given Burns was never particularly fond of laborious agriculture.[43] Similarly in Milwaukee, the orator emphasised how Burns was "not only a poet, but a man, in every sense of the word" and thus he (Burns) "could not look back and recall a single violation of his truth or honesty".[44] In Charleston, South Carolina, one of the speakers, J. L. Petigru, rather tenuously conflated Burns's "moral and intellectual renown" with Scotland's "martial powers".

In a statement that foreshadowed elements of Civil War-era Confederate rhetoric (as the Confederacy fought to maintain troop morale against a better-equipped enemy), Petigru described how "Scotland had asserted a rank far beyond mere members, or physical advantages and resources" and further emphasised the nation's "historic prestige of successful opposition against both Romans and Englishmen".[45] The statement appears to exert sympathy for Scotland as a smaller, threatened entity in a wider ruling imperium, a political feeling that was resonant, of course, in the Secessionist States of the South. In contrast to the sentimental, romanticised version of Scottish identity evident at some of the Northern celebrations, where Wallace and Bruce were evoked in ways that were safely remote both in space and time; the martial evocations of Scottish valour in Charleston were, arguably, more closely aligned with contemporary secessionism.[46]

W. D. Porter, President of The South Carolina Senate, concluded the evening by first toasting "The State of South Carolina" before praising the event for bringing together "native sons" with "those of Scottish birth", for "South Carolina has no jealousies of foreign birth or national feeling". Porter further emphasised how the centenary had created a "harmonizing feeling" and established "our unity as a people" by "assimilating our sympathies and enjoyments".[47] Clearly, commemorating Burns had served to unite a portion of the local Charleston community and promote common values. Despite Porter's harmonious effusions, however, it is less clear whether his sympathies would have extended towards enslaved African-Americans. Shortly after the centenary celebrations, Porter, writing in the *Charleston Mercury*, expressed his distaste for anti-slavery organisations describing them as a threat to the "institutions of the South". For Porter "this whole anti-slavery agitation" was against the "the well-being, the peace, nay the very lives of millions of human beings, white or black!"[48] While the Charleston celebrations may well have "assimilated" the "sympathies and enjoyments" of select Southern admirers of Burns, it is hard to imagine that the likes of Henry Ward Beecher, Frederick Douglass and other prominent abolitionists would have been met with the same sense of sympathy for articulating their own memories of the poet. This provides a further testament to how civic, local and regionally specific frameworks (rather than broader "national" ones) shaped American commemorations of the poet.

While toasts to "The Memory of Robert Burns" simultaneously rang out across several States in over 60 different locations on 25 January 1859, these respective memories were, evidently, invested with complex, often conflicting, layers of meaning and, moreover, communicated through multiple ways and means. As this discussion hopes to have illustrated, a comparative treatment of the US centenary celebrations serves to highlight the multifarious ways in which the poet was remembered and "preserved", be it through songs, paintings, material culture, busts, texts, marches, rites or otherwise. At the dawn of the nineteenth century, during the formative years of Burns's transatlantic popularity, memories of the poet were circulated through newspaper clippings, songs, American editions and perhaps even a minority of "communicative memories". Just under sixty years later, by 1859, the ways in which Burns and his works were remembered had been transformed by multiple processes of remediation that, as has been demonstrated, led to multiple, often divergent, appropriations across and within the USA.

In returning to Winter's theory of transnational memory sites, consider the multiple modes of commemorations outlined in the centenary indicative of the "Burnsian palimpsest", replete with visible but overwritten layers of memory relating to Burns. The above discussion has, of course, merely touched upon a small portion of these palimpsestuous memories; from biographical texts, suppers, statues, individual accounts and vastly contrasting public centenary celebrations. As the century progressed, new inscriptions would add further layers to the palimpsest, such as the continuing erection of statues, adoption and appropriation of songs or widely publicised commentaries by influential figures such as Walt Whitman, John Muir (1838–1914) and Andrew Carnegie (1835–1919). Pertaining to Winter's sense of a palimpsest being "reused or altered" but not erasing earlier inscriptions, these instances of commemoration allowed for a diversity of interpretations that underlined simultaneous, polyphonic meanings while, in some way, preserving the memory of Burns.

Where the naturalist, philosopher and saviour of "America's wild places" Muir would inscribe a memory of Burns as a most ecologically sensitive poet,[49] Carnegie promoted the poet as a symbol of egalitarian learning through his philanthropic contributions. Consistently, the Burnsian palimpsest, in accordance with the fluid nature of transnational sites of cultural memory, variously preserves contested narratives; divergent ideologies; plural identities; multiple appropriations and contradictory national histories; all the while, retaining a trace of the original memory source—Robert Burns.

In addition to underlining a plurality of Burns commemorations in nineteenth-century America, these contrasting appropriations also alert us to the advantages of sectional, or regionally specific, approaches *within* transnational and transatlantic literary contexts. Christopher Hanlon employs the term "Atlantic sectionalism" to describe how, in the antebellum period, assertions of transatlantic connectedness frequently "entwined polemics over states' rights and federalism, northern and southern lineage, secession and union, slavery and freedom".[50] On the specific issue of American slavery and its relationship to England, Hanlon further states:

> Public intellectuals in the United States could not but refer the terms of the national conflict over slavery to England—whose abolition of slavery throughout the empire in 1833 pressured conservative U.S. discourses as well as voices of liberal dissent—but rather than doing so directly and literally, these partisans tended to codify their antipathies for one another in terms of complicated engagements with various constructions of English history, race, geography, and political economy.[51]

Here, opposing sectional entities shored up political beliefs through a subjective transatlantic connection to a reconstituted mother country. Expanding this concept, the reception and memory of transatlantic literature (and literary figures) in nineteenth-century America might also benefit from a greater awareness of patterns of "Atlantic sectionalism". As demonstrated above, the subjective reconstruction of Burns by various parties provides a useful example of how the same poet was simultaneously appropriated to articulate conflicting sectional values. That is, strains of American identity were expressed through a connection, whether racial, ideological, or otherwise, to a transatlantic poet and his works.

What is clear, in the specific case of Burns, is that the popular and abiding narrative of him being remembered as the embodiment of "national American" values must evolve to consider the sectional intricacies of transatlantic literature in the nineteenth century.

NOTES

1. *Chronicle of the Hundredth Birthday of Robert Burns*, 571.
2. Benedict Anderson, *Imagined Communities: Reflections on the Origins and Spread of Nationalism* (1983). Rev. ed. (London and New York: Verso, 1991).
3. Rigney, "Embodied Communities", 94–95.
4. Leith Davis, "The Robert Burns 1859 Centenary: Mapping Transatlantic (Dis)Location", in *Robert Burns and Transatlantic Culture*, eds. Alker, Davis, and Nelosn, 201.
5. Winter, "Palimpsests", 170.

6. Alex Tyrrell, "Paternalism, Public Memory and National Identity in Early Victorian Scotland: The Robert Burns Festival at Ayr in 1844", *History* 90, no. 297 (2005): 43.

7. Hagen Schulze, "Foreword", in *Memory, History, and Colonialism: Engaging with Pierre Nora in Colonial and Postcolonial Contexts*, eds. Indra Sengupta and Hagen Schulze (London: German Historical Institute, 2009).

8. Tyrrell, "Paternalism, Public Memory and National Identity", 43.

9. Davis, "The Robert Burns 1859 Centenary", 188.

10. Pittock and Whatley, "Poems and Festivals, Art and Artefact", 58.

11. *Celebration of the Hundredth Anniversary of the Birth of Robert Burns*, 3.

12. See David Waldstreicher, *In the Midst of Perpetual Fetes: The Making of American Nationalism, 1776–1820* (Virginia: University of North Carolina Press, 1997), 1–14.

13. Schulze, "Foreword".

14. Winter, "Palimpsests", 167.

15. Indra Sengupta, "Locating *lieux de memoire*: A (Post)colonial Perspective", in *Memory, History, and Colonialism*, eds. Sengupta and Schulze, 4.

16. Winter, "Palimpsests", 168–169.

17. Ibid., 176–170.

18. See also Sarah Dillon, *The Palimpsest: Literature, Criticism, Theory* (London: Continuum, 2007). Dillon traces the initial metaphorical use to Thomas De Quincy's essay "The Palimpsest", first published in Blackwood's Magazine (1845) as part of his *Suspiria De Profundis*.

19. See Gesa Mackenthum, "America's Troubled Postcoloniality: Some Reflections from Abroad", *Discourse* 22, no. 3 (2000): 34.

20. Eric Cheyfitz, "Savage Law: The Plot Against American Indians in *Johnson and Graham's Lessee v M'Intosh* and *The Pioneers*", in *Cultures of United States Imperialism* (Durham: Duke University Press, 1993), 118.

21. Peter Hulme, "Including America", *Ariel* 26, no. 1 (1995): 122.

22. Mackenthum, "America's Troubled Postcoloniality", 37.

23. Ibid., 36.

24. *Chronicle of the Hundredth Birthday of Robert Burns*, 549.

25. See "Auld Acquaintance for the New Year: Burns's Auld Lang Syne". Accessed 16 December 2015, http://blogs.loc.gov/folklife/2013/12/auld-acquaintance-for-the-new-year-burnss-auld-lang-syne/.

26. *Chronicle of the Hundredth Birthday of Robert Burns*, 568.

27. Ibid., 567.

28. Ibid., 559.

29. For a discussion of the "British Burns", see Robert Crawford, *Devolving English Literature* (Edinburgh: Edinburgh University Press, 2000), 88.

30. Pittock and Whatley, "Poems and Festivals, Art and Artefact", 65–67.

31. *Chronicle of the Hundredth Birthday of Robert Burns*, 584.

32. Ibid., 571.

33. Davis, "The Robert Burns 1859 Centenary", 201.

34. *Chronicle of the Hundredth Birthday of Robert Burns*, 590.

35. Ibid., 573.

36. Ibid., 564.

37. Ibid., 597.

38. Ibid., 556.

39. Ibid., 583.

40. Ibid., 580.

41. Rigney, "Plentitude, Scarcity and the Circulation of Cultural Memory", 11.

42. *Chronicle of the Hundredth Birthday of Robert Burns*, 583.

43. Ibid., 604.

44. Ibid., 571.

45. Ibid., 560.

46. For a discussion of Scottish identity in relation to martial symbolism and "patriot valour" see also Murray G. H. Pittock, *Scottish Nationality* (Hampshire: Palgrave, 2001), 77–80.

47. *Chronicle of the Hundredth Birthday of Robert Burns*, 564.

48. *Charleston Mercury*, 30th October (1860).

49. Mary Colwell, *John Muir: The Scotsman Who Saved America's Wild Places* (Oxford: Lion Books, 2014), 128–129.

50. Ibid.

51. Christopher Hanlon, *America's England: Antebellum Literature and Atlantic Sectionalism* (Oxford: Oxford University Press, 2013), Preface.

CHAPTER 8

Afterword: The (Trans)National Poet

> We twa hae paidl'd in the burn,
>   Frae morning sun till dine;
> But seas between us braid hae roar'd,
>   Sin auld lang syne
>   —"Auld Lang Syne" (17–20) (1788)[1]

Every year as the clock turns midnight on 31 December in Times Square, New York, "Auld lang syne" bellows across the symbolic centre of the city as an estimated one million people, in addition to billions of others celebrating worldwide, bid a collective farewell to the departing year by attempting to sing (or at least hum along to) Burns's version of, in his own words, an "exceedingly expressive"[2] old Scottish song. Even among those who might associate the song with the poet, Burns's inspired lyrical adaptations and additions remain largely overlooked and forgotten. Yet pertinent to this book, a brief reference to a neglected verse of Burns's best-known song serves as a fitting reminder of why we must continue to reconsider the poet and his works in transnational contexts.

Lamenting on an old friendship affected by migration, space, time and geo-physical separation in verses three and four, Burns's description of how "seas between us braid hae roar'd" is one of many reminders that the poet lived in and responded to a transnational "world of encounters"[3] on the Atlantic periphery (as also demonstrated by the American works addressed in Chapter 2 and several other proleptic emigration

© The Author(s) 2018
A. Sood, *Robert Burns and the United States of America*,
https://doi.org/10.1007/978-3-319-94445-6_8

211

poems discussed elsewhere).[4] A transnational perspective of Burns, then, need not merely be considered a compound product of twenty-first-century scholarship. Rather, it but also serves to articulate how the world was perceived and delineated in the late eighteenth and nineteenth centuries, a period particularly abundant in material, institutional, intellectual and literary connections. To ignore these connections when considering the life, work and broader reception of Burns would involve (to borrow a term from Paul Giles) a process of "radical dehistoricization"[5] that overlooks our overlapping cultural cross-currents. Displacing Burns from his status as the "National Bard" of Scotland has not only provided fresh insights into his poetry, but also revealed much about the sociocultural interconnections that facilitated his relationship with—and rise to prominence in—the USA, c.1786–1866. Indeed, instances of transnational encounters and exchange have permeated the chapters of this book.

Though the revolutionary events that Burns wrote about in "When Guilford Good" may have severed parliamentary ties, new lines of cultural, intellectual and literary exchange continued to evolve and flourish throughout the nineteenth century, as evidenced in Part I of this book through discussion of how a thriving transatlantic reprint trade facilitated the spread of Burns's work, and Parts II and III through analysis of notable literary connections and objectified commemorations. The introduction to this book playfully gestured towards a subtle permutation of Burns's sobriquet from "Scotland's National Bard" to "The Transnational Poet of Scotland". Though this fresh theoretical baptism might not displace long-established popular monikers, the complex and multifarious connections between Burns and the USA surely suggest that future critical studies of the poet should not be restricted by singular national paradigms, leaving much work to be done on the reception and influence of Burns in other transnational contexts.

Perhaps one of the most interesting observations of this book is the extent to which—despite the transnational focus—concepts of the "nation", in a wide plurality of forms, pervaded Burns's nineteenth-century American reception. Indeed, magnifying the connections between a relatively new nation (America) and a poet self-described as the national "Scotch Bard"[6] has been particularly apt for assessing concepts of the "nation" in a transnational, cross-border literary context. Burns's popularity in the USA has most commonly been attributed to his kinship with "national American" ideals of freedom, egalitarianism and individual liberty.

This common claim, bolstered by notable writers, poets, critics and biographers, has persisted from the mid-nineteenth century right through to the present day. As noted in Chapter 6, Ralph Waldo Emerson, speaking in 1859, emphatically conflated Burns's songs with the "Declaration of Independence"[7]; A few decades later, Walt Whitman described Burns as "essentially a Republican" who would have been "at home in the Western United States"[8]; and in 1974, critic Donald. A. Low suggested that "Fellow-feeling with Burns was instinctive" for Americans as his "praise of independence vindicated their own recent historic choice",[9] and even the more recent groundbreaking work of Murray Pittock and Robert Crawford frequently refers back to the idea that Burns was broadly considered to be a friend to "democratic America"[10] and "liberty in the United States".[11]

While there is evidence to substantiate this common conflation, it also wrongly assumes, when stated without qualification, a "spatiotemporal unity"[12] for nineteenth-century American nationhood. That is, in stating that Burns was popularly received due to his kinship with the perceived ideals of the "American nation", there lies an implicit, inaccurate suggestion of the nation as a unified, all-containing entity and central frame of reference. Saskia Sassen suggests that "nation-states" have rarely achieved "spatiotemporal unity" and thus the "national", upon closer inspection, reveals itself to be composed of "multiple spatialities and temporalities" that might be, at best, composed into some form of comprehensible order. When applied to the case of America, Sassen's observations are further complicated by the fact that the country, by its very constitution, was (and still is) a federal republic of semi-autonomous states rather than a singular "nation-state", arguably making a "national" spatiotemporal unity even more rare.

This idea was perhaps most obvious in Chapter 7 where centenary commemorations of Burns differed between Southern confederate states and the largely abolitionist North, demonstrating a plurality of spatially disparate national values and civic identities that impacted upon the preservation of a literary figure. As our understanding of historical American nationalisms continues to evolve, then, so too does our understanding of Burns's reception and nineteenth-century legacy. Anatol Lieven has recently suggested that students of American nationalism "have never properly addressed the development of Southern identity before 1865" or before the region's "particular nationalism" was "reincorporated into that of the United States as a whole" after the Civil War.[13] Similarly, Paul Quigley's study, *Shifting Grounds: Nationalism and the American South, 1848-1865*, discusses white Southern identity and its (dis)connections with more widely held conceptions of nineteenth-century American national identity.[14]

In addition to the divergent centenary celebrations held on the cusp of the Civil War, Burns's earlier reception was equally affected by complex and multifarious conceptions of the American nation. As discussed in Chapter 3, for example, the contextual suggestion of Burns as the "Heaven-Taught ploughman" in the early nineteenth-century periodical press chimed with streams of Anti-Federalist, agrarian thought, whereby national progress could only be achieved by avoiding the corruption of hierarchal governance and an urban market economy. This view of progress was, of course, quite different to contemporary Federalist challenges that sought to develop commerce in order for civic advancement. Here lies an earlier example of where national "spatiotemporal unity" was notably absent and, crucially, impacted upon the early appearance and American reception of Burns's poems.[15]

Further complicating the significance of the nation in regard to Burns's American reception were the (predominantly diasporic) associations of Burns with perceived Scottish or indeed British nationalism. The selective associations of Burns with "plaid and the tartan"[16] or the Union Jack, for example, hardly framed the poet as a beacon of American Revolutionary fervour or Republican ideals. Even more convoluted were Robert Dinsmoor and David Bruce's poetic articulations of the Ulster-Scots American experience.

Here, a more literal sense of transnational relations—entwining Scotland, Ulster and America—are deeply embedded within literary reception, yet Dinsmoor's repeated emphasis on his "bless'd land" ("To Mrs. Agnes Park", 31–36) (America) renders an "American national" reading as equally viable. The underlying point here is that any conceptual national, or indeed transnational, perspective must be considered as partial rather than central and definitive. A transnational approach, then, should not result in the negation of national perspectives; nor should it overshadow the relevance of other cultural contexts, that are not necessarily aligned with the nation. In other words, the validity of the nation as an analytical frame should not so much be displaced by transnational approaches, but rather be encompassed *within* them along with other equally valid frames of reference useful for literary scholars and cultural historians.

Opposing Benedict's Anderson's now-famous suggestion—in *Imagined Communities*—that literature is integral to both nation-formation and sustenance, Wai-Chee Dimock insists that literature "outlives the scope of the nation" and thus unsettles, rather than upholds "territorial sovereignty" and regimes of simultaneity.[17] One example of this might be the critical backlash directed towards Scottish national readings of Burns in the nineteenth-century USA. There was, at times, a perceived distaste for the "unequivocal eulogy" and "strong biases" expressed by Scottish readers and critics ("one must have been born a Scotsman to relish with *goût* the writings of Burns"),[18] thus both disrupting Burns's "territorial sovereignty" as a Scottish poet while also prompting fresh frames of analysis in a new space.

Dimock's conception of "Deep Time" (literature as circulating in "denationalized space")[19] certainly allows for fresh insights when considering a poet such as Burns who, as evidenced, occupied several cultural frames over eighty years within a single nation. Yet wholly adopting the concept of "Deep Time", or "denationalized space", also misses the significance of, for example, Burns being considered a "friend" to "national American ideals" or as a uniting national symbol for the Scottish diaspora. We might, then, adjust Dimock's phrasing accordingly. Literature does not so much "outlive the scope of the nation", but rather outlives "the scope of nations" in the plural, whereby fluid and multifarious reincarnations of national identities (within and across geopolitical boundaries) might be included as credible, but not dominant, units of analysis among many others.

"Owre the Sea" Today

Whether through echoes of New Year songs, annual suppers, statues, lakes or the advent of new editions, various sites of memory continue to invoke and commemorate Robert Burns and his works in the twenty-first-century USA. New, Web-based umbrella platforms such as the "Robert Burns Association of North America" remain dedicated to "the preservation and appreciation of the life, works and philosophy" of Burns,[20] while celebratory events and conferences continue to be held across the country, with promotion, membership and cohesion more accessible than ever before in a digital age of instantaneous interconnectivity.[21] Arguably more so than any other eighteenth-century British writer, Burns's memory continues to be remediated across and beyond academic circuits in America. The transatlantic media convergences that led to Burns's initial American popularity, it seems, continue to evolve, overlap, and preserve the poet and his works.

Pertinently, much Burns scholarship also continues to emanate from the USA. Coinciding with the Scottish government's 2009 "Year of Homecoming" campaign (for which the bicentenary of Burns's birth was the focal point), the American Folklife Center at the Library of Congress, Washington, DC, presented a free public symposium on Burns's life and work, which included talks on his "impact on America and American culture".[22] Picking up the baton from the likes of J. DeLancey Ferguson, Franklyn Bliss Snyder and G. Ross Roy, North American scholars such as Leith Davis, Carol McGuirk and Corey Andrews continue to be counted among the world's most prominent contemporary Burns critics. As recently as 2014, for example, McGuirk added to a considerable body of Burns research with her latest book *Reading Robert Burns: Texts, Contexts, Transformations*, while just months later Corey Andrews published *The Genius of Scotland: The Cultural Production of Robert Burns, 1785–1834* (2015). Going by current publication rates, then, the tradition of much fruitful Burns scholarship being written and researched in America (and by American scholars) remains strong.

On an institutional level, the University of South Carolina continues to be a vital organ in Burns scholarship. The 5000+Burns materials held at the university's Thomas Cooper Library, first collected by W. Ormiston Roy and inherited by his grandson G. Ross Roy (whom the collection is named after) remains an invaluable resource for scholars, evidenced most recently by the music holdings being of substantial aid to the recent Oxford University Press edition of *The Scots Musical Museum*, edited by Murray Pittock. Thanks to the rigorous work of Elizabeth Sudduth, the collection is now catalogued and divided into "Typescripts"; "Printed Materials"; "Burnsiana"; "Art, Prints, Posters and Photographs"; "Sound, Film and Video Recordings"; and "Realia and Cultural Objects"; thus further illustrating the importance of mixed-media convergences in relation to both the poet's reception and ongoing cultural memory. Significantly, the majority of "American editions" listed in Appendix 1 can also be found in the collection, with most others catalogued in the equally rich William R. Smith Collection, based at the Library of the Supreme Council, 33. S. J., Washington, DC.[23]

With an abundance of fresh resources and the dawn of several reinvigorated critical studies, it seems a new era of Burns Studies is well and truly underway in the USA. With that, I shall leave the final words to one of America's first great canonical poets, or, as some would have it, the "American Burns" himself:

> No more these simple flowers belong
>   To Scottish maid and lover:
> Sown in the common soil of song,
>   They bloom the wide world over.
>   John Greenleaf Whittier, "Burns" (1–4)[24]

NOTES

1. *The Poems and Songs*, 1:443
2. *Letters*, 1:342.
3. Doyle, "Notes Toward a Dialectical Method", 195.
4. See also Liam McIlvanney, "Editorial: Burns and the World," *International Journal of Scottish Literature* 6 (Spring/Summer 2010).
5. Paul Giles, "'To Gird this Watery Globe": Freneau, Barlow and American Neoclassical Poetry' in *Transatlantic Literary Studies, 1660–1830*, ed. Bannet and Manning, 140.
6. For a recent discussion of the "Heaven-Taught Ploughman" and "Scotch Bard" personae, see *The Genius of Scotland*, 35–37.
7. *Celebration of the Hundredth Anniversary of the Birth of Robert Burns*, 36.
8. Walt Whitman, *November Boughs* (Philadelphia: David McKay, 1888), 57.
9. *The Critical Heritage*, 44.
10. *The Bard*, 6.
11. Pittock, "Introduction: Global Burns", 19.
12. Saskia Sassen, "Spatialities and Temporalities of the Global: Elements for a Theorization," *Public Culture* 12, no. 11 (2000): 215.
13. *America Right or Wrong: An Anatomy of American Nationalism*, 108.
14. Paul Quigley, *Shifting Grounds: Nationalism and the American South, 1848–1865* (Oxford: Oxford University Press, 2011).
15. For discussion of the complex interrelationship between commerce, agriculture and "virtue" in post-revolutionary America, see *The Machiavellian Moment*, 506–553.

16. *The Knickerbocker*, August 2 (1833): 148–149.
17. Wai Chee Dimock, "Literature and the Planet," *Publications of the Modern Language Association of America* 116, no. 1 (2001): 175.
18. *Life of Robert Burns*, 5.
19. See Wai Chee Dimock, *Through Other Continents: American Literature Across Deep Time* (Princeton: Princeton University Press, 2008).
20. "Robert Burns Association of North America". Accessed 18 October 2015. http://www.rbana.com/.
21. See Sharon Alker and Holly Faith Nelson, "Transatlanticism and Beyond: Robert Burns and the World Wide Web," in *Robert Burns and Transatlantic Culture*, ed. Alker, Davis and Nelson, 247–261.
22. "Folklife Symposium". Accessed 18 October 2015. http://www.loc.gov/folklife/Symposia/Burns/.
23. See Larissa P. Watkins, eds., *Burnsiana: A Bibliography of the William R. Smith Collection in the Library of the Supreme Council, 33°, S.J.* (Delaware and Washington: Oak Knoll Press & Library of the Supreme Council, 2008).
24. *The Complete Poetical Works of John Greenleaf Whittier*, 196.

Appendix A

With the advent of new technologies, manuscript discoveries and fresh scholarly investigation, the bibliography of Robert Burns is currently in a state of revision. J. W. Egerer's seminal *A Bibliography of Robert Burns* (1964) remains an immensely useful resource for tracking Burns editions from 1786 through 1953. However, as Patrick Scott has recently noted, Egerer's bibliography also has "significant limitations both for textual editing and in coverage of Burns and publishing history".[1] For example, Egerer only lists items (individual poems, songs, letters) making their first appearance in each separate entry, thus making it difficult to determine textual variances between editions. This is of particular significance to reprinted American editions from 1786 through 1866.

As discussed in Part II of this book, American reprints, though predominantly based on contemporary British editions, often contained textual variations and idiosyncrasies, some more significant than others. Analysis of John and Archibald Maclean's 1788 New York reprinting of *Poems, Chiefly in The Scottish Dialect* (in Chapter 3), reveals, for example, the uncensored inclusion of political figures from the American War in Burns's "A Fragment"[2] (omitted from both the 1787 "Edinburgh editions"[3] and 1788 Philadelphia edition). Similarly, Craig Lamont has documented incongruities between the 1798 Edinburgh edition of *Poems, Chiefly in the Scottish Dialect* (two volumes) and the Philadelphia edition (two volumes in one) of the same year.[4] Indeed, Lamont's recent work on a new free online resource, *A Bibliography of Robert Burns for the*

A. Sood, *Robert Burns and the United States of America*, https://doi.org/10.1007/978-3-319-94445-6

21st Century: 1786–1802, marks the first step in providing the additional kinds of information—full contents lists and textual variants of every single edition—that might help to provide a fuller picture of Burnsian print culture.

In the vein of an enumerative bibliography, this Appendix lists, rather than describes minutely, known American editions (books) of Burns's poetry up to 1866. In addition to providing quantitative evidence of the distribution of Burns's poetry, it is hoped this checklist will also aid future scholars involved in projects dedicated to tackling the complexity of Burnsian print culture on both sides of the Atlantic. In the words of Burns's most influential bibliographer to date, the only sure fact about any bibliography "is that it is never finished".[5]

The checklist has been compiled from the following bibliographic sources: James Gibson and James McKie, *The Bibliography of Robert Burns, with Bibliographical and Biographical Notes, and Sketches of Burns Clubs, Monuments and Statues* (Kilmarnock: J. McKie, 1881); J. W. Egerer, *A Bibliography of Robert Burns* (Edinburgh and London: Oliver and Boyd, 1964); Larissa P. Watkins, *A Bibliography of the William R. Smith Collection in the Library of the Supreme Council, 33, S. J.* (Delaware: Oak Knoll Press, 2008); and Elizabeth Sudduth, *The G. Ross Roy Collection of Robert Burns: An Illustrated Catalogue* (Columbia: The University of South Carolina Press, 2009). Secondary searches have also been made in the following digital databases: *HathiTrust*; *Worldcat*; *Early American Imprints, Series I*; *Eighteenth Century Collections Online*; and the *Mitchell Library, National Library of Scotland* and *Library of Congress* online catalogues. All entries have been viewed by the author—in the form of at least one physical or digital edition—with the exception of those marked (*), which rely solely on the authority of previous bibliographers.

Chronological Checklist of Burns Print Editions in the United States of America: 1788–1866

Poems, Chiefly in the Scottish Dialect. By Robert Burns. Philadelphia: Peter Stewart and George Hyde, 1788.

Poems, Chiefly in the Scottish Dialect. By Robert Burns. To Which Are Added, Scots Poems, Selected from the Works of Robert Fergusson. New York: J. and A. M'Lean, 1788.

The Scots, Musical Museum. Being a Collection of the Most Favorite Scots Tunes Adapted to the Voice, Harpsicord, and Piano-Forte. Philadelphia: John Aitken, 1797.

Poems, Chiefly in the Scottish Dialect. By Robert Burns. From the latest European Edition. Two Volumes in One. Philadelphia: Patterson & Cochran, 1798.

Poems, Chiefly in the Scottish Dialect. By Robert Burns. To which are Added, Scots Poems, Selected from the Works of Robert Fergusson. New York: John Tiebout, 1799.

Poems, Chiefly in the Scottish Dialect. A New Edition, which Includes All the Poems and Songs in that Printed at Edinburgh in 1787 Under the Authors Own Inspection; Also His Life Appendix, Containing His Other Select Pieces. Berwick Upon Tweed & Boston: H. Richardson for J. White & Co., 1801.

The Works of Robert Burns. With an Account of His Life, and a Criticism on His Writings. In Four Volumes. To which are Prefixed, Some Observations on the Character and Conditions of the Scottish Peasantry. Philadelphia: Thomas Dobson, 1801.

Poems, Chiefly in the Scottish Dialect. By Robert Burns. Wilmington: Bonsal and Niles, 1804.

The Poetical Works of Robert Burns. With the Author's Life Written by Himself. Philadelphia: Benjamin Johnson, Jacob Johnson, & Robert Johnson, 1804.

The Works of Robert Burns. With an Account of His Life, and a Criticism on His Writings. In Three Volumes. To which are Prefixed, Some Observations on the Character and Conditions of the Scottish Peasantry. Philadelphia: William Fairbairn, 1804.

The Poetical Works of Robert Burns. Together with an Appendix, and a Concise History of His Life. Philadelphia: Peter Stewart, 1807.

Letters Addressed to Clarinda, &c. Never before Published in America; with a Choice Selection of Poems and Songs. By Robert Burns. Philadelphia: John B. Austin, 1809.

Reliques of Robert Burns. Consisting Chiefly of Original, Letters, Poems, and Critical Observations on Scottish Songs. Collected and published by R. H. Cromek. Philadelphia and New York: Bradford and Inskeep, Baltimore: Coale and Thomas, Boston: Oliver C. Greenleaf, 1809.

The Poetical Works of Robert Burns. To which is Prefixed His Life, as Written by Himself, and Continued or Commented on by Others. Philadelphia: Benjamin Chapman, 1811.

Poems, Chiefly in the Scottish Dialect. By Robert Burns. Baltimore: A. Miltenberger, 1812.

Letters Addressed to Clarinda, &c. Philadelphia: 1812.*

The Poetical Works of Robert Burns. A New Edition. Alexandria: John A. Stewart, 1812.

Reliques of Robert Burns. Philadelphia: 1813.*

The Works of Robert Burns. With an Account of His Life, and a Criticism on His Writings. In Four Volumes. To which are Prefixed, Some Observations on the Character and Conditions of the Scottish Peasantry. Baltimore: F. Lucas, Jun, and J. Cushing, 1814.

Reliques of Robert Burns. Philadelphia: 1814.*

Poems, Chiefly in The Scottish Dialect. By Robert Burns. Baltimore: F. Lucas, Jun, and J. Cushing, 1815.

The Poetical Works of Robert Burns. Including Several Poems not to be Found in any Other Edition. Also, the Author's Life, Written by Himself, and Extracts from Some of His Letters. In Two Volumes. Salem, NY: J.P. Reynolds, 1815.

The Poetical Works of Robert Burns. To which is Prefixed His Life, as Written by Himself, and Continued or Commented on by Others. Philadelphia: Benjamin Chapman, 1815.

The Works of Robert Burns. With an Account of His Life, and a Criticism on His Writings. In Four Volumes. To which are Prefixed, Some Observations on the Character and Conditions of the Scottish Peasantry. Baltimore: F. Lucas, Jun, and J. Cushing, 1815.

The Works of Robert Burns. With an Account of His Life, and a Criticism on His Writings. In Four Volumes. To which are Prefixed, Some Observations on the Character and Conditions of the Scottish Peasantry. Baltimore: F. Lucas, Jun, and J. Cushing, 1816.

Reliques of Robert Burns (Philadelphia: 1817).*

Letters Addressed to Clarinda, Etc. By Robert Burns. First American Edition. Washington City: J. M'Laughlin, 1818.

The Poetical Works of Robert Burns. With an Account of His Life and Correspondence with Mr. Thomson. In Two Volumes. To which is Added a New and Complete. Philadelphia: Benjamin Warner, 1818.

The Scottish Minstrel: Being a complete Collection of Burns' Songs. Together with His Correspondence with Mr. Thomson, To which is Added a New and Complete Glossary. Philadelphia: Benjamin Warner, 1818.

Burns' Select Works, Prose. Volume One. New York: R. & W. A. Bartow, 1820.

The Letters of Robert Burns. Chronologically Arranged from Dr. Currie's Collection. Two Volumes in One. Boston: Wells and Lily, 1820.

The Works of Robert Burns. With an Account of His Life. New York: R. & W. A. Bartow, 1821.

The Poetical Works of Robert Burns. With an Account of His Life and Correspondence with Mr. Thomson. In Two Volumes. Philadelphia: M'Carty & Davis, 1822.

The Works of the British Poets Edited by Robert Walsh, Jr. Vol. XXVIII. Boston: Charles Ewer and Timothy Bedlington, 1822.

The Poetical Works of Robert Burns. With Several Pieces Never before Published, Notes Illustrative of His Poems, and Definitions of All the Scottish Words and Phrases. To which is Prefixed, an Account of His Life: and also a View of His Character, by Gilbert Burns. Philadelphia: B. Chapman, 1823.

The Life and Works of Robert Burns. As Originally Edited by James Currie, M.D. To which is Prefixed a Review of the Life of Burns and of Various Criticisms on His Character and Writings. New York: S. King, 1824.

The Works of Robert Burns. With an Account of His Life. In Four Volumes. New York: W. A Bartow, 1824.

The Poetical Works of Robert Burns. In Two Volumes. New York: D. Mallon, 1825.

The Poetical Works of Robert Burns. Including Several Pieces Not Inserted in Dr. Currie's Edition, Exhibited Under a New Plan of Arrangement, and Preceded by a Life of the Author, and a Complete Glossary. In Two Volumes. New York: William Borradaile, 1826.

The Works of Robert Burns. With an Account of His Life, and a Criticism on His Writings, To which are Prefixed, Some Observations on the Character and Conditions of the Scottish Peasantry, by James Currie, M.D. A New Edition, with Many Additional Poems and Songs, and an Enlarged and Corrected Glossary. New York: William Borradaile, 1826.

The Works of Robert Burns. With an Account of His Life, and a Criticism on His Writings, To which are Prefixed, Some Observations on the Character and Conditions of the Scottish Peasantry, by James Currie, M.D. A New Edition, with Many Additional Poems and Songs, and an Enlarged and Corrected Glossary, from the Last London Edition of 1825. Philadelphia: J. Crissy and J. Grigg, 1828.

The Poetical Works of Robert Burns. Including Several Pieces Not Inserted in Dr. Currie's Edition, Exhibited Under a New Plan of Arrangement, and Preceded by a Life of the Author, and a Complete Glossary. In Two Volumes. Philadelphia: J. Yarding, 1829.

The Works of Robert Burns. With an Account of His Life, and a Criticism on His Writings, To which are Prefixed, Some Observations on the Character and Conditions of the Scottish Peasantry, by James Currie, M.D. A New Edition, with Many Additional Poems and Songs, and an Enlarged and Corrected Glossary, from the last London edition of 1825. Philadelphia: J. Crissy and J. Grigg, 1829.

The Works of Robert Burns. With an Account of His Life, and a Criticism on His Writings, To which are Prefixed, Some Observations on the Character and Conditions of the Scottish Peasantry, by James Currie, M.D. A New Edition, Four Volumes Complete in One, with Many Additional Poems and Songs, and an Enlarged Corrected Glossary. New York: S. & D.A. Forbes, 1830.

The Complete Works of Robert Burns. With an Account of His Life, and a Criticism on His Writings, with Observations on the Character and Conditions of the Scottish Peasantry, and a Copious Glossary, by James Currie, M.D. Four Volumes in One. New York: S. King, 1831.

Life of Robert Burns by J. G. Lockhart. With an Essay on His Writings, Prepared for this Edition. New York: W. Stodart, 1831.

The Works of Robert Burns. With an Account of His Life, and a Criticism on His Writings, To which are Prefixed, Some Observations on the Character and Conditions of the Scottish Peasantry, by James Currie, M.D. A New Edition, with Many Additional Poems and Songs, and an Enlarged and Corrected Glossary, from the Last London edition of 1825. Philadelphia: J. Crissy and J. Grigg, 1831.

The Works of Robert Burns. With an Account of His Life, and a Criticism on His Writings, To which are Prefixed, Some Observations on the Character and Conditions of the Scottish Peasantry, by James Currie. A New Edition, with Many Additional Poems and Songs, from the Latest London Editions, Embellished with Thirty-three Engravings on Wood. New York: J. Booth and Sons, 1832.

The Works of Robert Burns. Containing His Life by John Lockhart, the Poetry and Correspondence of Dr, Currie's Edition, Biographical Sketches of the Poet by Himself, Gilbert Burns, Professor Stewart, and Others, Essay on Scottish Poetry, Including the Poetry of Burns, by Dr Currie, Burns's Songs, from Johnson's "Musical Museum, and "Thomson's Select Melodies", Select Scottish Songs of the Other Poets, from the Best Collections, with Burns's Remarks. Forming, in One Work, the Truest

Exhibition of the Man and the Poet, and the Fullest Edition of His Poetry and Prose Writing Hithereto Published. New York: William Pearson, 1832.

The Works of Robert Burns. Containing His Life by John Lockhart, the Poetry and Correspondence of Dr, Currie's Edition, Biographical Sketches of the Poet by Himself, Gilbert Burns, Professor Stewart, and Others, Essay on Scottish Poetry, Including the Poetry of Burns, by Dr Currie, Burns's Songs, from Johnson's "Musical Museum, and "Thomson's Select Melodies", Select Scottish Songs of the Other Poets, from the Best Collections, with Burns's Remarks. New York: Leavitt & Allen Bros, 1832.

The Works of Robert Burns. With an Account of His Life, and a Criticism on His Writings, To which are Prefixed, Some Observations on the Character and Conditions of the Scottish Peasantry, by James Currie, M.D. A New Edition, with Many Additional Poems and Songs, and an Enlarged and Corrected Glossary, from the Last London edition of 1825. Philadelphia: J. Crissy and J. Grigg, 1832.

The Works of Robert Burns. With an Account of His Life, and a Criticism on His Writings, To which are Prefixed, Some Observations on the Character and Conditions of the Scottish Peasantry, by James Currie, M.D. A New Edition, Four Volumes Complete in One, With Many Additional Poems and Songs, from the Latest London of 1829. Philadelphia: James Locken, 1832.

The Works of Robert Burns. With an Account of His Life, and a Criticism on His Writings, To which are Prefixed, Some Observations on the Character and Conditions of the Scottish Peasantry, by James Currie, M.D. A New Edition, Four Volumes Complete in One, With Many Additional Poems and Songs, and an Enlarged and Corrected Glossary. Philadelphia: J. Crissy and J. Grigg, 1833.

The Poetical Works of Robert Burns. Including Several Pieces Not Inserted in Dr. Currie's Edition, Exhibited Under a New Plan of Arrangement, and Preceded by a Life of the Author, and a Complete Glossary. In Two Volumes. [In One] Boston: James B. Dow, 1834.

The Works of Robert Burns. With His Life by Allan Cunningham. In Four Volumes. Boston: Hilliard, Gray, and Company, 1834.

The Works of Robert Burns. With an Account of His Life, and a Criticism on His Writings, To which are Prefixed, Some Observations on the Character and Conditions of the Scottish Peasantry, by James Currie, M.D. A New Edition, Four Volumes Complete in One, With Many

Additional Poems and Songs, and an Enlarged and Corrected Glossary. Philadelphia: J. Crissy and J. Grigg, 1834.

The Works of Robert Burns. With an Account of His Life, and a Criticism on His Writings, To which are Prefixed, Some Observations on the Character and Conditions of the Scottish Peasantry, by James Currie, M.D. Philadelphia: J. Locken, 1835.

The Works of Robert Burns. Containing His Life by John Lockhart, the Poetry and Correspondence of Dr, Currie's Edition, Biographical Sketches of the Poet by Himself, Gilbert Burns, Professor Stewart, and Others, Essay on Scottish Poetry, Including the Poetry of Burns, by Dr Currie, Burns's Songs, from Johnson's "Musical Museum, and "Thomson's Select Melodies", Select Scottish Songs of the Other Poets, from the Best Collections, with Burns's Remarks. Forming, in One Work, the Truest Exhibition of the Man and the Poet, and the Fullest Edition of His Poetry and Prose Writing Hitherto Published. New York: William Pearson, 1835.

The Works of Robert Burns. With an Account of His Life, and a Criticism on His Writings, To which are Prefixed, Some Observations on the Character and Conditions of the Scottish Peasantry, by James Currie, M.D. Including Additional Poems, Extracted from the Late Edition Edited by Allan Cunningham. Philadelphia: J. Crissy and Charles Desilver, 1835.

The Poetical Works of Robert Burns. With a Sketch of His Life, by James Currie, M.D, with Many Additional Poems and Songs, and an Enlarged and Corrected Glossary. In Two Volumes. New York: C. Wells, 1836.

The Works of Robert Burns. Containing His Life by John Lockhart, the Poetry and Correspondence of Dr, Currie's Edition, Biographical Sketches of the Poet by Himself, Gilbert Burns, Professor Stewart, and Others, Essay on Scottish Poetry, Including the Poetry of Burns, by Dr Currie, Burns's Songs, from Johnson's "Musical Museum, and "Thomson's Select Melodies", Select Scottish Songs of the Other Poets, from the Best Collections, with Burns's Remarks. Forming, in One Work, the Truest Exhibition of the Man and the Poet, and the Fullest Edition of His Poetry and Prose Writing Hitherto Published. New York: World Publishing House, 1836.

The Works of Robert Burns. Containing His Life by John Lockhart, the Poetry and Correspondence of Dr, Currie's Edition, Biographical Sketches of the Poet by Himself, Gilbert Burns, Professor Stewart, and Others, Essay on Scottish Poetry, Including the Poetry of Burns, by Dr Currie,

Burns's Songs, from Johnson's "Musical Museum, and "Thomson's Select Melodies", Select Scottish Songs of the Other Poets, from the Best Collections, with Burns's Remarks. Forming, in One Work, the Truest Exhibition of the Man and the Poet, and the Fullest Edition of His Poetry and Prose Writing Hitherto Published. Hartford: Judd Loomis and Co., 1836.

The Works of Robert Burns. With an Account of His Life, and a Criticism on His Writings, To which are Prefixed, Some Observations on the Character and Conditions of the Scottish Peasantry, by James Currie, M.D. Philadelphia: J. Crissy and J. Grigg, 1836.

The Works of Robert Burns. With an Account of His Life, and a Criticism on His Writings, To which are Prefixed, Some Observations on the Character and Conditions of the Scottish Peasantry, by James Currie, M.D. Including Additional Poems, Extracted from the Late Edition Edited by Allan Cunningham. Philadelphia: J. Crissy, 1837.

The Works of Robert Burns. Containing His Life by John Lockhart, the Poetry and Correspondence of Dr, Currie's Edition, Biographical Sketches of the Poet by Himself, Gilbert Burns, Professor Stewart, and Others, Essay on Scottish Poetry, Including the Poetry of Burns, by Dr Currie, Burns's Songs, from Johnson's "Musical Museum, and "Thomson's Select Melodies", Select Scottish Songs of the Other Poets, from the Best Collections, with Burns's Remarks. Forming, in One Work, the Truest Exhibition of the Man and the Poet, and the Fullest Edition of His Poetry and Prose Writing Hitherto Published. Hartford: Judd Loomis and Co., 1837.

The Works of Robert Burns. With an Account of His Life, and a Criticism on His Writings, To which are Prefixed, Some Observations on the Character and Conditions of the Scottish Peasantry, by James Currie, M.D. Including Additional Poems, Extracted from the Late Edition Edited by Allan Cunningham. Philadelphia: J. Crissy, 1838.

The Works of Robert Burns. Containing His Life by John Lockhart, the Poetry and Correspondence of Dr, Currie's Edition, Biographical Sketches of the Poet by Himself, Gilbert Burns, Professor Stewart, and Others, Essay on Scottish Poetry, Including the Poetry of Burns, by Dr Currie, Burns's Songs, from Johnson's "Musical Museum, and "Thomson's Select Melodies", Select Scottish Songs of the Other Poets, from the Best Collections, with Burns's Remarks. Forming, in One Work, the Truest Exhibition of the Man and the Poet, and the Fullest Edition of His Poetry and Prose Writing Hitherto Published. New York: Robinson & Franklin, 1839.

The Works of Robert Burns. With an Account of His Life, and a Criticism on His Writings, To which are Prefixed, Some Observations on the Character and Conditions of the Scottish Peasantry, by James Currie, M.D. Including Additional Poems, Extracted from the Late Edition Edited by Allan Cunningham. Philadelphia: J. Crissy, 1839.

The Life and Land of Burns by Allan Cunningham. With Contributions by Thomas Campbell ESQ. To which is Prefixed an Essay on The Genius and Writings of Burns, by Thomas Carlyle ESQ. New York: J. & H. G. Langely, 1841.

The Complete Poetical Works of Robert Burns. With Explanatory and Glossarial Notes; and a Life of the Author, by James Currie, Abridged. The First Complete American Edition. New York: D. Appleton & Co., 1842.

The Works of Robert Burns. With an Account of His Life, and a Criticism on His Writings, To which are Prefixed, Some Observations on the Character and Conditions of the Scottish Peasantry, by James Currie, M.D. Including Additional Poems, Extracted from the Late Edition Edited by Allan Cunningham. Philadelphia: J. Crissy, 1842.

Correspondence Between Burns and Clarinda. With a Memoir of Mrs. M'Lehose, (Clarinda.) Arranged and Edited by her Grandson, W.C. M'Lehose. New York: Robert P. Bixby & Co., 1843.

The Complete Poetical Works of Robert Burns. With Explanatory and Glossarial Notes, and a Life of the Author, by James Currie. The Second Complete American Edition. New York: D. Appleton & Co., 1843.

The Complete Poetical Works of Robert Burns. With Explanatory and Glossarial Notes, and a Life of the Author, by James Currie. The Second Complete American Edition. Philadelphia: George S. Appleton, 1843.

The Poetical Works of Robert Burns. With a Sketch of His Life, by James Currie, M.D, with Many Additional Poems and Songs, and an Enlarged and Corrected Glossary. In Two Volumes. New York: Edward Kearny, 1843.

The Works of Robert Burns. With an Account of His Life, and a Criticism on His Writings, To which are Prefixed, Some Observations on the Character and Conditions of the Scottish Peasantry, by James Currie, M.D. A New Edition, Four Volumes Complete in One, With Many Additional Poems and Songs, and an Enlarged and Corrected Glossary. Philadelphia: J. Locken, 1843.

Letters Addressed to Clarinda, &c. New York: 1843.*

The Complete Poetical Works of Robert Burns. With Explanatory and Glossarial Notes, and a Life of the Author, by James Currie. The Second Complete American Edition. New York: D. Appleton & Co., 1844.

The Works of Robert Burns. With an Account of His Life, and a Criticism on His Writings, To which are Prefixed, Some Observations on the Character and Conditions of the Scottish Peasantry, by James Currie, M.D. A New Edition, Four Volumes Complete in One, With Many Additional Poems and Songs, and an Enlarged and Corrected Glossary. Philadelphia: J. Locken, 1844.

The Works of Robert Burns. With an Account of His Life, and a Criticism on His Writings, To which are Prefixed, Some Observations on the Character and Conditions of the Scottish Peasantry, by James Currie, M.D. Including Additional Poems, Extracted from the Late Edition Edited by Allan Cunningham. Philadelphia: J. Crissy, 1845.

The Complete Poetical Works of Robert Burns. With Explanatory and Glossarial Notes; and a Life of the Author, by James Currie, Abridged. The Second Complete American Edition. New York: D. Appleton & Co., 1846.

The Works of Robert Burns. Containing His Life by John Lockhart, the Poetry and Correspondence of Dr, Currie's Edition, Biographical Sketches of the Poet by Himself, Gilbert Burns, Professor Stewart, and Others, Essay on Scottish Poetry, Including the Poetry of Burns, by Dr Currie, Burns's Songs, from Johnson's "Musical Museum, and "Thomson's Select Melodies", Select Scottish Songs of the Other Poets, from the Best Collections, with Burns's Remarks. Forming, in One Work, the Truest Exhibition of the Man and the Poet, and the Fullest Edition of His Poetry and Prose Writing Hitherto Published. Boston: Otis, Broaders, and Company, 1846.

The Poetical Works of Robert Burns. Including Several Pieces not Inserted in Dr. Currie's Edition, Exhibited Under a New Plan of Arrangement, and Preceded by a Life of the Author, and a Complete Glossary. In Two Volumes. Boston: Timothy Bedlington, 1846.

The Works of Robert Burns. With an Account of His Life, and a Criticism on His Writings, To which are Prefixed, Some Observations on the Character and Conditions of the Scottish Peasantry. Philadelphia: Henry F. Anners, 1846.

The Works of Robert Burns. With an Account of His Life, and a Criticism on His Writings, To which are Prefixed, Some Observations on the Character and Conditions of the Scottish Peasantry, by James Currie,

M.D. *Including Additional Poems, Extracted from the Late Edition Edited by Allan Cunningham.* Philadelphia: J. Crissy, 1846.

The Works of Robert Burns. With an Account of His Life, and a Criticism on His Writings, To which are Prefixed, Some Observations on the Character and Conditions of the Scottish Peasantry, by James Currie, M.D. A New Edition, Four Volumes Complete in One, With Many Additional Poems and Songs, and an Enlarged and Corrected Glossary. Philadelphia: J. Locken, 1846.

The Complete Poetical Works of Robert Burns. With Explanatory and Glossarial Notes, and a Life of the Author, by James Currie. The Second Complete American Edition. New York: D. Appleton & Co., 1847.

The Complete Poetical Works of Robert Burns. With Explanatory and Glossarial Notes, and a Life of the Author, by James Currie. The Second Complete American Edition. Philadelphia: George S. Appleton, 1847.

The Poetical Works of Robert Burns. With a Glossary and Life of The Author, By James Currie M.D. Including Additional Poems, Extracted from the Late Edition Edited by Allan Cunningham. Cincinnati: J.A. & U.P. James, 1847.

The Works of Robert Burns. Containing His Life by John Lockhart, the Poetry and Correspondence of Dr, Currie's Edition, Biographical Sketches of the Poet by Himself, Gilbert Burns, Professor Stewart, and Others, Essay on Scottish Poetry, Including the Poetry of Burns, by Dr Currie, Burns's Songs, from Johnson's "Musical Museum, and "Thomson's Select Melodies", Select Scottish Songs of the Other Poets, from the Best Collections, with Burns's Remarks. Forming, in One Work, the Truest Exhibition of the Man and the Poet, and the Fullest Edition of His Poetry and Prose Writing Hitherto Published. Boston: Otis, Broaders, and Company, 1847.

The Works of Robert Burns. With an Account of His Life, and a Criticism on His Writings, To which are Prefixed, Some Observations on the Character and Conditions of the Scottish Peasantry, by James Currie, M.D. Including additional poems extracted from the late edition of Allan Cunningham. Philadelphia: Crissy and Markley, 1847.

Robert Burns, As a Poet, And as a Man. By Samuel Tyler of the Maryland Bar. New York: Baker & Scribner, 1848.

The Poetical Works of Robert Burns. Including Several Pieces not Inserted in Dr. Currie's Edition, Exhibited Under a New Plan of Arrangement, and Preceded by a Life of the Author, and a Complete Glossary. Two Volumes in One. Boston: Phillips and Sampson, 1848.

The Works of Robert Burns. With an Account of His Life, and a Criticism on His Writings, To which are Prefixed, Some Observations on the Character and Conditions of the Scottish Peasantry, by James Currie, M.D. Including additional poems extracted from the late edition of Allan Cunningham. Philadelphia: Crissy and Markley, 1848.

The Complete Poetical Works of Robert Burns. With Explanatory and Glossarial Notes; and a Life of the Author, by James Currie, Abridged. The Only Complete American Edition. New York: D. Appleton & Co., 1849.

The Complete Poetical Works of Robert Burns. With Explanatory and Glossarial Notes, and a Life of the Author, by James Currie. The Second Complete American Edition. Philadelphia: George S. Appleton, 1849.

The Poetical Works of Robert Burns. With a Sketch of His Life, by James Currie, M.D, with Many Additional Poems and Songs, and an Enlarged and Corrected Glossary. In Two Volumes. [In One]. New York: Leavitt & Allen, 1849.

The Poetical Works of Robert Burns. With a Glossary and Life of The Author, By James Currie M.D. Including Additional Poems, Extracted from the Late Edition Edited by Allan Cunningham. Cincinnati: J.A. & U.P. James, 1849. *The Poetical Works of Robert Burns. Including Several Pieces not Inserted in Dr. Currie's Edition, Exhibited Under a New Plan of Arrangement, and Preceded by a Life of the Author, and a Complete Glossary. Two Volumes in One.* Boston: Phillips and Sampson, 1849.

The Works of Robert Burns. Containing His Life by John Lockhart, the Poetry and Correspondence of Dr, Currie's Edition, Biographical Sketches of the Poet by Himself, Gilbert Burns, Professor Stewart, and Others, Essay on Scottish Poetry, Including the Poetry of Burns, by Dr Currie, Burns's Songs, from Johnson's "Musical Museum, and "Thomson's Select Melodies", Select Scottish Songs of the Other Poets, from the Best Collections, with Burns's Remarks. Forming, in One Work, the Truest Exhibition of the Man and the Poet, and the Fullest Edition of His Poetry and Prose Writing Hitherto Published. New York: Leavitt, Trow & Co., 1849.

The Works of Robert Burns. With an Account of His Life, and a Criticism on His Writings, To which are Prefixed, Some Observations on the Character and Conditions of the Scottish Peasantry, by James Currie, M.D. Four Volumes Complete in One, with Many Additional Poems and Songs, and an Enlarged and Corrected Glossary. A New Edition—from the last London Edition. Philadelphia: J. Locken, 1849.

The Poetical Works of Robert Burns. Including Several Pieces Not Inserted in Dr. Currie's Edition, Exhibited Under a New Plan of Arrangement, and Preceded by a Life of the Author, and a Complete Glossary. Two Volumes in One. Boston: Phillips and Sampson, 1850.

The Works of Robert Burns. With an Account of His Life, and a Criticism on His Writings, To which are Prefixed, Some Observations on the Character and Conditions of the Scottish Peasantry, by James Currie, M.D. Including Additional Poems, Extracted from the Late Edition. Edited by Allan Cunningham. Philadelphia: Crissy & Markley, 1850.

The Complete Works of Robert Burns. Containing His Poems, Songs and Correspondence, with a New Life of the Poet and Notices, Critical and Biographical, by Alan Cunningham. Philadelphia: George S. Appleton, 1851.

The Complete Works of Robert Burns. Containing His Poems, Songs and Correspondence, with a New Life of the Poet and Notices, Critical and Biographical, by Alan Cunningham. New York: D. Appleton & Co., 1851.

The Works of Robert Burns. With an Account of His Life, and a Criticism on His Writings, To which are Prefixed, Some Observations on the Character and Conditions of the Scottish Peasantry, by James Currie, M.D. Including Additional Poems, Extracted from the Late Edition. Edited by Allan Cunningham. Philadelphia: Crissy & Markley, 1851.

The Complete Poetical Works of Robert Burns. With an Account of His Life. The only complete American Edition. Containing His poems, Songs and Correspondence, with a New Life of the Poet and Notices, Critical and Biographical, by Alan Cunningham. New York: D. Appleton & Co., 1852.

The Life and Works of Robert Burns. Edited by Robert Chambers. In four volumes. New York: Harper & Brothers, 1852.

The Poetical Works of Robert Burns. With a Sketch of His Life, by James Currie, M.D, with Many Additional Poems and Songs, and an Enlarged and Corrected Glossary. In Two Volumes. [In One]. New York: Leavitt & Allen, 1852.

The Poetical Works of Robert Burns. Including Several Pieces Not Inserted in Dr. Currie's Edition, Exhibited Under a New Plan of Arrangement, and Preceded by a Life of the Author, and a Complete Glossary. Two Volumes in One. Boston: Phillips and Sampson, 1852. *The Works of Robert Burns. Containing His Life by John Lockhart, the Poetry and Correspondence of Dr, Currie's Edition, Biographical Sketches of the Poet by Himself, Gilbert Burns, Professor Stewart, and Others, Essay on Scottish Poetry, Including the Poetry of Burns, by Dr Currie, Burns's Songs, from Johnson's "Musical Museum, and "Thomson's Select Melodies", Select Scottish Songs of the Other Poets, from the Best Collections, with Burns's Remarks. Forming, in One Work, the Truest Exhibition of the Man and the Poet, and the Fullest Edition of His Poetry and Prose Writing Hitherto Published.* New York: Leavitt & Allen, 1852.

The Complete Poetical Works of Robert Burns. With an Account of His Life. The only complete American Edition. Containing His poems, Songs and Correspondence, with a New Life of the Poet and Notices, Critical and Biographical, by Alan Cunningham. New York: D. Appleton & Co., 1853.

The Complete Works of Robert Burns, Containing His Poems, Songs and Correspondence, with a New Life of the Poet and Notices, Critical and Biographical, by Alan Cunningham. Boston: Phillips, Sampson, and Company, 1853.

The Poetical Works of Robert Burns. Including Several Pieces not Inserted in Dr. Currie's Edition, Exhibited Under a New Plan of Arrangement, and Preceded by a Life of the Author, and a Complete Glossary. Two Volumes in One. Boston: Phillips and Sampson, 1853.

The Works of Robert Burns. With an Account of His Life, and a Criticism on His Writings, To which are Prefixed, Some Observations on the Character and Conditions of the Scottish Peasantry, by James Currie, M.D. Including Additional Poems, Extracted from the Late Edition. Edited by Allan Cunningham. Cincinnati: J. A. & U. P. James, 1853.

The Works of Robert Burns. Containing His Life by John Lockhart, the Poetry and Correspondence of Dr, Currie's Edition, Biographical Sketches of the Poet by Himself, Gilbert Burns, Professor Stewart, and Others, Essay on Scottish Poetry, Including the Poetry of Burns, by Dr Currie, Burns's Songs, from Johnson's "Musical Museum, and "Thomson's Select Melodies", Select Scottish Songs of the Other Poets, from the Best Collections, with Burns's Remarks. Forming, in One Work, the Truest Exhibition of the Man and the Poet, and the Fullest Edition of His Poetry and Prose Writing Hitherto Published. New York: Leavitt & Allen, 1853.

The Complete Works of Robert Burns, Containing His Poems, Songs and Correspondence, with a New Life of the Poet and Notices, Critical and Biographical, by Alan Cunningham. Boston: Phillips, Sampson, and Company, 1854.

The Life and Works of Robert Burns. Edited by Robert Chambers. In four volumes. New York: Harper & Brothers, 1854.

The Life and Works of Robert Burns. In Four Volumes. Edited by Robert Chambers. Philadelphia: Lippincott, Grambo & Co., 1854.

The Poetical Works of Robert Burns. Including Several Pieces not Inserted in Dr. Currie's Edition, Exhibited Under a New Plan of Arrangement, and Preceded by a Life of the Author, and a Complete Glossary. Two Volumes in One. Boston: Phillips and Sampson, 1854.

The Complete Poetical Works of Robert Burns. With Explanatory and Glossarial Notes, and a Life of the Author, by James Currie, M.D. New York: D. Appleton & Co., 1855.

The Complete Works of Robert Burns. Containing His Poems, Songs and Correspondence, with a New Life of the Poet and Notices, Critical and Biographical, by Alan Cunningham. Boston: Phillips, Sampson, and Company, 1855.

The Complete Works of Robert Burns. Containing His Poems, Songs and Correspondence, with a New Life of the Poet and Notices, Critical and Biographical, by Alan Cunningham. New York: C Derby, 1855.

The Poetical Works of Robert Burns. With a Sketch of His Life, by James Currie, M.D, with Many Additional Poems and Songs, and an Enlarged and Corrected Glossary. In Two Volumes. [In One]. New York: Leavitt & Allen, 1855.

The Poetical Works of Robert Burns. With a Life of the Author, and an Essay on the Genius and Writings of Burns, by A. Cunningham, Esq., Carefully Revised, and Rendered Perfectly Intelligble to the General Reader by a Copious Glossary. New York: William H. Murphy, 1855.

The Poetical and Prose Works of Robert Burns. With life, notes and correspondence; by A. Cunningham, esq. With original pieces from the collection of Sir Egerton Brydges, bart. Hartford: William Jas. Hammersley, 1855.

The Complete Poetical Works of Robert Burns. With an Account of His Life. The only complete American Edition. Containing His poems, Songs and Correspondence, with a New Life of the Poet and Notices, Critical and Biographical, by Alan Cunningham. New York: D. Appleton & Co., 1856.

The Poetical Works of Robert Burns. Including Several Pieces not Inserted in Dr. Currie's Edition, Exhibited Under a New Plan of Arrangement, and Preceded by a Life of the Author, with Notes, and a Complete Glossary, Illustrated. Boston: Phillips, Sampson, and Company, 1856.

The Poetical Works of Robert Burns. With Life, Notes, and Glossary, by A. Cunningham, Esq., with Many Illustrations on Steel. Philadelphia: Willis P. Hazard, 1856.

The Complete Poetical Works of Robert Burns. With an Account of His Life. The only complete American Edition. Containing *His* Poems, Songs and Correspondence, with a New Life of the Poet and Notices, Critical and Biographical, by Alan Cunningham. New York: D. Appleton & Co., 1856.

The Complete Works of Robert Burns, Containing His Poems, Songs and Correspondence, with a New Life of the Poet and Notices, Critical and Biographical, by Alan Cunningham. Boston: Phillips, Sampson, and Company, 1857.

The Complete Poetical Works of Robert Burns. With Explanatory and Glossarial Notes, and a Life of the Author, by James Currie. The Only Complete American Edition. New York: D. Appleton & Co., 1857.

The Poetical Works of Robert Burns. With Life, Notes, and Glossary, by A. Cunningham, Esq., with Many Illustrations on Steel. Philadelphia: Willis P. Hazard, 1857.

The Poetical Works of Robert Burns. Including Several Pieces not Inserted in Dr. Currie's Edition, Exhibited Under a New Plan of Arrangement, and Preceded by a Life of the Author, with Notes, and a Complete Glossary, Illustrated. Boston: Phillips, Sampson, and Company, 1857.

The Poetical Works of Robert Burns. With Memoir, Critical Dissertation, and Explanatory Notes, by Rev. George Gilfillan. Complete Two Volumes in One. New York: D. Appleton & Co., 1857.

The Works of Robert Burns. With an Account of His Life, and a Criticism on His Writings, To which are Prefixed, Some Observations on the Character and Conditions of the Scottish Peasantry, by James Currie, M.D. Including Additional Poems, Extracted from the Late Edition. Edited by Allan Cunningham. Cincinnati: J. A. & U. P. James, 1857.

The Works of Robert Burns. Containing His Life by John Lockhart, the Poetry and Correspondence of Dr, Currie's Edition, Biographical Sketches of the Poet by Himself, Gilbert Burns, Professor Stewart, and Others, Essay on Scottish Poetry, Including the Poetry of Burns, by Dr Currie, Burns's Songs, from Johnson's "Musical Museum, and "Thomson's Select Melodies", Select Scottish Songs of the Other Poets, from the Best Collections, with Burns's Remarks. Forming, in One Work, the Truest Exhibition of the Man and the Poet, and the Fullest Edition of His Poetry and Prose Writing Hitherto Published. New York: Leavitt & Allen, 1857.

Poems and Songs of Robert Burns. Illustrated with Numerous Engravings. New York: D. Appleton & Co., 1858.

The Complete Works of Robert Burns, Containing His Poems, Songs and Correspondence, with a New Life of the Poet and Notices, Critical and Biographical, by Alan Cunningham. Boston: Phillips, Sampson, and Company, 1858.

The Complete Poetical Works of Robert Burns. With Explanatory and Glossarial Notes, and a Life of the Author, by James Currie, M.D. The Only Complete American Edition. New York: D. Appleton & Co., 1858.

The Poetical Works of Robert Burns. With Critical and Bibliographical Notices, by Allan Cunningham, and a Glossary. Elegantly illustrated by Schmolze. Philadelphia: E. H. Butler and Co., 1858.

The Poetical Works of Robert Burns. With a Sketch of His Life, by James Currie, M.D, with Many Additional Poems and Songs, and an Enlarged and Corrected Glossary. In Two Volumes. [In One] New York: Leavitt & Allen, 1858.

The Poetical Works of Robert Burns. With Critical and Biographical notes by Allan Cunningham. Philadelphia: E.H. Butler, 1858.

The Works of Robert Burns. With an Account of His Life, and a Criticism on His Writings, To which are Prefixed, Some Observations on the Character and Conditions of the Scottish Peasantry, by James Currie, M.D. Including Additional Poems, Extracted from the Late Edition. Edited by Allan Cunningham. Cincinnati: J. A. & U. P. James, 1858.

The Complete Poetical and Prose Works of Robert Burns. With Life and Correspondence by A. Cunningham, esq. With original pieces from the collection of Sir Egerton Brydges, bart. New York: S. A. Rollo & Co., 1859.

The Poetical Works of Robert Burns. Including Several Pieces not Inserted in Dr. Currie's Edition, Exhibited Under a New Plan of Arrangement, and Preceded by a Life of the Author, with Notes, and a Complete Glossary, Illustrated. Boston: Phillips, Sampson, and Company, 1859.

The Poetical Works of Robert Burns. With Life, Notes, and Glossary, by A. Cunningham, Esq., with Many Illustrations on Steel. Philadelphia: G.G Evans & Co., 1859.

The Complete Works of Robert Burns. Containing His Poems, Songs and Correspondence, with a new life of the poet, and notices, critical and biographical by Allan Cunningham, elegantly illustrated. Boston: Crosby, Nichols, Lee & Co., 1860.

The Life and Works of Robert Burns. Edited by Robert Chambers. New York: Harper & Brothers, 1860.

The Poetical Works of Robert Burns. With Life, Notes, and Glossary, by A. Cunningham, Esq., with Many Illustrations on Steel. Philadelphia: Jas. B. Smith & Co., 1860.

The Works of Robert Burns. Containing His Life by John Lockhart, the Poetry and Correspondence of Dr, Currie's Edition, Biographical Sketches of the Poet by Himself, Gilbert Burns, Professor Stewart, and Others, Essay on Scottish Poetry, Including the Poetry of Burns, by Dr Currie, Burns's Songs, from Johnson's "Musical Museum, and "Thomson's Select Melodies", Select Scottish Songs of the Other Poets. New York: Leavitt & Allen, 1860.

The Poetical Works of Robert Burns. Including Several Pieces not Inserted in Dr. Currie's Edition, Exhibited Under a New Plan of Arrangement, and Preceded by a Life of the Author, with Notes, and a Complete Glossary. Boston: Crosby, Nichols, Lee & Company, 1861.

The Poetical Works of Robert Burns. Including Several Pieces not Inserted in Dr. Currie's Edition, Exhibited Under a New Plan of Arrangement, and Preceded by a Life of the Author, with Notes, and a Complete Glossary. Boston: Crosby, Nichols, Lee & Company, 1863.

The Poetical Works of Robert Burns. With a Sketch of the Author's Life. Boston: Little, Brown and Company, 1863.

Tam o' Shanter and Souter Johnny: A Poem. Illustrated by Thomas Landseer. Philadelphia: Mass & Vogdes, 1864.

The Poetical Works of Robert Burns. With a Sketch of the Author's Life. Boston: Little, Brown and Company, 1864.

The Poetical Works of Robert Burns. Including Several Pieces not Inserted in Dr. Currie's Edition, Exhibited Under a New Plan of Arrangement, and Preceded by a Life of the Author, with Notes, and a Complete Glossary. Boston: Crosby, Nichols, Lee & Company, 1864.

The Poetical Works of Robert Burns. With Critical and Biographical References. Philadelphia: E.H Butler, 1864.

The Complete Poetical Works of Robert Burns. With an Original Memoir by William Gunnyon, with Portrait and Illustrations on Wood by Eminent Artists. 3rd edition. Philadelphia: J.B. Lippincoot & Co., 1865.

The Complete Poetical Works of Robert Burns. Containing His Poems, Songs and Correspondence, with a New Life of the Poet, and Notices, Critical and Biographical by Allan Cunningham. New York: Oliver S. Felt; Boston: Crosby & Ainsworth, 1865.

The Poetical Works of Robert Burns. With a Sketch of the Author's Life. Boston: Little, Brown and Company, 1865.

The Complete Poetical Works of Robert Burns. With Explanatory and Glossarial Notes, and a Life of the Author, by James Currie, M.D. The Only Complete American Edition. New York: D. Appleton & Co., 1865.

The Complete Poetical Works of Robert Burns. Containing His Poems, Songs and Correspondence, with a New Life of the Poet, and Notices, Critical and Biographical by Allan Cunningham. New York: Oliver S. Felt; Boston: Crosby & Ainsworth, 1866.

The Complete Poetical Works of Robert Burns. With an Original Memoir by William Gunnyon, with Portrait and Illustrations on Wood by Eminent Artists. Philadelphia: J.B. Lippincoot & Co., 1866.

The Complete Poetical Works of Robert Burns. With an Original Memoir by William Gunnyon, with Portrait and Illustrations on Wood by Eminent Artists. New York: American News Company, 1866.

The National Edition of The Works of Robert Burns. Comprising the Poems, Songs, and Letters, with the biographies of Currie and Lockhart, and a general introduction edited by William Wallace, illustrated with twenty-four-full-page plates. London; Paris; New York; Cassell, Petter, Galpin, 1866.

The Poetical Works of Robert Burns. Including Several Pieces not Inserted in Dr. Currie's Edition, Exhibited Under a New Plan of Arrangement, and Preceded by a Life of the Author, with Notes, and a Complete Glossary. Boston: Crosby & Ainsworth; New York: Oliver S. Felt, 1866.

The Poetical Works of Robert Burns. Edited by the Rev. Robert Aris Wilmott. Illustrated by John Gilbert. New Edition. London; New York: George Rutledge and Sons, 1866.

The Poems of Robert Burns & The Songs of Robert Burns. In Two Volumes. Boston: Ticknor & Fields, 1866.

NOTES

1. Patrick Scott, "'Not in Egerer"? (Some of) What We Still Don't Know about Burns Bibliography", *Studies in Scottish Literature* 43, no. 9 (2017): 313.
2. See Robert Burns, *Poems Chiefly in the Scottish Dialect, to which are added Scots Poems selected from the works of Robert Fergusson* (New York: J & A Maclean, 1788), 225.

3. For more on the "two settings" of the Edinburgh printing see Patrick Scott and Craig Lamont, "'Skinking" and "Stinking": The Printing and Proofing of Robert Burns's *Poems, Chiefly in the Scottish Dialect* (Edinburgh, 1787)', *Book Collector* 65, no. 4 (2016): 601–616.
4. Craig Lamont, "Towards a New Bibliography of Robert Burns", *Studies in Scottish Literature* 43, no. 9 (2017): 307.
5. J. W. Egerer, *A Bibliography of Robert Burns* (Edinburgh and London: Oliver and Boyd, 1964), 8.

Appendix B

Based on the checklist data in Appendix A, the following distribution maps chart the number of editions distributed per location in three different stages up to 1866. In cases where the same edition lists multiple publishers in different locations, I have counted them separately. For example, for the following entry, I have counted separate entries for Philadelphia, New York, Baltimore and Boston respectively:

Reliques of Robert Burns (Philadelphia and New York: Bradford and Inskeep, Baltimore: Coale and Thomas, Boston: Oliver C. Greenleaf, 1809.

© The Editor(s) (if applicable) and The Author(s), under exclusive license to Springer International Publishing AG, part of Springer Nature 2018
A. Sood, *Robert Burns and the United States of America*,
https://doi.org/10.1007/978-3-319-94445-6

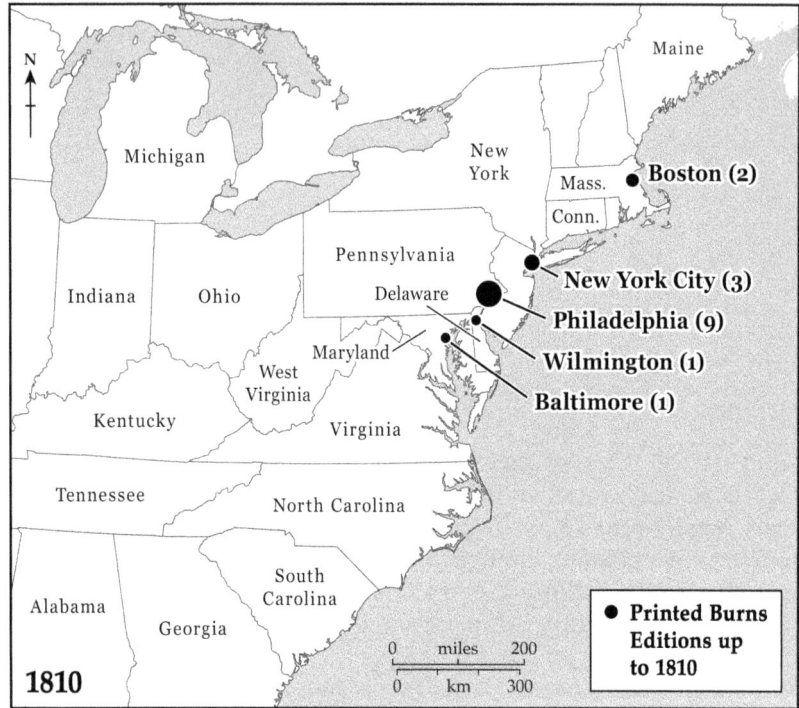

Fig. B.1 American Burns Editions by Location up to 1810

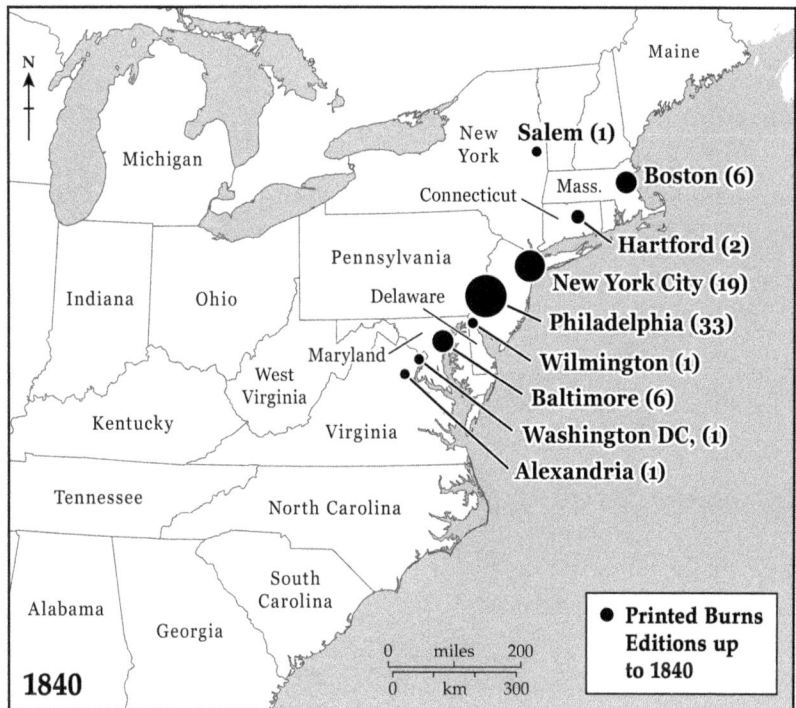

Fig. B.2   American Burns Editions by Location up to 1840

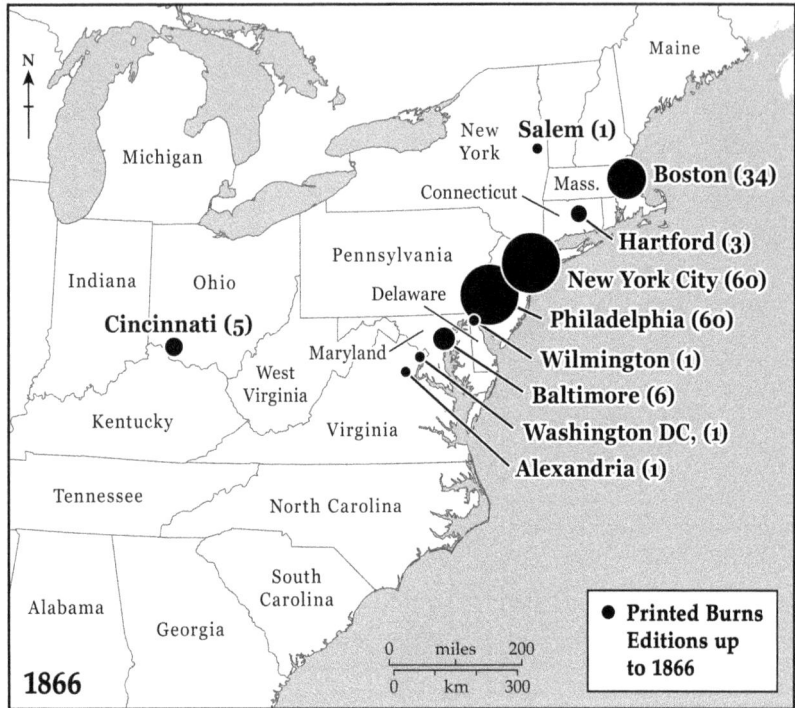

Fig. B.3   American Burns Editions by Location up to 1866

BIBLIOGRAPHY

Abel, Darrel, *Democratic Voices and Vistas: American Literature from Emerson to Lanier*. Lincoln: iUniverse, 2002.

"About Anti Slavery Bugle." Accessed 31 December 2015. http://chroniclingamerica.loc.gov/lccn/sn83035487/.

Albany Spectator, 12 December 1804.

Albertone, Manuela, *National Identity and the Agrarian Republic: The Transatlantic Commerce of Ideas Between America and France (1750–1830)*. Surrey and Burlington: Ashgate, 2014.

Alker, Sharon, and Holly Faith Nelson, "Transatlanticism and Beyond: Robert Burns and the World Wide Web." In *Robert Burns and Transatlantic Culture*, edited by Sharon Alker, Leith Davis and Holly Faith Nelson, 247–261. Farnham, Burlington: Ashgate, 2012.

Allmendinger Jr., David F, "New England Students and the Revolution in Higher Education, 1800–1900." *History of Education Quarterly* 11, no. 4 (1971): 381–389.

"The American Dialect Association." Accessed 20 September 2015. http://www.americandialect.org/.

"America's Historical Imprints, Series I." Accessed 29 November 2015. http://www.readex.com/content/early-american-imprints-series-i-evans-1639-1800.

The American Register: Or General Repository of History, Politics and Science 4, 1809.

The American Review of History and Politics, and General Repository of State Papers 1, 1811.

The American Review and Literary Journal 1, 1801.

"American Time Capsule: Three Centuries of Broadsides and Other Printed Ephemera." Accessed 31 January 2015. http://memory.loc.gov/cgibin/ampage?collId=rbpe&fileName=rbpe07/rbpe077/07701000/rbpe07701000.db&recNum=1&itemLink=r?ammem/rbpebib:@field(NUMBER+@band(rbpe+07701000))&linkText=0.

"Angelou on Burns." Accessed 2 January 2016. http://movingimage.nls.uk/film/7076.

Annan, Kofi, "Inaugural Robert Burns Memorial Lecture of 13 January 2004." Accessed 2 January 2016. http://www.un.org/press/en/2004/sgsm9112.doc.htm.

The Athenaeum 173, 1831.

The Aurora, January 1801.

Anderson, Benedict, *Imagined Communities: Reflections on the Origin and Spread of Nationalism [1983]*, Rev. 2nd ed. London, New York: Verso, 1991.

Anderson, John Jr., ed. *Catalogue of Manuscripts, Books and Autographs from the Library of the Late John Greenleaf Whittier*. New York: Taylor, 1903.

Andrews, Corey E. ""Almost the Same, But Not Quite": English Poetry by Eighteenth-Century Scots." *Eighteenth Century: Theory and Interpretation* 47, no. 1 (2006): 59–79.

———. ""Ev'ry Heart Can Feel": Scottish Poetic Responses to Slavery in the West Indies, from Blair to Burns." *International Journal of Scottish Literature* 4 (spring/summer, 2008). Accessed 7 January 2016. http://www.ijsl.stir.ac.uk/issue4/andrews.htm.

———. "The Genius of Scotland: Robert Burns and *His* Critics." *International Journal of Scottish Literature* no. 6 (2010): 1–16.

———. "Venders, Purchasers, Admirers: Burnsian "Men of Action" from the Nineteenth to the Twenty-First Century." *Scottish Literary Review* 2, no. 1 (2010): 97–115.

———. ""Far-fam'd RAB": Scottish Labouring-Class Poets Writing in the Shadow of Robert Burns, 1785–1792." *Studies in Hogg and His World* 23 (2013): 41–67.

———. *The Genius of Scotland: The Cultural Production of Robert Burns, 1785–1834*. Leiden and Boston: Brill and Rodopi, 2015.

Armenti, Peter, "Abraham Lincoln and Poetry." Accessed 24 January 2016. http://www.loc.gov/rr/program/bib/lincolnpoetry.

Aron, Cindy S., "The Evolution of the Middle Class." In *A Companion to 19th—Century America*, edited by William Barney, 178–195. Malden & Oxford: Blackwell, 2008.

Assmann, Jan, "Communicative and Cultural Memory." In *Cultural Memory Studies: An International and Interdisciplinary Handbook*, edited by Astrid Erill and Angsar Hunning, 109–118. Berlin, New York: De Gruyter, 2008.

Assmann, Jan, and John Czaplicka, "Collective Memory and Cultural Identity." *New German Critique* 65 (1995): 125–133.

Ballantine, James, ed. *Chronicle of the Hundredth Birthday of Robert Burns.* Edinburgh and London: A. Fullarton & Co., 1859.

Bambery, Chris, "How Would Robert Burns Vote in the Scottish Referendum." Accessed 10 September 2015. http://www.theguardian.com/commentisfree/2014/jul/23/robert-burns-vote-scottish-referendum-identity.

Bannet, Eve Tavor and Susan Manning, eds. *Transatlantic Literary Studies, 1660–1830.* Cambridge: Cambridge University Press, 2011.

Bailyn, Bernard, ed. *The Debate on the Constitution: Federalist and Antifederalist Speeches, Articles, and Letters During the Struggle over Ratification.* New York: The Library of America, 1993.

Baranuik, Carol, *James Orr: Poet and Irish Radical.* London: Routledge, 2014.

Barger, M. Susan and William B. White, *The Daguerreotype: Nineteenth Century Technology and Modern Science.* Baltimore: John Hopkins University Press, 2000.

Barney, William, ed. *A Companion to 19th—Century America.* Malden & Oxford: Blackwell, 2008.

Bayly, Christopher Alan, *Imperial Meridian: The British Empire and the world, 1780–1830.* London: Longman, 1989.

Beach, Christopher, *The Cambridge Introduction to Twentieth-Century American Poetry.* Cambridge: Cambridge University Press, 2003.

Bell, Eleanor and Gavin Miller, eds. *Scotland in Theory.* Amsterdam: Rodopi, 2004.

Bell, Ternece, ed. *The Federalist: With Letters of Brutus.* Cambridge: Cambridge University Press, 2003.

Beveridge, Albert J., *Abraham Lincoln,* 2 Vols. Boston: Houghton Mifflin, 1928.

Blair, Kirsty and Mina Gorji, *Class and the Canon: Constructing Labouring-Class Poetry and Poetics, 1780–1900.* London: Palgrave Macmillan, 2012.

Blassingame, John, ed. *The Frederick Douglass Papers,* vol. 5. New Haven: Yale University Press, 1979.

Bloomfield, Robert, *The Farmer's Boy, A Rural Poem by Robert Bloomfield.* Baltimore: Thomas, Andrews & Butler, 1803.

Bold, Valentina, "Janet Little "the Scotch Milkmaid" and "Peasant Poetry,"" *Scottish Literary Journal* 20, no. 2 (1993): 21–30.

———. "Inmate of the Hamlet: Burns as Peasant Poet." In *Love and Liberty: A Bicentenary Celebration,* edited by Kenneth Simpson, 43–52. East Lothian: Tuckwell Press, 1997.

Boggs, Colleen Glenney, "Transatlantic Romanticisms." In *Transatlantic Literary Studies 1660–1830,* edited by Eve Tavor Bannet and Susan Manning, 219–238. Cambridge: Cambridge University Press, 2011.

Bourdieu, Pierre, *The Field of Cultural Production: Essays on Art and Literature*. New York: Columbia University Press, 1993.

The British Critic 10, 1818.

Brown, Charles Brockden, *Memoirs of Charles Brockden Brown, the American Novelist, Author of Weiland*, edited by William Dunlap. London: Henry Colburn, 1822.

Brown, Nikki, ""Send Back the Money!" Frederick Douglass's Anti-Slavery Speeches in Scotland and the Emergence of African American Internationalism." Accessed 2 January 2016. http://www.iash.ed.ac.uk/star/archive/Papers/Brown_Douglass.

Brown, Rhona, "Robert Burns and Robert Fergusson." In *The Edinburgh Companion to Robert Burns*, edited by Gerard Carruthers, 86–97. Edinburgh: Edinburgh University Press, 2009.

———. "Allan Ramsay, Robert Fergusson and Robert Burns." In *Burns and Other Poets*, edited by Fiona Stafford and David Sergeant, 22–38. Edinburgh: Edinburgh University Press, 2012.

———. ""Guid Black Prent": Robert Burns and the Contemporary Scottish and American Periodical Press." In *Robert Burns and Transatlantic Culture*, edited by Sharon Alker, Leith Davis and Holly Faith Nelson, 71–87. Farnham, Burlington: Ashgate, 2012.

———. *Robert Fergusson and The Scottish Periodical Press*. Farnham: Ashgate, 2012.

Brown, Stephen and Warren McDougall, eds. *The Edinburgh History of the Book in Scotland Volume 2: Enlightenment and Expansion 1707–1800*. Edinburgh: Edinburgh University Press, 2007.

Bryant, William Cullen, *A History of the Celebration of Robert Burns's 110th Natal Day, at the Metropolitan Hotel, New York*. Jersey City: John H. Lyon, 1869.

Bryant II, William Cullen, "The Genesis of "Thanatopsis,"" *The New England Quarterly* 21, no. 2 (1948): 163–184.

Bryers, Chris, "Augustan American Verse." In *The Oxford Handbook of Early American Literature*, edited by Kevin J. Hayes, 189–215. New York: Oxford University Press Inc., 2008.

Bruce, David, *Poems Chiefly in the Scottish Dialect, Originally Written Under the Signature of the Scots-Irishman, By a Native of Scotland*. Washington: John Colerick, 1801.

Buchan, Earl of, "Letter to Robert Burns [1 February 1787]." Digitised MS Accessed 20 November 2015. http://www.burnsscotland.com/items/l/letter-addressed-to-robert-burns.aspx.

Bueltmann, Tanja, *Clubbing Together: Ethnicity, Civility and Formal Sociability in the Scottish Diaspora to 1930*. Liverpool University Press, 2014.

Burke, Tim, "Labour, Education and Genius." In *Fickle Man: Robert Burns in the 21st Century*, edited by Johnny Rodger and Gerard Carruthers, 13–24. Dingwall: Sandstone Press, 2009.

Burns, Robert, *Poems, Chiefly in The Scottish Dialect*. Edinburgh: William Creech, 1787. Note: For a full bibliographic record of the American Burns editions referenced in this book, see Appendix A.

Calder, Jenni, *Scots in the USA*. Edinburgh: Luath Press ltd, 2014.

Carlyle, Thomas, *On Heroes, Hero-Worship and the Heroic in History*. London: Chapman and Hall, 1840.

Carruthers, Gerard, *Robert Burns*. Tavistock: Northcote House, 2005.

———. "Robert Burns and Slavery." In *Fickle Man: Robert Burns in the 21st Century*, edited by Johnny Rodger and Gerard Carruthers, 163–176. Dingwall: Sandstone Press, 2009.

———. *Scottish Literature*. Edinburgh: Edinburgh University Press, 2009.

———. ed. *The Edinburgh Companion to Robert Burns*. Edinburgh: Edinburgh University Press, 2009.

———. "Burns and Ireland." *International Journal of Scottish Literature* 6 (Spring/Summer, 2010). http://www.ijsl.stir.ac.uk/issue6/carruthers.pdf. Accessed 21 March 2017.

———. "Burns's Political Reputation in North America." In *Robert Burns and Transatlantic Culture*, edited by Sharon Alker, Leith Davis and Holly Faith Nelson, 87–99. Farnham, Burlington: Ashgate, 2012.

———. "The Myth-Eaten Corpse of Robert Burns." Accessed 20 September 2015. http://blog.oup.com/2015/01/robert-burns-appropriation/.

———. "In Search of Highland Mary." Accessed 7 January 2016. http://www.electricscotland.com/familytree/frank/burns_lives128.htm.

Carruthers, Gerard, David Goldie, and Alistair Renfrew, eds. *Beyond Scotland: New Contexts for Twentieth-Century Scottish Literature*. Amsterdam: Rodopi, 2004.

Carruthers, Gerard, and Norman R. Paton, "Did Robert Burns Write The Tree of Liberty." In *Fickle Man: Robert Burns in the 21st Century*, edited by Johnny Rodger and Gerard Carruthers, 242–257. Dingwall: Sandstone Press, 2009.

Carruthers, Gerard and Pauline Mackay, "Re-reading James Currie; Robert Burns's First Editor." *John Clare Society Journal* 32 (2013): 73–84.

Carruthers, Mary, *The Book of Memory: A Study of Memory in Medieval Culture*. Cambridge: Cambridge University Press, 2008.

Carter, Nathaniel Hazeltine, *Letters from Europe, Comprising the Journal of a Tour Through Ireland, England, Scotland, France, Italy, and Switzerland in the years 1825, '26, and '27*. New York: G & C. & H. Carvill, 1829.

Celebration of the Hundredth Anniversary of the Birth of Robert Burns, By the Boston Burns club. January 25th, 1859. Boston: H.W. Dutton and son, 1859.

Charleston Mercury, 30 October 1860.

Commercial Advertiser, 8 December 1804.

Clair, William St., "Publishing, Authorship and Reading." In *The Cambridge Companion to Fiction in the Romantic Period*, edited by Richard Maxwell and Katie Trumpener, 23–46. Cambridge: Cambridge University Press, 2008.

Clark, David Lee, *Charles Brockden Brown: Pioneer Voice of America*. Durham: Duke University Press, 1952.

Classen, Albert, ed. *Rural Space in the Middle Ages and Early Modern Age: The Spatial Turn in Premodern Studies*. Berlin & Boston: De Gruyter, 2012.

Classen, Albert, and Connie Scarborough, eds. *Crime and Punishment in the Middle Ages and Early Modern Age: Mental-Historical Investigations of Basic Human Problems and Social Responses*. Berlin & Boston: De Gruyter, 2012.

"Collection Highlight: Robert Burns and Frederick Douglass." Accessed 2 January 2016. http://rbscp.lib.rochester.edu/4646.

Colwell, Mary, *John Muir: The Scotsman Who Saved America's Wild Places*. Oxford: Lion Books, 2014.

The Connecticut Gazette, 28 April 1775.

Corse, Sarah M., *Nationalism and Literature: The Politics of Culture in Canada and the United States*. Cambridge: Cambridge University Press, 1997.

Craig, David, *Scottish Literature and the Scottish People*. London: Chatto & Windus, 1961.

Crawford, Robert, *Devolving English Literature*. Edinburgh: Edinburgh University Press, 2000.

———. *The Bard: Robert Burns, A Biography*. London: Pimlico, 2009.

———. "America's Bard." In *Robert Burns and Transatlantic Culture*, edited by Sharon Alker, Leith Davis and Holly Faith Nelson, 99–117. Farnham, Burlington: Ashgate, 2012.

Crawford, Robert, ed. *Robert Burns and Cultural Authority*. Iowa City: University of Iowa Press, 1997.

Crawford, Thomas, *Burns: A Study of The Poems and Songs*. Stanford: Stanford University Press, 1960.

Cromek, R.H., ed. *Reliques of Robert Burns*. London: T. Cadell and Davies, 1808.

Crowley, John W., "James Russell Lowell's The Biglow Papers [First Series]: A Critical," (Review) *The New England Quarterly* 51, no. 2 (1978): 279–281.

Cumming, Mark, *The Carlyle Encyclopedia*. Madison: Farleigh Dickinson University Press, 2004.

Currie, James, ed. *The Works of Robert Burns; With an Account of His Life, and a Criticism on His Writings*, 4 Vols. J.M'creery, 1800.

Currie, James, "James Currie to Cadell and Davies, 7 Dec, 1797." Accessed 5 April 2016. http://jamescurrie.gla.ac.uk/details.php?id=55.

Currie, William Wallace, ed. *Memoir of The Life and Writings, and Correspondence of James Currie, M.D. F.R.S. of Liverpool*, 2 Vols. London: Longman, Rees, Orme, Brown and Green, 1831.

Cushman, Stephen, Clare Cavanagh, Jahan Ramazani, and Paul Rouzer, eds. *The Princeton Encyclopedia of Poetry and Poetics*. Princeton: Princeton University Press, 2012.

The Daily Dispatch, 4 November 1852.

———. 4 February 1853.

———. 15 October 1856.

———. 24 December 1859.

Davis, Leith, "Burns and Transnational Culture." In *The Edinburgh Companion to Robert Burns*, 150–163. Edinburgh: Edinburgh University Press, 2009.

———. "The Robert Burns 1859 Centenary: Mapping Transatlantic (Dis) location." In *Robert Burns and Transatlantic Culture*, edited by Sharon Alker, Leith Davis and Holly Faith Nelson, 187–209. Farnham, Burlington: Ashgate, 2012.

———. "James Currie's *Works of Robert Burns*: The Politics of Hypochondriasis." *Studies in Romanticism* 36, no. 1 (Spring, 1997): 46.

———. "Negotiating Cultural Memory: James Currie's *Works of Robert Burns*." Accessed 1 May 2016. http://www.ijsl.stir.ac.uk/issue6/davis.htm.

Darsey, James, *Prophetic Tradition and Radical Rhetoric in America*. New York: New York University Press, 1999.

"Database of Public Memorials to Robert Burns Worldwide." Accessed 30 December 2015. http://www.robertburnsmemorials.arts.gla.ac.uk/details.php?ID=8.

"David Bruce, American Poet." Accessed 29 December 2015. http://www.ulsterscotslanguage.com/en/texts/biography/david-bruce-ulster-scot-american-poet/.

Devine, T.M., *The Tobacco Lords: A Study of the Tobacco Merchants of Glasgow and Their Trading Activities*. Edinburgh: John Donald Publishers Ltd., 1975.

———. *Scotland's Empire 1600–1815*. London: Allen Lane, 2003.

Dickinson, Harry T., *British Pamphlets on The American Revolution, 1763–1785*. London: Pickering & Chatto, 2008.

"The Dictionary of Scots Language." Accessed 27 December 2015. http://www.dsl.ac.uk.

Dillon, Sarah, *The Palimpsest: Literature, Criticism, Theory*. London: Continuum, 2007.

Dinsmoor, Robert, *Incidental Poems: Accompanied with Letters…Together with a Preface, and Sketch of the Author's Life (Written By Himself)*. Haverhill: A. W. Thayer, 1828.

Dimock, Wai Chee, "Literature and The Planet." *Publications of the Modern Language Association of America* 116, no. 1 (2001): 173–188.

———. *Through Other Continents: American Literature Across Deep Time*. Princeton: Princeton University Press, 2008.

Dobson, David, *Scottish Emigration to Colonial America, 1607–1785*. Georgia: University of Georgia Press, 2004.

Douglas, David, ed. *The Journal of Sir Walter Scott*. 2 Vols. Edinburgh: David Douglas, 1890.

Douglass, Frederick, "Why Should A Colored Man Enlist?" Accessed 2 January 2016. http://rbscp.lib.rochester.edu/4396.

Doyle, Laura, "Notes Toward a Dialectical Method: Modernities, Modernisms, and the Crossings of Empire." *Literature Compass* 7, no. 3 (2010): 195–293.

Du Rant, Joseph, "Burns North and South, in mid 19th C American Newspapers." *The Burns Chronicle* (2016): 26–33.

Durey, Michael, *Transatlantic Radicals and the Early American Republic*. Lawrence: University Press of Kansas, 1997.

Dwight, John Sullivan, ed. *Select Minor Poems: Translated from the German of Goethe and Schiller*. Boston: Hilliard, Gray, and Company, 1839.

Dziennik, Matthew P., *The Fatal Land: War, Empire and the Highland Soldier in British America*. New Haven: Yale University Press, 2015.

The Edinburgh Review 33, 1820.

———. 96, 1828.

"Editing Robert Burns for the Twenty-First Century." Accessed 11 September 2015. http://burnsc21.glasgow.ac.uk/.

Edwards, Owen Dudley and George Shepperson, eds. *Scotland, Europe and the American Revolution*. London: Polygon, 1976.

"Edward Rushton, Blind Eye Witness." Accessed 28 December 2015. http://manuscriptsandmore.liv.ac.uk/?tag=edward-rushton.

Egerer, J.W., *A Bibliography of Robert Burns*. Edinburgh and London: Oliver and Boyd, 1964.

Eisner, Eric, *Nineteenth-Century Poetry and Literary Celebrity*. London: Palgrave Macmillan, 2009.

Enkvist, Nils Erik, "The Biglow Papers in Nineteenth-Century England." *The New England Quarterly* 26, no. 2 (1953): 219–236.

Erill, Astrid, and Angsar Hunning, eds. *Cultural Memory Studies: An International and Interdisciplinary Handbook*. Berlin, New York: De Gruyter, 2008.

———. *A Companion to Cultural Memory Studies*. Berlin: De Gruyter, 2010.

Estes, Dana, ed. *Among the Birds: Selections from the Standard Poets*. Boston: Dana Estes, 2009.

Farmer's Museum, or, Literary Gazette 8, no. 400, 1800.

"Federalism and The Tenth Amendment." Accessed 2 January 2016. https://www.gop.com/platform/we-the-people/.

Ferguson, J. DeLancey, "New Light on the Burns-Dunlop Estrangement." *Publication of the Modern Language Association (PMLA)* 44, no. 4 (1929): 1106–1115.

———. "In Defense of R.H. Cromek." *Philological Quarterly* 9 (1930): 239–248.

———. "The Earliest Obituary of Burns: Its Authorship and Influence." *Modern Philology* 32, no. 2 (1934): 179–184.

Ferguson, J. De Lancey, ed. *The Letters of Robert Burns*, 2 Vols. Oxford: Clarendon Press, 1931.

Ferguson, Frank, ed. *Ulster-Scots Writing: An Anthology*. Dublin: Four Courts Press, 2008.

Ferguson, Frank and Andrew R. Holmes, eds. *Revising Robert Burns and Ulster: Literature, Religion and Politics, c. 1770–1920*. Dublin: Four Courts Press, 2009.

Ferguson, Frank, and McReynolds, Alister, eds. *Robert Dinsmoor's Scotch-Irish Poems*. Belfast: Ulster Historical Foundation, 2012.

Friend, Craig Thompson and Lorri Glover, eds. *Southern Manhood: Perspectives on Masculinity in the Old South*. Athens: University of Georgia Press, 2004.

Garrett, Franklin M., *Atlanta and Environs: A Chronicle of Its People and Events, 1880s–1930s*. Athens: University of Georgia Press, 2010.

Garside, Peter, Peter Horfsall, and Richard D. Jackson, eds. *James Hogg, The Forest Minstrel* [1810]. Edinburgh: Edinburgh University Press, 2006.

Giles, Paul, *Virtual Americas: Transnational Fictions and the Transatlantic Imaginary*. Durham: Duke University Press, 2002.

———, ""To Gird this Watery Globe": Freneau, Barlow and American Neoclassical Poetry." In *Transatlantic Literary Studies, 1660–1830*, edited by Eve Tavor Bannet and Susan Manning, 139–153. Cambridge: Cambridge University Press, 2011.

Gilman, William H., and J.E. Parsons, eds. *The Journals and Miscellaneous Notebooks of Ralph Waldo Emerson*, 8 Vols. Cambridge, MA: Harvard University Press, 1970.

Glasgow Advertiser and Evening Intelligencer, 23 April 1792.

The Glasgow Magazine and Review 1, 1783.

"The Global Burns Network." Accessed 11 September 2015. http://www.gla.ac.uk/schools/critical/research/researchcentresandnetworks/globalburnsnetwork/.

Gitlin, Martin, *The Ku Klux Klan: A Guide to an American Sub-culture*. California: ABC-CLIO, 2009.

Goodman, Susan, *Republic of Words: The Atlantic Monthly and Its Writers, 1857–1925*. Hanover & London: University Press of New England, 2011.

Gordon, Sarah, "Rural and Agricultural Space in the Old French *Fabliaux* and the *Roman de Renart*." In *Rural Space in the Middle Ages and Early Modern*

Age: The Spatial Turn in Premodern Studies, edited by Albert Classen, 281–295. Berlin & Boston: De Gruyter, 2012.

Gould, Eliga H. and Peter S. Onuf, eds. *Empire and Nation: The American Revolution in the Atlantic World*. Baltimore: John Hopkin University Press, 2005.

Gray, Pauline Anne, "Prudes, Pirates and Bills of Suspension: The Correspondence of Burns and Clarinda." *The Burns Chronicle* (2005): 9–13.

Greene, Jack P., and Philip D. Morgan, eds. *Atlantic History: A Critical Appraisal* Oxford: Oxford University Press, 2008.

Griffin, Patrick, "The People with No Name: Ulster's Migrants and Identity in Formation in Eighteenth-Century Pennsylvania." *The William and Mary Quarterly* 58, no. 3 (2001): 587–614.

Gruesz, Kirsten Silva, *Ambassadors of Culture: The Transamerican Origins of Latino Writing*. Princeton: Princeton University Press, 2002.

Halbwachs, Maurice, *La mémoire Collective*. Paris: Presses Universitaires de France, 1950.

Haralson, Eric L., ed. *Encyclopedia of American Poetry: The Nineteenth Century*. London: Routledge, 2014.

Harder, Jayne Crane, "James Russell Lowell: Linguistic Patriot." *American Speech* 29, no. 3 (1954): 181–186.

Harvardinia 4, 1838.

Harvey, Samantha, *Transatlantic Transcendentalism: Coleridge, Emerson and Nature*. Edinburgh: Edinburgh University Press, 2013.

Hastings, Adam, *The Construction of Nationhood*. Cambridge: Cambridge University Press, 1997.

Haupt, Paul, "Alcohol In The Bible." *Journal of Biblical Literature* 36, nos. 1/2 (1917): 75–83.

Hayes, Kevin J., ed. *The Oxford Handbook of Early American Literature*. New York: Oxford University Press Inc., 2008.

Hemingway, Andrew, and Alan Wallach, eds. *Transatlantic Romanticism: British and American art and Literature, 1790/1860*. Amherst: University of Massachusetts Press, 2015.

Hill, Darper, ed., *The Satirical Etchings of James Gillray*. Mineola: Dover, 1976.

"The Historical Thesaurus of English of the Oxford English Dictionary." Accessed 27 December 2015. http://historicalthesaurus.arts.gla.ac.uk.

Hook, Andrew, *Scotland and America: A Study of Cultural Relations, 1750–1835*. Glasgow: Blackie, 1975.

———. "Scotland and America Revisited." In Owen Dudley Edwards and George Shepperson, eds. *Scotland, Europe and the American Revolution*, 83–88. London: Polygon, 1976.

———. "Philadelphia, Edinburgh and the Scottish Enlightenment." In *Scotland and America in the Age of the Enlightenment*, edited by Richard B. Sher and Jeffrey R. Smitten, 230–236. Edinburgh: Edinburgh University Press, 1990.

———. *From Goosecreek to Gandercleugh: Studies in Scottish-American Literary and Cultural History.* East Linton: Tuckwell Press, 1999.

———. "Troubling Times in the Scottish-American Relationship." In *Transatlantic Scots,* edited by Celeste Ray, 215–231. Tuscaloosa: University of Alabama Press, 2005.

———. "Down with that Flag." Accessed 2 January 2016. http://www.scottishreview.net/AHook148.html.

Hovey, Esther, "Burns' Songs American Connection." *The Burns Chronicle* (2001): 13–21.

Hovey, Serge, "The Retrieval and Performance of The Songs of Robert Burns." Undated Typewritten Document Retrieved from The University of Mississippi.

Hutton, Patrick, *History as an Art of Memory.* Hanover & London: University Press of New England, 1993.

———. "Sigmund Freud and Maurice Halbwachs: The Problem of Memory in Historical Psychology." *The History Teacher* 27, no. 2 (1994): 148–149.

Hunter, Clark, ed. *The Life and Letters of Alexander Wilson.* Philadelphia: The American Philosophical Society, 1983. *The Independent Journal,* 29 August 1787.

Ireland, Alexander, ed. *Ralph Waldo Emerson: His Life, Genius, And Writings.* London: Simpkin, Marshall, & Co., 1882.

Jay, Paul, *Global Matters: The Transnational Turn in Literary Studies.* Ithaca: Cornell University Press, 2010.

Jarrett, Gene Andrew, and Morgan, Thomas Lewis, eds. *The Complete Stories of Paul Laurence Dunbar.* Ohio: Ohio University Press, 2005.

"Jefferson and Liberty." Accessed 6 December 2015. http://www.folkways.si.edu/oscar-brand/for-jefferson-and-liberty-thomas-jefferson/childrens-historical-song/music/track/smithsonian.

Jefferson, Thomas, "Letter to W. S. Smith [13 November 1787]." http://www.loc.gov/exhibits/jefferson/105.html.

Jernegan, Marcus W, "Compulsory Education in the American Colonies: I. New England." *The School Review* 26, no. 10 (1918): 732–733.

Johnston, Francis, and William Hamilton, eds. *The Washingtoniana: Containing a Sketch of the Life and Death of the Late Gen. George Washington, with a Collection of Elegant Eulogies, Orations, Poems, & c., Sacred to His Memory.* Lancaster: William Hamilton, 1802.

Jung, C.G., *Memories, Dreams, Reflections [1962],* edited by Aniela Jaffe, translated by Richard Winston and Clara Winston. New York: Pantheon Books, 1973.

Jung, Sandro, ed. *Experiments in Genre in Eighteenth-Century Literature.* Ghent: Academic Scientific, 2011.

Kaestle, Carl F., "The History of Literacy and The History of Reading." In *Perspectives on Literacy: Civic Engagement and Service Learning Collection,* edited by Eugene R. Kingten, Barry M. Kroll and Mike Rose, 95–126. Carbondale: Southern Illinois University Press, 1988.

Kanter, James, "E.U. Nations Urged to Accept 160,000 Migrants." Accessed 11 September 2015. http://www.nytimes.com/2015/09/10/world/europe/europe-migrant-crisis-jean-claude-juncker.html?_r=0.

Kaplan, Fred, *Lincoln: The Biography of a Writer*. New York: Harper Collins, 2008, 49–86.

Katula, Richard A., *The Eloquence of Edward Everett: America's Greatest Orator*. New York: Peter Lang Publishing Inc., 2010.

Keating, Michael, *Nations Against the State: The New Politics of Nationalism in Quebec, Catalonia and Scotland*. Basingstoke: Macmillan, 1996.

Keith, Thomas, "Burns Statues—North America." *The Burns Chronicle* (2001): 71–84.

Kempshall, Matthew, *Rhetoric and the Writing of History*. Manchester: Manchester University Press, 2011.

Kerkering, John D., *The Poetics of National and Racial Identity in Nineteenth-Century American Literature*. Cambridge: Cambridge University Press, 2003.

Kidd, Colin, "Scottish Independence: Literature and Nationalism." Accessed 10 September 2015. http://www.theguardian.com/books/2014/jul/19/scottish-independence-literature-nationalism.

Killheffer, Marie, "A Comparison of the Dialect of "The Biglow Papers" with the Dialect of Four Yankee Plays." *American Speech* 3, no. 3 (1928): 222–236.

Kingten, Eugene R., Barry M. Kroll, and Mike Rose, *Perspectives on Literacy: Civic Engagement and Service Learning Collection*. Carbondale: Southern Illinois University Press, 1988.

Kinsley, James, ed. *The Poems and Songs of Robert Burns*, 3 Vols. Oxford: Clarendon Press, 1968.

The Knickerbocker, 2 August 1833.

Kovecses, Zoltan, *American English: An Introduction*. Peterborough: Broadview Press, 2000.

Lamont, Craig, "Towards a New Bibliography of Robert Burns." *Studies in Scottish Literature* 43, no. 9 (2017): 303–308.

"Labouring Class Poets Online Blog." Accessed 15 December 2015. https://lcpoets.wordpress.com/.

"Labouring Class Poets Online Database." Accessed 15 December 2015. https://laboringclasspoetsonline.omeka.net/.

LaFantasie, Glenn W., *Gettysburg Requiem: The Life and Lost causes of Confederate Colonel William C. Oates*. Oxford: Oxford University Press, 2006.

LaRocca, David, ed. *Estimating Emerson: An Anthology of Criticism from Carlyle to Cavell*. New York and London: Bloomsbury, 2013.

Laslett, Peter, ed. *John Locke, Two Treatises of Government [1689]*. Cambridge: Cambridge University Press, 2005.

Laver, Harry S., "Refuge of Manhood: Masculinity and the Militia Experience." In *Southern Manhood: Perspectives on Masculinity in the Old South*, edited by Craig Thompson Friend and Lorri Glover, 1–2. Athens: University of Georgia Press, 2004.

Leask, Nigel, "Irish Republicans and Gothic Eleutherarchs: Pacific Utopias in the Writings of Theobald Wolfe Tone and Charles Brocken Brown." *The Huntington Library Quarterly* 63, no. 3 (2000): 347–367.

———. "Burns and the Poetics of Abolition." In *The Edinburgh Companion to Robert Burns*, edited by Gerard Carruthers, 47–61. Edinburgh: Edinburgh University Press, 2009.

———. *Robert Burns and Pastoral: Poetry and Improvement in Late Eighteenth-Century Scotland*. Oxford: Oxford University Press, 2010.

———. ""Their Grove o' Sweet Myrtles": Robert Burns and the Scottish Colonial Experience." In *Robert Burns in Global Culture*, edited by Murray Pittock, 172–189. Lewisburg: Bucknell University Press, 2011.

———. "Was Burns a Labouring Class Poet?" In *Class and the Canon: Constructing Labouring-Class Poetry and Poetics, 1780–1900*, edited by Kirsty Blair and Mina Gorji, 6–33. London: Palgrave Macmillan, 2012.

———. ed. *The Oxford Edition of The Works of Robert Burns Volume I: Commonplace Books, Tour Journals, and Miscellaneous Prose*. Oxford: Oxford University Press, 2014.

Lentricchia, Frank, *Modernist Quartet*. Cambridge: Cambridge University Press, 1994.

Letters addressed to Clarinda, etc., by Robert Burns, the Ayrshire Poet, Never Before Published. Glasgow: Thomas Stewart, 1802.

Levine, Alan, *A Political Companion to Ralph Waldo Emerson*. Lexington: University Press of Kentucky, 2011.

Lieven, Anatol, *America Right or Wrong: An Anatomy of American Nationalism* London: Harper Perennial, 2005.

The Life and Land of Burns. New York: J. & H. G. Langely, 1841.

The Literary Magazine, and American Register 2, 1804.

———. 5, 1806.

Lindsay, Andrew O., ""Negro-Driver" or "Illustrious Exile": Revisiting Illustrious Exile: Journal of My Sojourn in the West Indies." Accessed 7 January 2016. http://www.ijsl.stir.ac.uk/issue4/lindsayOP.htm.

Livingston, Samuel Luther and Jacob Chester Chamberlain, eds. *A Bibliography of the First Editions in Book Form of the Writings of James Russell Lowell, Compiled Largely from the Collection Formed by the Late Jacob Chester Chamberlain, with Assistance from His Notes and Memoranda*. New York: The De Vinne Press, 1914.

The Literary Magazine, and American Register 2, 1804.

Lockhart, J.G., ed. *Life of Robert Burns*. New York: W. Stodart, 1831.

Lockwood, Allison, *Passionate Pilgrims: The American Traveler in Great Britain, 1800–1914*. New York: Cornwall Books, 1981.

Lora, Ronald and William Henry, eds. *The Conservative press in Eighteenth-and-Nineteenth-Century America*. Connecticut: Greenwood Publishing Group, 1999.

Low, Donald, ed. *Robert Burns: The Critical Heritage*. London : Routledge and Kegan Paul, 1974.

Lowell, James Russell, *Latest Literary Essays And Addresses*. London: Macmillan, 1891.

Lowell, James Russell, ed. *The Poetical works of John Keats with a memoir by James Russell Lowell*. New York: J. Miller, 187.

Ljungquist, Kent & Buford Jones, "The Identity of "Outis": A Further Chapter in the Poe-Longfellow War." *American Literature* 60, no. 3 (1988): 404–415.

Macaulay, Catherine, *History of England from the Revolution to the Present Time*. London: T. Cadell and J. Walter, 1778.

Mackay, Pauline and Murray Pittock, "Beyond Text: Burns, Byron and Their Material Culture Afterlife." *The Byron Journal* 39, no. 2 (2011): 149–162.

———. "Highland Mary: Objects and Memories." *Romanticism* 18, no. 2 (2012): 191–203.

Maclean, J. P., *An Historical Account of The Settlements of Scotch Highlanders in America Prior to the Peace of Paris in 1783 together with notices of Highland Regiments and Biographical Sketches*. Glasgow: John Mackay, 1900.

Macleod, Emma, *British Visions of America, 1775–1820*. London: Pickering & Chatto, 2013.

Maddox, David, "Was Robert Burns a Nat or Unionist." Accessed 31 December 2015. http://www.scotsman.com/news/politics/top-stories/scottish-independence-mps-gripped-by-the-question-was-rabbie-burns-a-nat-or-a-unionist-1-2077809.

Manning, Susan, "Burns and God." In *Robert Burns and Cultural Authority*, edited by Robert Crawford, 113–136. Iowa City: University of Iowa Press, 1997.

———. *Fragments of Union: Making Connections in Scottish and American Writing*. New York: Palgrave Macmillan, 2002.

———. ""Grounds for Comparison": The Place of Style in Transatlantic Romanticism." In *Wordsworth in American Literary Culture*, edited by Joel Pace and Matthew Scott, 19–42. Basingstoke and New York: Palgrave Macmillan, 2005.

———. *Poetics of Character: Transatlantic Encounters 1700–1900*. Cambridge: Cambridge University Press, 2013.

———. "Robert Burns's Transatlantic Afterlives" in *Robert Burns and Transatlantic Culture,* edited by Sharon Alker, Leith Davis and Holly Faith Nelson, 149–169. Farnham, Burlington: Ashgate, 2012.

Marchand, Ernest, "Literary Opinions of Charles Brockden Brown." *Studies in Philology* 31, no. 4 (1934): 541–566.

Marshall, P. J., *Remaking The British Atlantic: The United States and the British Empire After American Independence*. Oxford: Oxford University Press, 2012.

May, Henry F., *The Enlightenment in America*. Oxford: Oxford University Press, 1976.

Maxwell, Richard and Katie Trumpener, eds. *The Cambridge Companion to Fiction in the Romantic Period*. Cambridge: Cambridge University Press, 2008.

McAleer, John, *Ralph Waldo Emerson: Days of Encounter*. Boston: Little, Brown and Company, 1984.

McCarthy, Angela, *Irish Migrants in New Zealand, 1840–1937: 'The Desired Haven'*. Woodbridge: Boydell Press, 2005.

McCue, Kirsteen, "'Magnetic Attraction": The Transatlantic Songs of Robert Burns and Serge Hovey.' In *Robert Burns and Transatlantic Culture*, edited by Sharon Alker, Leith Davis and Holly Faith Nelson, 233–247. Farnham, Burlington: Ashgate, 2012.

McGinn, Clark, "Vehement Celebrations: The Global Celebration of the Burns Supper Since 1801." In *Robert Burns and Global Culture*, edited by Murray Pittock, 189–203. Lewisburg: Bucknell University Press, 2011.

———. ""Every honour except canonisation": The global development of the Burns Supper, 1801 to 2009." Unpublished Ph.D. Thesis, University of Glasgow, 2013.

———. "Burns and Slavery." Accessed 2 January 2015. http://www.electricscotland.com/familytree/frank/burns_lives92.htm#sdendnote43anc.

———. "Early American Burns Celebrations." *The Burns Chronicle* (2015): 47–59.

———. Clark McGinn, "The Scotch Bard and "The Planting Line": New Documents on Burns and Jamaica." *Studies in Scottish Literature* 43, no. 2 (2017): 265.

McGuirk, Carol, *Robert Burns and the Sentimental Era*. Athens: University of Georgia Press, 1985.

———. "George Thomson and Robert Burns: With Friends Like These." *Eighteenth Century Scotland* 9 (1995): 16–20.

———. "Haunted By Authority: Nineteenth-Century American Constructions of Robert Burns and Scotland." In *Robert Burns and Cultural Authority*, edited by Robert Crawford, 136–159. Iowa City: University of Iowa Press, 1997.

———. ed. *Critical Essays on Robert Burns*. New York: G.K. Hall & Co., 1998.

———. *Reading Robert Burns: Texts, Contexts, Transformations*. London: Pickering & Chatto, 2014.

McIlvanney, Liam, *Burns the Radical: Poetry and Politics in Late Eighteenth-Century Scotland*. Edinburgh: Tuckwell Press, 2002.

———. "Editorial: Burns and The World." *International Journal of Scottish Literature* 6 (Spring/Summer, 2010): 1–16.

McWhiney, Grady, *Cracker Culture: Celtic Ways in the Old South*. Tuscaloosa: University of Alabama Press, 1988.

Melish, John, *Travels in the United States of America*. Philadelphia: Thomas & George Palmer, 1812.

Mitchell, L. G., *Charles James Fox*. Oxford: Oxford University Press, 1992.

"Modern Day Slavery in Focus." Accessed 4 January 2016. http://www.theguardian.com/global-development/series/modern-day-slavery-in-focus.

Mole, Tom, ed. *Romanticism and Celebrity Culture*. Cambridge: Cambridge University Press, 2012.

The Monthly Anthology and Boston Review 3, 1806.

Montgomery, Michael, "The Rediscovery of The Ulster Scots Languages" in *Englishes Around the World: General Studies, British Isles, North America*, edited by Edgar Werner Schneider, 211–266. Amsterdam: John Benjamins Press, 1997.

Moody, T. W., "The Ulster Scots in Colonial and Revolutionary America: Part II." *Studies: An Irish Quarterly Review* 34, no. 134 (1945): 85–94.

Moreland, Kim Ileen, *The Medievalist Impulse in American Literature: Twain, Adams, Fitzgerald, and Hemingway*. Charlottesville, University of Virginia Press, 1996.

Morris, Michael, "Robert Burns: Recovering Scotland's Memory of the Black Atlantic." *Journal for Eighteenth-Century Studies* 37, no. 3 (2014): 343–359.

———. *Scotland and the Caribbean, c. 1740–1833: Atlantic Archipelagos*. London: Routledge, 2015.

Morrison, Leonard A., *Rambles in Europe: In Ireland, Scotland, England, Belgium, Germany, Switzerland, and France*. Boston: Cupples, Upham & Co., 1887.

Moreno, Beatriz González Moreno and Margarita Rigal Aragón, eds. *A Descent Into Edgar Allan Poe and His Works: The Bicentennial*. Bern: Peter Lang, 2010.

Muller, Gilbert H., *William Cullen Bryant: Author of America*. Albany: State University of New York Press, 2010.

Nairn, Tom, *Faces of Nationalism: Janus Revisited*. London, New York: Verso, 1997.

The New York American 2, no. 588, 1822.

———. 9, no. 857, 1829.

New-York Daily Advertiser, 3 February 1818.

New York Daily Gazette, 11 November 1791.

The New York Magazine: or, Literary Repository 1, 1790.

———. 4, 1793.

———. New Series 1, 1796.

The New York Review 4, 1839.

The New York Times, 15 Febraury 1854.

New York Weekly Tribune 5, no. 45, 1846.

The North American Review and Miscellaneous Journal 7, 1818.

————. 34, 1832.

Newcomb, John Timberman, *Would Poetry Disappear?: American Verse and the Crisis of Modernity.* Columbus: Ohio State University Press, 2004.

Noble, Andrew, "Burns, Scotland, and the American Revolution." In *Robert Burns and Transatlantic Culture,* edited by Sharon Alker, Leith Davis and Holly Faith Nelson, 31–55. Farnham, Burlington: Ashgate, 2012.

Noble, Andrew and Patrick Scott Hogg, eds. *The Canongate Burns: The Complete Poems and Songs of Robert Burns.* Edinburgh: Canongate, 2001.

Nora, Pierre, "Between Memory and History: Les Lieux de Mémoire." *Representations* 26 (1989): 7–24.

————. ed. *Realms of Memory,* translated by Arthur Goldhammer. New York: Columbia University Press, 1996.

Nurhussein, Nadia, *Rhetorics of Literacy: The Cultivation of American Dialect.* Columbus: The Ohio State University Press, 2013.

O' Rourke, Donny, ed. *Ae Fond Kiss: The Love Letters of Robert Burns and Clarinda: Love Letters of Burns and Clarinda.* Edinburgh: Mercat Press, 2000.

Orr, Jennifer, ""The Diel's Awa Wi' The Exciseman": Robert Burns the Giver of Guns to Revolutionary France?" In *Fickle Man: Robert Burns in the 21st Century,* edited by Johnny Rodgers and Gerard Carruthers, 257–266. Dingwall: Sandstone Press, 2009.

————. "Constructing the Ulster Labouring-Class Poet: The Case of Samuel Thomson." In *Class and the Canon: Constructing Labouring-Class Poetry and Poetics, 1780–1900,* edited by Kirsty Blair and Mina Gorji, 35–54. London: Palgrave Macmillan, 2012.

"Our Founding Novelist." Accessed 8 December 2015. https://www.neh.gov/humanities/2010/januaryfebruary/feature/our-founding-novelist.

"Oxford Dictionary of National Biography." Accessed 18 January 2013. http://www.oxforddnb.com.

"Oxford English Dictionary Online." Accessed 17 September 2015. http://www.oed.com/.

Pace, Joel and Matthew Scott, eds. *Wordsworth in American Literary Culture.* Basingstoke and New York: Palgrave Macmillan, 2005.

Painter, Anna M., "American Editions of The *Poems* of Burns Before 1800." *The Library* 4, no. 12 (1932): 434–456.

"The Pennsylvania Packet and Daily Advertiser." Accessed 26 September 2015. http://www.nls.uk/collections/rarebooks/acquisitions/singlebook.cfm/idfind/80.

The Pennsylvania Packet, 25 September 1775.
———. 26 October 1787.
———. 16 July 1788.
———. 25 December 1790.
Peterson, Merrill D., ed. *Thomas Jefferson: Writings*. New York: Library of America, 1984.
The Philadelphia Monthly Magazine; or, Universal Repository of Knowledge and Entertainment 1, no. 2, 1798.
———. 2, no. 7, 1798.
Pickard, John B., ed. *The Letters of John Greenleaf Whittier: 1828–1845*. 3 Vols. Cambridge, MA: Belknap Press of Harvard University Press, 1975.
Pittock, Murray, *Scottish Nationality*. Hampshire: Palgrave, 2001.
———. ""A Long Farewell to All My Greatness": The History of The Reputation of Robert Burns." In *Robert Burns and Global Culture*, edited by Murray Pittock, 25–46. Lewisburg: Bucknell University Press, 2011.
———. "Introduction: Global Burns." In *Robert Burns in Global Culture*, edited by Murray Pittock, 13–25. Lewisburg: Bucknell University Press, 2011.
———. ed. *Robert Burns in Global Culture*. Lewisburg: Bucknell University Press, 2011.
———. "Slavery as Political Metaphor in Scotland and Ireland in the Age of Burns." In *Robert Burns and Transatlantic Culture*, edited by Sharon Alker, Leith Davis and Holly Faith Nelson, 19–31. Farnham, Burlington: Ashgate, 2012.
———. ed., *The Oxford Edition of The Works of Robert Burns, Volumes II and III: The Scots Musical Museum*. Oxford: Oxford University Press, 2018.
Pittock, Murray, and Christopher A. Whatley, "Poems and Festivals, Art and Artefact." *The Scottish Historical Review* 93, no. 236 (2014): 56–79.
Pocock, J.G.A., *The Machiavellian Moment: Florentine Political Thought and the Atlantic Republican Tradition*. Princeton: Princeton University Press, 1975.
Port Folio, 5, 1805.
———. New Series 1, 1806.
Post, Loretta J., *Scenes in Europe; or, Observations by an Amateur Artist*. Cincinnati, OH: Hitchcock & Walden, 1874.
Quigley, Paul, *Shifting Grounds: Nationalism and the American South, 1848–1865* Oxford: Oxford University Press, 2011.
Radcliffe, David Hill, "Imitation, Popular Literacy, and "The Cottar's Saturday Night"". In *Critical Essays on Robert Burns*, edited by Carol McGuirk, 251–281. New York: G.K. Hall & Co., 1998.
Ramsay, Allan, *The Ever Green, Being a Collection of Scots Poems*. Oxford: Oxford University, 1724.
Ray, Celeste, ed. *Transatlantic Scots*. Tuscaloosa: University of Alabama Press, 2005.

Read, Dennis M., *R.H. Cromek, Engraver, Editor and Entrepreneur*. Farnham and Burlington: Ashgate Publishing, 2011.

Read, James H., "The Limits of Self Reliance: Emerson, Slavery and Abolition." In *A Political Companion to Ralph Waldo Emerson*, edited by Alan Levine, 152–184. Lexington: University Press of Kentucky, 2011.

The Republican Journal, August 14, 1797.

Rhys, Ernest, ed. *James Russell, The Biglow Papers*. London: The Walter Scott Publishing Company, 1892.

Rice, Alan, *Radical Narratives of the Black Atlantic*. London: Continuum, 2003.

Richardson, Thomas C., 'John Lockhart's Burns: Stirring "National Enthusiasm,"' *Studies in Scottish Literature* 30, no. 1 (1998): 157–166.

Richardson, W., "Letter to S. Rose, 1 Jan, 1787" MS. University of Glasgow Special Collections, MS Gen 520/2.

Rigney, Ann, "Plenitude, Scarcity and the Circulation of Cultural Memory." *Journal of European Studies* 35, no. 1 (2005): 11–28.

———. "Embodied Communities: Commemorating Robert Burns, 1859." *Representations* 115, no. 1 (2011): 71–101.

———. *The Afterlives of Walter Scott: Memory on the Move*. Oxford: Oxford University Press, 2012.

"Robert Burns at 250." Accessed 18 October 2016. http://www.loc.gov/folklife/Symposia/Burns/.

"The Robert Burns Association of North America." Accessed 18 October 2016. http://www.rbana.com/.

"Robert Burns Beyond Text." Accessed 30 December 2015. www.gla.ac.uk/robertburnsbeyondtext.

"Robert Burns Conference, University of Glasgow, 2009." Accessed 2 January 2016. http://www.gla.ac.uk/media/media_105067_en.pdf.

"Robert Burns: Inventing Tradition and Securing Memory, 1796–1909." Accessed 11 September 2015. http://www.gla.ac.uk/schools/critical/research/researchcentresandnetworks/robertburnsstudies/ourresearch/burns/.

"Robert Burns Public Memorials—Missing, Destroyed or Undiscovered." Accessed 2 January 2016. http://www.gla.ac.uk/media/media_196586_en.pdf.

Roberts, Timothy Mason, *Distant Revolutions: 1848 and the Challenge to American Exceptionalism*. Charlottesville: University of Virginia Press, 2009.

Robotham, John, "The Reading of Robert Burns." *Bulletin of the New York Public Library* 74, no. 9 (1970): 561–576.

Rocks, James E., "Whittier's "Snow-Bound": "The Circle of Our Hearth" and the Discourse on Domesticity." *Studies in the American Renaissance* (1993): 339–353.

Rodger, Johnny and Carruthers, Gerard, eds. *Fickle Man: Robert Burns in the 21st Century*. Dingwall: Sandstone Press, 2009.

Rowe, John Carlos, "Nineteenth-Century United States Literary Culture and Transnationality." *Publications of The Modern Language Association of America (PMLA)* 118, no. 1 (2003): 78–89.

Roy, G. Ross, ed. *Robert Burns & America: A Symposium*. Thomas Cooper Library, University of South Carolina; Kircaldy, Scotland : Akros Publications, 2001.

Roy, G. Ross, and J. Delancey Ferguson, eds. *The Letters of Robert Burns*, 2 Vols. Revised 2nd edition. Oxford: Clarendon Press, 1985.

Rusk, Ralph L., *The Life of Ralph Waldo Emerson*. New York: Columbia University Press, 1957.

Rushton, Edward, *Poems*. London: J.M'creery, 1806.

Russell, Nicolas, "Collective Memory Before and After Halbwachs." *The French Review* 79, no. 4 (2006): 792–804.

The Salem Gazette 1, no. 16, 1823.

Sales Catalogue for Puttock and Simpson, May 1861.

"Salmond launches SNP General Election Campaign." Accessed 31 December 2015. http://www.snp.org/media-centre/news/2005/jan/salmond-launches-snp-general-election-campaign.

Sanborn, Franklin B., *The Personality of Emerson*. New York: Hasker House Publishers, 1971.

Sassen, Saskia, "Spatialities and Temporalities of the Global: Elements for a Theorization." *Public Culture* 12, no. 1 (2000): 215–232.

Sassi, Carla, "Glocalising Scottish Literature: A Call for New Strategies of Reading." Accessed 10 September 2015. http://www.arts.gla.ac.uk/ScotLit/ASLS/SWE/TBI/TBISupp/TBISupp1/Sassi.html.

The Scottish Minstrel: Being a Complete Collection of Burns' Songs. Philadelphia: Benjamin Warner, 1818.

Scharnhorst, Gary, "Whitman on Robert Burns: An Early Essay Recovered." *The Walt Whitman Quarterly Review* 13, no. 3 (1996): 217–220.

Schneider, Edgar Werner, ed. *Englishes Around the World: General Studies, British Isles, North America*. Amsterdam: John Benjamins Press, 1997.

Schoene, Berthold, ed. *The Edinburgh Companion to Contemporary Scottish Literature*. Edinburgh: Edinburgh University Press, 2007.

Scott, Patrick, ""Not in Egerer"? (Some of) What We Still Don't Know about Burns Bibliography." *Studies in Scottish Literature* 43, no. 9 (2017): 309–320.

Scudder, H.E., ed. *The Complete Poetical Works of Whittier*. Boston: Houghton Mifflin, 1894.

Select Reviews, and Spirit of the Foreign Magazines 2, 1809.

Sengupta, Indra and Hagen Schulze, eds. *Memory, History, and Colonialism: Engaging with Pierre Nora in Colonial and Postcolonial Contexts*. London: German Historical Institute, 2009.

Sher, Richard B., and Jeffrey R. Smitten, eds. *Scotland and America in the Age of the Enlightenment*. Edinburgh: Edinburgh University Press, 1990.

———. *The Enlightenment and the Book: Scottish Authors and Their Publishers in Eighteenth-Century Britain, Ireland and America*. Chicago: University of Chicago Press, 2008.

Simpson, Kenneth, ed. *Love and Liberty: Robert Burns; a Bicentenary Celebration*. East Lothian: Tuckwell Press, 1997.

———. "Poetic Genre and National Identity: Ramsay, Fergusson, and Burns." *Studies in Scottish Literature* 30 (1998): 31–42.

Simpson, David, *The Politics of American English, 1776–1850*. Oxford: Oxford University Press, 1986.

Singh, Amritjit and Peter Schmidt, eds. *Postcolonial Theory and the United States: Race, Ethnicity, and Literature*. Mississippi: University Press of Mississippi, 2008.

"Songs Along the Campaign Trail." Accessed 4 January 2015. http://www.npr.org/templates/story/story.php?storyId=95408459.

Skinner, Andrew S., "Adam Smith and the American Revolution." *Presidential Studies Quarterly* 7, no. 2/3 (1977): 75–87.

Sloan, Douglas, *The Scottish Enlightenment and the American College Ideal*. New York: Teachers College Press of Columbia University, 1971.

Sloane, David. E. E., "Dialect, Doggerel, and Local Colour: Comic Traditions and the Rise of Realism in Popular Poetry." In *The Cambridge History of American Poetry*, edited by Alfred Bendixen and Stephen Burt, 445–469. New York: Cambridge University Press, 2015.

Smith, Craig R. and David M. Hunsaker, *The Four Freedoms of the First Amendment* Longrove: Waveland Press, 2003.

Smith, Jeremy J., "Copia Verborum: The Linguistic Choices of Robert Burns." *Review of English Studies* 58, no. 233 (2007): 73–88.

"Smithsonian Institution, Inventory of American Art." Accessed 31 January 2015. http://www.AmericanArt.si.edu.

Snyder, Alan K., *Defining Noah Webster: A Spiritual Biography*. Fairfax: Allegiance Press, 2002.

Snyder, Franklyn Bliss, *Life of Robert Burns*. New York: Macmillan, 1932.

Sood, Arun, "An American Trove of Burnsiana: The William R. Smith Collection." *The Burns Chronicle* (2015): 39–46.

———. ""A Modern Poet on the Scotch Bard": Walt Whitman's 1875 Essay on Robert Burns." *The Walt Whitman Quarterly Review* 32, no. 4 (2015): 230–236.

Sorby, Angela, *Schoolroom Poets: Childhood, Performance and the Place of American Poetry, 1865–1917*. Durham: University of New Hampshire Press, 2005.

Spritzer, Lorraine Nelson, *The Belle of Ashby Street: Helen Douglas Mankin and Georgia Politics*. Athens: University of Georgia Press, 2008.

Stafford, Fiona, and David Sergeant, eds. *Burns and Other Poets*. Edinburgh: Edinburgh University Press, 2012.

St Clair, William, *The Reading Nation in The Romantic Period*. Cambridge: Cambridge University Press, 2004.

Szasz, Ferenc Morton, *Abraham Lincoln and Robert Burns: Connected Lives and Legends*. Carbondale: Southern Illinois University Press, 2008.

Taylor, Scott L., *"Judicium Dei, Vulgaris Popularisque Sensus:* Survival of Customary Justice and Resistance to Its Displacement by the "New" *Ordines iudiciorum* as Evidenced by Francophonic Literature of the High Middle Ages."* In *Crime and Punishment in the Middle Ages and Early Modern Age: Mental-Historical Investigations of Basic Human Problems and Social Responses*, edited by Albrecht Classen and Connie Scrarborough, 109–130. Berlin: De Gruyter, 2012.

Toorn, Karel van der, Bob Becking, Bob and Pieter Willem van deer Horst, eds. *Dictionary of Deities and Demons in the Bible*. Michigan: Wm. B. Eerdmans Publishing, 1999.

"Thomas Muir of Huntershill: Father of Scottish Democracy." Accessed 19 November 2015. http://www.thomasmuir.co.uk/thomasmuir250.html.

Thomson Gallagher, Carol, *The Scots Who Built New York*. New York: St Andrew's Society of the State of New York, 2006.

Thompson, Todd N., "From Brahmin to Biglow (and Back Again): James Russell Lowell as Temporary Satirist." *A Journal of the American Renaissance* 58, no. 2 (2012): 154–184.

Trumpener, Katie, *Bardic Nationalism: The Romantic novel and the British Empire*. Princeton: Princeton University Press, 1997.

Twain, Mark, *Life on the Mississippi [1883]*. Oxford: Oxford University Press, 1996.

Tyler, Samuel, *Robert Burns, As a Poet, And as a Man*. New York: Baker & Scribner, 1848.

———. *Discourse of the Baconian Philosophy [1844]*. London: Forgotten Books, 2013.

Tyrrell, Alex, "Paternalism, Public Memory and National Identity in Early Victorian Scotland: The Robert Burns Festival at Ayr in 1844." *History* 90, no. 297 (2005): 42–61.

Tytler, James, *The Rising of the Sun in the West, or The Origin and Progress of Liberty*. Salem: William Carlton, 1795.

Verhoven, Wil, "Transatlantic Utopianism." In *Transatlantic Literary Studies 1660–1830*, edited by Eve Taylor Bannet and Susan Manning, 28–46. Cambridge: Cambridge University Press, 2011.

———. *Americomania and the French Revolution Debate in Britain, 1789–1802*. Cambridge: Cambridge University Press, 2013.

Van Kugt, William E., *British Buckeyes: The English, Scots and Welsh in Ohio, 1700–1900*. Kent: Kent State University Press, 2006.

Wade, Wyn Craig, *The Fiery Cross: The Ku Klux Klan in America*. Oxford: Oxford University Press, 1998.

Waldstreicher, David, *In The Midst of Perpetual Fetes: The Making of American Nationalism, 1776–1820*. University of North Carolina Press, 1997.

Wallace, Gavin, "Voyages of Intent: Literature and Cultural Politics in Post-Devolution Scotland." In *The Edinburgh Companion to Contemporary Scottish Literature*, edited by Gerard Carruthers, 17–28. Edinburgh: Edinburgh University Press, 2009.

Washington, George, "Letter to David C. Claypoole [7 August 1782]." Accessed 26 November 2015. http://founders.archives.gov/documents/Washington/99-01-02-09057.

Waterman, Bryan, "Charles Brockden Brown, Revised and Expanded." *Early American Literature* 40, no. 1 (2005): 173–191.

Watkins, Larissa P., ed. *Burnsiana: A Bibliography of the William R. Smith Collection in the Library of the Supreme Council, 33, S.J.* Delaware and Washington: Oak Knoll Press & Library of the Supreme Council, 2008.

Werkmesiter, Lucyle, "Robert Burns and the Daily Press." *Modern Philology* 63, no. 4 (1966): 322–335.

Whatley, Harlan Douglas, Duncan A. Bruce and Randall Lenox Taylor, *Two Hundred Fifty Years 1756–2006: The History of Saint Andrew's Society of The State of New York*. New York: Saint Andrew's Society of The State of New York, 2008.

Whatley, Christopher A., ""It Is Said That Burns Was a Radical" Contest, Concession, and the Political Legacy of Robert Burns, ca. 1796–1859." In *The Journal of British Studies* 50, no. 3 (2011): 639–666.

———. *Immortal Memory: Burns and the Scottish People*. Edinburgh: Birlinn Ltd., 2016.

Whelan, Kevin, *The Tree of Liberty: Radicalism, Catholicism, and the Construction of Irish Identity 1760–1830*. Cork: Cork University Press, 1996.

Whitman, Walt, *November Boughs*. Philadelphia: David McKay, 1888.

Whittier, John Greenleaf, *The Poetical Works of John Greenleaf Whittier*. London: Macmillan, 1874.

Whyte, Christopher, "Masculinities in Contemporary Scottish Fiction." *Forum for Modern Language Studies* 34, no. 2 (1998): 274–285.

Whyte, Ian, *Scotland and the Abolition of Black Slavery, 1756–1838*. Edinburgh: Edinburgh University Press, 2006.

Wilson, David. A, *United Irishmen, Unites States: Immigrant Radicals in the Early Republic*. Ithaca: Cornell University Press, 1998. Wilson, Frances, ed. *Byromania: Portraits of the Artist in Nineteenth and Twentieth Century Culture*. London: Macmillan, 1999.

Winick, Stephen, "Auld Acquaintance for the New Year." Accessed 26 November 2015. http://blogs.loc.gov/folklife/2013/12/auld-acquaintance-for-the-new-year-burnss-auld-lang-syne/.

Yates, Francis, *The Art of Memory*. London: The Bodley Head, 2014.

Young, Elizabeth, *Black Frankenstein: The Making of an American Metaphor*. New York: New York University Press, 2008.

Young, Linda, *Middle-Class Culture in the Nineteenth Century: America, Australia, and Britain*. New York: Palgrave Macmillan, 2002.

Young, Ronnie, "Genius, Men, and Manners: Burns and Eighteenth- Century Scottish Criticism." *Scottish Studies Review* 9 (2008): 129–147.

Index